Arrowhead Mills® COOKBOOK

Vicki Rae Chelf

AVERY PUBLISHING GROUP INC.
Garden City Park, New York

Front cover carved wooden image: Robert Wade
Front cover photograph: Mary McCulley
Editor: Rick Mastelli
Designer: Deborah Fillion
Illustrations: Vicki Rae Chelf
Photographs: ©Rick Mastelli
Copy Editor: Betsy Strauch
Production: Image & Word, Montpelier, VT
Printer: Paragon Press, Honesdale, PA

Library of Congress Cataloging-in-Publication Data

Chelf, Vick Rae.
    Arrowhead Mills cookbook : Vicki Rae Chelf.
        p.   cm.
    Includes index.
    ISBN 0-89529-546-6 :
    1. Cookery (Natural foods).   2. Vegetarian cookery.   I. Arrowhead
Mills.   II. Title.
TX741.C47   1993
641.5′63—dc20
                                                                93-17146
                                                                CIP

Printed in the United States of America

10 9 8 7 6 5 4 3 2

Contents

Foreword

Vickie Chelf has proven, once again, how easy and exciting it is to use whole natural foods. I'm sure you'll find as we did that her recipes are not only tasty and nutritious but attractive and economical as well.

Here at Arrowhead Mills, we have been committed for more than thirty years to natural foods, organic farming, and the connection between our well-being and that of the earth. We have cultivated relationships with scores of independent organic farmers, from Texas to the Dakotas, whose work improves the land as it feeds our people. Our mission is to provide these farmers with a premium for the very best certified organic grains, beans, and seeds, clean them thoroughly, and sell them in forms as close to their natural state as possible.

Now, we are putting an equal effort into providing easy-to-prepare and ready-to-eat foods of great taste and convenience as well as the information necessary to make the most of all natural foods. This book will provide you with ideas and inspiration for using natural foods, serving as a guide to their fun, taste, and nutrition.

—*Frank Ford*
Chairman of the Board
Arrowhead Mills

Acknowledgments

When Rudy Shur, from Avery Publishing Group, asked me to write this book, I was thrilled, not only because I have used and loved Arrowhead Mills products for many years, but because the first Arrowhead Mills Cookbook, *The Deaf Smith Country Cookbook,* was one of the books that I learned to cook with. I am very proud to have had the opportunity to work with Frank and Marjorie Ford, the founders of Arrowhead Mills. They are true pioneers in the natural foods movement, and they continue to be a major force in educating the American public about healthy food and sustainable agriculture.

I would like to thank Rudy for suggesting that I do this project, and the Fords for being so helpful in answering any questions I had about their products. I would like to thank Patty Marie Davis, a good cook as well as a wonderful person, for the recipes that she contributed. I would also like to thank my dear friend Dominique Biscotti, who is a naturopath and the owner of Le Pommier Fleuri natural foods store in Ste-Agathe, Quebec. Dominique has contributed recipes, ideas, and moral support, not only in this book but in almost all my other books as well. Other people who have contributed recipes and inspiration are my friends Amy Warren and Louise Hammel.

No list of acknowledgments is complete without mentioning all of my cooking students, whose ideas and questions keep me learning and trying new things. Last but not least, I would like to thank my husband, Jean Renoux, who tried every single recipe that I made!

This book is dedicated to Frank and Marjorie Ford and to John Robbins, who have been an inspiration, not only to me but to many others with their commitment to making this a healthier and more peaceful world.

—Vicki Rae Chelf

Introduction

A whole world of healthy and delicious foods is just waiting to be rediscovered. The variety we can add to our diets by using grains, beans, seeds, and the products made from them is nothing new. These foods have sustained mankind all over the world since the beginning of agriculture. They are the traditional foods of almost every culture. It is time we recognize their place in our own kitchens.

Natural foods cooking has come a long way in the past twenty years. Without sacrificing nutrition, we can now make dishes that will please even the most discriminating palate, meals that are, nevertheless, simple and easy enough for everyday fare. Natural foods are also naturally beautiful. By combining grains, beans, and seeds with an abundance of colorful fruit and vegetables, we can make dishes as attractive as those served in any fine restaurant.

Nutrition is, of course, important, and that's where natural foods excel. By eating these basic foods, which have undergone little processing, we will be doing what health experts today are recommending—cutting down on fat and cholesterol, eating more fruits and vegetables, and adding fiber to our diet. And if these are organically grown foods (foods that have been grown, harvested, stored, processed, and packaged without using synthetically compounded fertilizers, pesticides, or growth regulators), we'll be limiting our consumption of harmful substances.

Besides the nutritional and culinary appeal, cooking with natural foods is simpler today and finding the ingredients is easier than ever. Natural foods stores are everywhere; many large supermarkets have natural foods sections. Combining grains, beans, and seeds with seasonal vegetables and fruits costs much less than eating processed foods. In our fast-paced world, food preparation should be fast and easy. Cooking with natural foods has an old reputation for being very time-consuming, but this is no longer true. I cook not because I love cooking but because I want to feel good, look good, and eat foods of high quality. I also believe that the foods I make at home from natural ingredients taste better than any processed food I can buy. However, I don't want to spend hours in the kitchen, nor is that necessary. With a little practice, it is possible to make beautiful meals in thirty minutes or less, and that is what this book is all about.

Throughout the years that I have been eating natural foods, I have had to develop preparation methods that fit into a busy schedule. For six years I owned and operated a natural foods store and restaurant. During that time I wrote four cookbooks and taught weekly cooking classes. I also ran competitively, did lots of cross-country skiing, and renovated a 150-year-old-house. Since then, I have received a diploma in fine arts, and I continue to write, teach, and pursue a career as a visual artist. Needless to say, I cannot spend my days cooking. In this book, I'll be sharing the practical knowledge I've acquired from twenty years of cooking, so that you, too, can easily make healthy, attractive meals.

I've tried to make this book easy to use. If you are new to natural foods, please read Chapter 1 before you try the recipes. It contains tips on shopping for and storing natural foods as well as a glossary of ingredients that offers background on all the most commonly used natural foods. If you come across an ingredient in a recipe that you are unfamiliar with, look it up in the glossary to understand what it is and how it's used.

The recipes in this book are divided into general types of food, from breakfasts to dessert. Within the chapters, similar dishes are grouped together—for example, all the croquettes and burgers are next to each other, and so are the recipes for quiches and vegetable pies. I hope you'll experiment with variations within these categories. Success will come from getting to know your ingredients. So keep trying, and enjoy the possibilities.

If you are just learning to cook, this book represents an important opportunity. By starting out with natural foods, you will develop habits that will benefit you throughout your life. You are laying the foundation for radiant health and glowing beauty.

If you've tried natural foods cooking before and given it up because of taste or lack of practicality, it's time to try again. The recipes in this book are nothing like the natural foods recipes of the past. They are tastier, lighter, and easier to make. We might call this cooking "la nouvelle cuisine naturelle," because it contains so many exotic-sounding ingredients—quinoa, seitan, tempeh, miso, and arame, to name a few. But these are not really new foods; they are ancient foods that we have rediscovered. Let's simply call the result "healthy cooking" and enjoy it.

1. USING NATURAL FOODS

How many times have you heard that natural foods are expensive and no better than supermarket products? Is this true? What are natural foods, anyway? Just because something is natural doesn't mean it's good for you. Toadstools and poison ivy are natural! Using the word "natural" to sell everything from soap to ice cream underscores how artificial our world has become; on a label the word means little. Therefore, with natural foods, as with anything else, to get the value for your money, you need to be an informed consumer.

To better understand natural foods, let's replace the term "natural" with "traditional." Throughout most of history, people have eaten whole grains, beans, seeds, seasonal fruits, and vegetables—natural foods. It is only in this century that food has changed radically. We, as a species, however, are biologically the same as we were a thousand years ago, and the long-term effects that some of these new, overly refined, artificially colored, and chemically preserved foods have on our bodies are just being discovered. We do know that refined foods are less nutritious than whole foods, even when "enriched." Health experts agree that we should eat more whole grains, beans, fruits, and vegetables: traditional foods with a proven track record. No one who values health would recommend eating more junk food.

Traditional foods are more nutritious mainly because they are less processed. That's also why they are less expensive. Grains and beans have always been a bargain. They are powerhouses of nutrition, including fiber, trace minerals, and vitamins, while being low in fat, low in sodium, and cholesterol-free. When combined with each other, the various amino acids available in grains and beans complement one another to form complete proteins that rival those of meat or dairy products, and at far less cost. In fact, grains and beans are so inexpensive that you can buy them organically grown, as they are commonly available in natural foods stores, and still spend very little money. Produced without the use of chemical fertilizers, pesticides, herbicides, or growth regulators, organically grown foods taste better and, measured by their nutritional value, can be less expensive than other foods.

Seasonal fruits and vegetables are also relatively inexpensive, a much better buy than imported, out-of-season produce. Seasonal produce is also likely to be of higher quality because it's fresher. Other foods that are often good buys in natural foods stores include bulk nuts, seeds, dried fruits, and herbs. Some traditional foods such as tofu, soymilk, tempeh, seitan, sea vegetables, nut and seed butters, whole grain flours and meals, mechanically pressed oils, misos, and tamari do involve processing. Nevertheless, they offer good nutritional value because they remain whole foods. These, too, are readily available and frequently fresher in natural foods stores because their turnover of these foods is greater.

A category of foods that is definitely more expensive than similar foods in supermarkets is natural convenience foods—cookies, candy bars, ready-to-eat breakfast cereals, chips, sauces, breads, juices, mixes, and canned and frozen foods. Though they are certainly not staples, they can come in handy.

When buying convenience foods in a natural foods store, read the labels just as you would in a supermarket. Not all foods in a natural foods store are nutritious. Look out for sugar in all its disguises, such as glucose, corn syrup, and brown or turbinado sugar. You may want to avoid sugar altogether, but most people can enjoy whole-food sweeteners, such as honey, maple syrup, and molasses, in moderation. If amounts are not given, note that ingredients are listed in order of quantity. Steer clear of foods whose main ingredients are sweeteners; they represent empty calories.

For the same reason, look out for white flour, that is, flour whose nutrients have been depleted by refining. It may be unbleached, but if you think you are getting whole grain flour when a package says "wheat flour" or "rye flour," you are wrong. The label must read "whole wheat flour," or "whole rye flour" to really be whole grain.

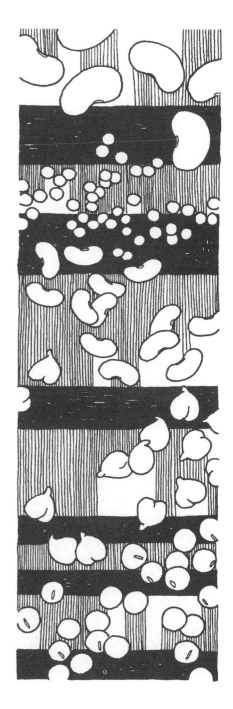

"Natural" convenience foods can also be high in fat and sodium, substances we should limit in our diets.

Read labels closely when comparing foods. If you find two similar foods marketed with different prices, see whether the higher price reflects higher-quality ingredients, such as organically grown flours, natural flavorings, and nonhydrogenated oils.

I prefer shopping in natural foods stores because I believe that many individuals in the natural foods business are genuinely concerned with the quality of the products they sell as well as with our environment. When I spend my money to encourage high-quality products and sustainable (organic) agriculture, it helps to assure me not only of pure, healthy food, but of rich, healthy farmland for future generations. It's like voting for what I believe in every time I shop. I've noticed, too, that the more people vote this way, the more accessible and the less expensive healthful food becomes.

A Glossary of Natural Foods

Adzuki beans (*ad-ZOO-kee*)—Also called **aduki,** these small, round, dark red beans have a somewhat less "beany" taste than do other legumes. In Japan, the only legume more popular is the soybean. Adzukis are excellent for sprouting, and they cook more quickly than most other beans. They are especially good when cooked with the sea vegetable kombu and with winter squash.

Agar-agar (*AH-gr–AH-gr*)—You shouldn't have trouble introducing this versatile sea vegetable into your family's diet, as it is odorless, tasteless, and colorless. Agar-agar (or simply agar) is used as a jelling agent in desserts, aspics, jams, etc. There are thousands of wonderful ways to employ it, but in this book I have used it mostly for desserts. Agar-agar is available in bar, powder, and flake form. In these recipes, I specify flakes.

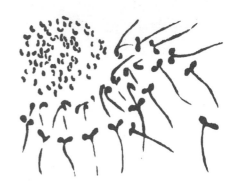

Alfalfa seeds—Sprouting these tiny brown seeds will give you fresh, home-grown produce the year around. All that's needed is the seed, water, a jar, and a screen (see page 74). Alfalfa sprouts are delicious in salads, sandwiches, and tacos. They contain protein, calcium, iron, and B-complex vitamins, as well as vitamin C. They are very low in fat and calories.

Amaranth (*AM-ah-ranth*)—With its exceptional nutritional qualities and versatility, this ancient "Food of the Aztecs" is rapidly gaining in popularity. A tiny grain, about half the size of millet, amaranth is high in protein (including lysine and methionine), fiber, iron, calcium, and phosphorus. Cooked amaranth seeds (one part seeds in three parts water, simmered for 25 minutes) can be eaten like porridge. Uncooked seeds can be added to cookie, muffin, and quick-bread batter to give added nutrition and a crunchy texture. Amaranth seeds can also be popped like popcorn in a dry skillet.

    Amaranth flour combines well with other flours to make many delicious, smooth-textured baked goods, such as quick breads, muffins, pancakes, and cookies. Amaranth flour does not contain gluten. It has a golden color and a rather strong flavor, but a little of it will give baked goods more protein and a light texture. Try substituting 5 to 15 percent amaranth flour for the flour a recipe calls for.

Amasake (*ah-mah-SAH-kay*)—Literally, "sweet sake," amasake is made from rice that has been inoculated with koji (a special bacterium) and allowed to ferment for several hours. It becomes delectably sweet and creamy and comes in several flavors, including plain, almond, and mocha. Amasake is used in making desserts and beverages. It makes cakes moist and light and also may be eaten plain or with fruit. Amasake can be found in the freezer section of most large natural foods stores.

Anasazi beans (*ah-nah-SAH-zee*)—Red-and-white-speckled Anasazi beans are considered the Native American bean; the name means "the ancient ones." They are a superior source of protein, iron, phosphorus, and thiamine and contain calcium and many other essential nutrients, too. Anasazi beans are unusually flavorful: sweeter and mealier than other beans. They are a tasty, colorful addition to any natural kitchen. Anasazis cook more rapidly than pintos, to which they are related.

Arame (*AH-rah-may*)—This is a mild-flavored, quick-cooking sea vegetable. Rinsed and soaked for 5 minutes, the thin, black strands of a small handful of arame will add an exotic note to any vegetable stir-fry. As with other sea vegetables, arame is rich in minerals, including calcium, iron, phosphorus, potassium, and iodine.

Arrowroot—The tuberous root of a tropical plant, arrowroot is dried and ground into a fine powder and used as a thickener. It may be substituted for cornstarch measure for measure. Many health-conscious cooks prefer arrowroot to cornstarch because it is produced by a fairly simple, traditional method, whereas cornstarch is chemically bleached and treated.

Baking powder—Most commercial baking powders contain aluminum, which is toxic. Rumford brand baking powder, which can be found in most supermarkets, along with those brands found in natural foods stores do not contain aluminum.

Barley—Thought to be the oldest cultivated grain, barley is available in several forms. Most grown in the United States is processed. The unprocessed grain has a thick hull and tough outer layers (called aleurone cells). While an asset for malting, these layers make cooking and digestion difficult. For this reason, barley is **pearled,** that is, scoured with abrasives. Arrowhead Mills pearls only some of the outer layers away, leaving most of the beneficial bran and germ intact; mass-market barleys are pearled up to six times, reducing the protein and vitamin content. Pearled barley can be added to casseroles, used to thicken soups or stews, or served alone.

Barley flakes are produced from grains of lightly pearled barley that are gently toasted, then flaked in a roller mill. They can be used like oat flakes (or oatmeal) or added to soups, casseroles, or bread recipes for the texture and pleasing taste of barley without the long cooking time.

Barley flour is wonderful in cakes, cookies, muffins, and quick breads. It gives a deliciously light and moist texture, combining beautifully with wheat or oat flour. Barley flour can be used in wheat-free diets, but it does contain some gluten and, therefore, shouldn't be eaten by persons with gluten allergies.

Black beans—The black (or **turtle**) bean is closely related to the kidney bean. Though the seed coat is black, the inside is white. Black beans contain high amounts of potassium and phosphorus and are also a good source of calcium and magnesium. Vitamins A, B_1, B_2, and niacin are also present. Black beans are excellent in soups and in Mexican dishes.

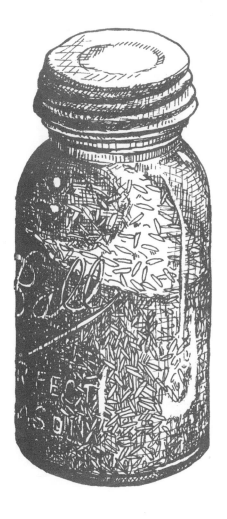

Brown rice—Rice is a staple for more than half the Earth's people. Brown rice is the whole rice kernel from which only the inedible hull has been removed. The bran layer is left intact, making brown rice higher in fiber, vitamins, and minerals than white rice. Because the oil in brown rice is in the surface bran layers, the rice should be stored in a cool, dry place (preferably under refrigeration).

Arrowhead Mills **long grain brown rice** is certified organic. It cooks to a firm, fluffy texture, and the grains remain separate. This texture and its mild, nutty flavor make it a good all-purpose rice. It's especially good in pilafs, rice salads, and as a bed for vegetable and bean dishes.

Though its ancestry may be traced to northern India (it's traditionally used in Indian cookery), **Basmati rice** is grown domestically in California and (by Arrowhead Mills) in Texas, Arkansas, and Louisiana. Basmati's special appeal lies in its exceptionally nutty flavor and enticing fragrance. Like other long grain brown rices, Basmati cooks up firm and fluffy and can be used in any recipe that calls for long or medium grain rice.

Medium grain brown rice cooks to a fluffy texture like long grain but is slightly more tender and has a nuttier, sweeter flavor. Medium grain rice is also a good all-purpose rice and works especially well in baked goods or as a stuffing.

The kernels of **short grain brown rice** are almost round and cook to a dense, chewy texture. It is sweeter than both long and medium grain brown rice and becomes sticky if cooked to more than just done. It's a good choice for rice puddings and may also be used in baked goods, stuffings, or Oriental dishes that are eaten with chopsticks.

Brown rice flour provides the taste and nutrition of brown rice in breads, cookies, muffins, and other baked goods. It contains no gluten and thus is tolerated by most people. Rice flour must be complemented by wheat flour in yeast-risen recipes.

Buckwheat—A traditional ingredient in Russian and Ukrainian cuisines, buckwheat is also used in French Canadian cooking. Buckwheat seeds are called **groats,** and when prepared, **kasha.** The groats are available raw (white) or toasted (brown). Buckwheat's hearty flavor is especially welcome during the winter months. Although not a cereal grain botanically, it is used as such and is similar in nutrients to wheat, with significant amounts of thiamine, riboflavin, calcium, and phosphorus.

Buckwheat flour is milled from whole, toasted buckwheat. It is relatively heavy, gluten-free, and most commonly used in making hearty buckwheat pancakes and waffles.

Bulgur (*BUL-gr*)—Bulgur wheat is whole grain wheat that has been partially cooked, dried, and then cracked. It has a delicious, nutty flavor and is very versatile and quick-cooking as well as nutritious. It is often used in Middle Eastern and European dishes, such as tabouli and pilafs.

Carob (*KAR-ub*)—Although carob does not taste exactly like chocolate, it is often used as a substitute. It contains less fat than chocolate, no caffeine, and because of its natural sweetness (unlike chocolate's natural bitterness) less sweetener is needed when carob is used in place of chocolate in a recipe. But carob is an excellent food in its own right. The rich, brown powder comes from grinding the dried pods of a Mediterranean locust tree. Carob is also sold as chips, but check the ingredients; some brands are made mostly of sugar and saturated fat.

Chick peas—Also called garbanzo beans or ceci, chick peas have long been popular in Middle Eastern and Mediterranean cuisines, as well as Indian cookery. When the cooked and mashed beans are mixed with tahini (sesame purée), garlic, lemon, and salt, they make an excellent high-protein, high-fiber dip or sandwich spread known as hummus. Chick peas are also excellent added to salads, mixed with grains, or served as a side dish. These large, round, yellow beans should be soaked overnight and take longer to cook than most other beans.

Garbanzo flour is made by toasting and then milling whole chick peas. It's great for making marvelous Mediterranean, Middle Eastern, and Indian dishes. The flour can be used in the same way as cooked and ground beans to create a host of quick, nutritious, and delicious dishes in minutes, such as instant hummus and falafel. Gluten-free and high in protein, garbanzo flour can be combined in small amounts with other flours in muffins and breads. Used alone, it is a good thickener for soups, stews, and sauces.

Concentrated fruit sweetener—Usually more than one type of fruit is combined to produce this syrup so that there is no predominant flavor. Concentrated fruit sweetener is sweeter than malt or rice syrup, but not as sweet as honey. It can be used measure for measure in recipes that call for a liquid sweetener.

I use Mystic Lake Dairy concentrated mixed-fruit sweetener, which is 30 percent fructose, 18 percent glucose, and 16 percent sucrose. Fructose is assimilated more slowly than glucose or sucrose, and it, therefore, has a more moderate effect on blood sugar levels and can be eaten by many who cannot eat other sugars.

Corn—As with other grains, corn comes in several forms that are found in natural foods stores. **Corn grits,** which are coarsely ground from white or yellow corn, are a versatile food known mainly in the South, but they are a delicious and nourishing addition to any meal, no matter where they are served. Grits make a superb breakfast dish or can be included in casseroles, breads, or burgers.

Milled from whole yellow corn, **yellow cornmeal** has been one of Arrowhead Mills' best-known and well-liked products for more than twenty years. It is used mainly for making delicious breads, polenta, and breakfast porridge.

Native Americans of the Hopi tribe were instrumental in developing blue corn, now available in natural foods stores as **blue cornmeal.** This colorful and flavorful food is open-pollinated (not a hybrid) and contains 20 percent more protein than yellow or white corn. It has a slightly sweeter and nuttier flavor than regular cornmeal. The satiny-smooth interior of the blue corn kernel and the deep blue layers of beneficial bran add up to a colorful, versatile, nutritious food. Use it like yellow or white cornmeal.

High-lysine cornmeal is ground from a special variety of corn that has 30 to 40 percent more lysine than regular corn. It has a better balance of some of the limiting amino acids (lysine, tryptophan, and methionine) than milk, beef, or soybeans. Additional bonuses are its

naturally sweet taste, slightly crunchy texture, nutty flavor, and high fiber content. As easy to use as regular cornmeal, high-lysine cornmeal's nutritional excellence, intriguing aroma, and special taste make it a very exciting food.

Couscous (*COOSS-COOSS*)—A staple of Tunisian and Moroccan cuisine, couscous is a light, quick-cooking wheat product similar to pasta. It makes an excellent vegetable bed or salad ingredient. Until recently in the United States, the only couscous available was highly refined. Now, however, whole wheat couscous may be purchased in natural foods stores.

Date sugar—This natural sweetener is made simply by grinding dried dates to a consistency similar to that of coarse brown sugar. Less sweet than sucanat, maple syrup, or honey but sweeter than malt or rice syrup, date sugar gives a rich moistness to baked goods.

Egg replacer—Vegetarian egg replacer is a white powder made from potato starch, tapioca flour, leavening, and carbohydrate gum. It contains no fat and is mixed with water to use in recipes as a substitute for eggs. I have successfully used it in veggie loaves and burgers, as well as cakes, muffins, and other baked goods.

Flaxseed—Flaxseed contains several essential nutrients, including phosphorus and calcium. The seeds are usually added to bread doughs, cooked cereals, or muesli. Though they have little flavor, they are commonly used because, being mucilaginous, they aid in digestion and are somewhat laxative.

Fruit, dried—Adding dried fruit to baked goods, desserts, and cereals is a good way to sweeten them without adding refined sugars. Dried fruits also make an excellent, high-fiber, energy-rich snack. Just make sure to brush your teeth after eating dried fruits because they stick to the teeth and cause cavities.

Most of the dried fruits in the supermarket and even some in natural foods stores are processed with sulfur dioxide, a poisonous gas. Although using it to treat food is considered harmless by the FDA, it is unnecessary because its only function is cosmetic: It helps keep the fruit from turning brown. Dried fruits are also sometimes treated with potassium sorbate or sorbic acid, or they are dipped in sugar to keep them soft and fresh.

For untreated, dried fruits, read the label carefully. If you are buying in bulk from a natural foods store, ask how the fruit has been processed.

Garbanzo—See **Chick peas.**

Gluten (*GLOO-tn*)—Wheat gluten is the natural protein derived from wheat. It is basically wheat flour with the starch removed. The addition of gluten to your bread dough will produce consistent, uniform, well-risen loaves. Arrowhead Mills Vital Wheat Gluten is extracted from wheat through a water-washing procedure. The process is entirely mechanical with no chemicals used or added. **Gluten flour** is refined wheat flour with some gluten added. Gluten flour is much less concentrated than Vital Wheat Gluten and more is needed to yield the same effect.

Gluten can also be mixed with liquid and seasoning, kneaded, and then cooked to form seitan, a meat-style vegetable protein.

Groats—See **Buckwheat.**

Honey—Honey has long been regarded as a health food. Today, however, most nutritionists maintain that being primarily glucose, it is no better than white sugar. But honey contains traces of vitamins and minerals, which sugar does not. Sugar, brown or white, is the result of much chemical and mechanical refining, whereas honey is a natural product. Honey is sweeter than cane sugar, maple syrup, molasses, malt, date sugar, and sucanat and, therefore, less of it will create the same degree of sweetness in a recipe. Lighter colors of honey, such as clover or orange blossom, are usually milder tasting than the darker wildflower or buckwheat honeys and are usually better to use in cooking.

Kanten (*KAN-ten*)—A jelled dessert of Japanese origin made from agar-agar, kanten can include fruit or adzuki beans. Served chilled, kanten is a cool, refreshing alternative to conventional gelatin desserts.

Kasha (*KAH-shah*)—See **Buckwheat.**

Koji (*KOH-jee*)—A bacteria culture (similar to yogurt culture) that is used to make miso and amasake, koji is sold in larger natural foods stores. Instructions for using koji are included on the package.

Kombu (*KOM-BU*)—This wide, thick, dark green sea vegetable is sold in strips about six inches long. A strip can be rinsed and added to a pot of soup, stew, rice, beans, or any other slow-cooking dish. When the kombu is tender, remove it from the pot, chop it, and stir it back in. Kombu more than doubles in size when cooked, and, like all sea vegetables, it enriches whatever it is cooked with.

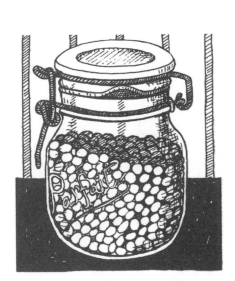

Kudzu—A white starch made from the roots of the wild kudzu vine, kudzu is used as a thickening agent for sauces and puddings in the same way as cornstarch and arrowroot are. Macrobiotic cooks prefer it because of its claimed medicinal qualities. However, it is more expensive than arrowroot or cornstarch and somewhat more difficult to use because it comes in chunks.

Lentils—The more familiar **green lentil** is one of the oldest foods known to humans. Lentils are nutritionally comparable to most other beans; that is, they are high in protein, phosphorus, potassium, and iron. They also contain zinc and copper, as well as B vitamins and vitamin A. Lentils are good in a variety of soups, stews, casseroles, loaves, stuffings, and patties. Lentils cook more quickly than most other legumes and are also very easy to sprout.

Red lentils are sometimes called "the beans of the future," in reference to their growing popularity. Just 100 grams of red lentils supply the same amount of protein as 134 grams of beef, without the fat and cholesterol. Red lentils cook faster than green—in about 15 to 20 minutes.

Malt—A natural sweetener made from sprouted barley, malt can be purchased either as a syrup or a powder. Malt is less sweet than honey, maple syrup, sucanat, or molasses, and is preferred by many persons because it is metabolized relatively slowly and has a rich flavor, like caramel. Liquid malt can be substituted measure for measure for honey or molasses, though the results will be much less sweet. To substitute malt syrup for maple syrup, add liquid to the recipe because malt syrup is much thicker than maple syrup.

Maple syrup—A natural sweetener with an exquisite flavor, maple syrup is made in the spring by collecting and boiling down the sap of the sugar maple tree. Maple syrup is a very concentrated food—forty gallons of sap are needed to make one gallon of syrup. Maple syrup may be substituted measure for measure for honey or molasses in recipes.

Millet—One of the oldest foods known to humans, millet offers an excellent balance of proteins. It is higher in B vitamins than most other grains, and is also high in iron, potassium, and calcium. The most alkaline of grains, millet is also one of the most easily digested. It is used in many of the same ways as rice, though it is fluffier and cooks in half the time.

Millet flour contains no gluten and, therefore, can be used by persons with gluten allergies. It may be used in pancakes, muffins, cookies, and other quick breads.

Mirin (*MEER-in*)—A sweet Japanese cooking wine made from rice, mirin can be used to flavor sauces, marinades, and desserts.

Miso (*MEE-soh*)—A savory fermented paste that offers concentrated nutrition as well as flavor, miso is made from soybeans and/or grains, sea salt, and koji. High in sodium, miso is usually eaten in small quantities, traditionally as a base for soups and sauces. It can also be used to season pâtés, dips, salad dressings, and all sorts of other dishes.

The numerous varieties of miso, commonly made from rice, barley, or soybeans, range from a sweet white or yellow through savory reds to a dark and pungent chocolate brown. Yellow or white miso is mild and does not alter the color of foods that it is mixed with. It is especially nice for seasoning light-colored dishes, cream soups, and mock dairy dishes. Dark miso is fermented longer and is a bit saltier and stronger flavored. It is good in hearty winter soups and in grain dishes. I use white (rice) miso and red (barley) miso most often, because I like their mild flavor.

Miso is highly esteemed in Japan both for its culinary uses and for its medicinal properties. (Miso has been found to contain protease inhibitors, which are believed to suppress the action of the enzymes suspected of promoting cancer.) Miso soup is a traditional Japanese breakfast, and macrobiotic healers recommend easily digestible miso broth for a variety of ailments. To preserve the benefits of the "friendly bacteria" and enzymes contained in unpasteurized miso (they aid in digestion), it should be added at the end of cooking.

Natto miso is a deliciously sweet and salty condiment made from barley, soybeans, koji, kombu, sea salt, and ginger. As the fermentation time for natto miso is shorter than that for other types of miso, the grains and strips of kombu that it contains are still whole and not broken down into a paste. Natto miso is usually served alongside salads or other dishes. It can also be lightly spread over bread for use in sandwiches or added to stir-fries and grain dishes. Natto miso is not used as a soup base.

Muesli (*MYOU-slee*)—This cereal, consisting of mixed grains, fruits, and nuts, was designed by a Swiss doctor as an ideal breakfast. The raw grains are soaked in water or milk to soften them rather than being baked with added oil, as is granola.

Mung beans—These small, round, green beans are wonderful for sprouting or cooking. They are most commonly known in their sprouted form as Chinese bean sprouts. These can be added to salads and sandwiches or used as a vegetable in Oriental dishes. Raw

mung bean sprouts are a good source of vitamins A and C and some B vitamins. They also contain potassium, phosphorus, calcium, iron, and zinc.

Natto miso (*NAH-toh MEE-soh*)—See **Miso.**

Nuts—Nuts are good sources of protein, some B vitamins, vitamin E, iron, calcium, and phosphorus. Rich in fat, nuts should be eaten in moderation. In natural foods cooking, nuts are employed in a variety of ways. Not only are they delightful in baked goods and desserts, they can also be used to build main dishes such as veggie burgers and meatless loaves. Nuts are also interesting in soups, salads, sauces, and beverages. Always refrigerate shelled nuts, because they will go rancid very quickly in a warm place. When nuts become rancid, they are both bad-tasting and bad for you.

Any nut can be ground into **nut butter**. Peanut (not actually a nut, but rather a legume) butter is the most familiar, but that is because of the product supermarkets sell in great quantities: a blend of peanuts, salt, sugar, and hydrogenated vegetable oil. Arrowhead Mills peanut butter consists only of unblanched, sun-dried Valencia peanuts, which are grown on composted soil without herbicides or pesticides on the high plains of Eastern New Mexico. This and other nut butters are good with bread or toast and can also be used in sauces, pâtés, and main dishes. Natural nut butters tend to separate into oil and solids, but refrigerating them after mixing will minimize this separation while keeping the oil from turning rancid.

Oats—Oats are highest in protein of all common grains and are rich in eight vitamins as well as iron, calcium, and phosphorus. They are high in dietary fiber and contain a natural antioxidant that delays rancidity. **Whole oat groats** can be used in place of barley in slow-cooking soups and stews, or even used like rice. Cooking times are about the same.

Oat bran is the edible outer covering of the whole oat groat. Recognized as one of the richest sources of fiber, Arrowhead Mills oat bran is 22 percent dietary fiber, one-third of which is soluble. (Soluble fiber helps to lower cholesterol.) It is easily added to muffins and is a good-tasting, quick hot cereal. Oat bran can also be used in the same ways as wheat bran.

Oat flakes are made from whole oats that have had only their hulls removed: they are briefly dry-heated, then run through rollers to flatten them. Arrowhead Mills oat flakes are thicker than most rolled oats or oatmeal and are less gummy when cooked.

The delicious flavor of **oat flour** makes it ideal for a variety of uses, from baked goods to veggie burgers and meatless loaves. It gives a moistness and sweetness to breads, pancakes, cakes, muffins and cookies. It is wonderful in pie crusts. The natural antioxidant in oats makes baked goods made with oat flour stay fresh longer.

Oils—Look for oils that have been mechanically extracted by low heat; they're usually labeled "unrefined" and are of the best quality. Cheaper oils, processed in huge quantities, are extracted by chemical solvents and/or very high heat, which destroys flavor. Avoid oils, especially generic "vegetable oils," that are odorless, flavorless, and colorless; they have been highly filtered, bleached, and chemically treated.

Arrowhead Mills offers seven fresh oils: canola, flaxseed, hazelnut, olive, safflower, sesame, and sunflower. They are made from certified organic nuts or seeds that are pressed slowly using a process that protects the oils from damaging light, heat, and oxygen during manufacturing. No chemicals are used.

My favorite oil for seasoning and gentle sautéing is olive oil. Hazelnut oil lends a special gourmet flavor to a salad. Safflower, sesame (light, not toasted), sunflower, peanut, and canola oils have high smoking points and therefore are good for stir-frying as well as baking and general uses. Dark or toasted sesame oil is strong-flavored and used as a seasoning. All unrefined oils should be kept in the refrigerator. Olive oil will solidify in the refrigerator, but it will reliquefy in just a few minutes in a warm place.

Peanut butter—See **Nut butters.**

Peas, dried—The familiar **split green pea** contains more than 20 percent protein and is highly digestible. It cooks to a mush and is best suited for soups, stews, and stick-to-the-ribs purées. **Split yellow peas,** which taste milder than green peas, can be used in the same ways.

Pinto beans—This spotted pink and brown, mild-flavored bean, traditional to Southwest cookery, is high in phosphorus, calcium, iron, and potassium. It also contains a fair amount of B vitamins. Pintos are a good source of protein, especially when served with grains, and can be used in any bean dish.

Quinoa (*KEEN-wa*)—A small, hearty, disc-shaped grain, brown to gold in color, quinoa is one of the finest sources of protein in the entire vegetable kingdom—an almost ideal balance of amino acids, along with a good complement of calcium, phosphorus, iron, B vitamins, and vitamin E. Cooked, it remains granular rather than becoming mushy and has an attractively nutty taste. Quinoa can be

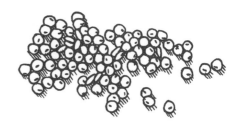

used in casseroles, as a bed for vegetable and bean dishes, or in place of rice in many recipes. Quinoa cooks quickly, in 15 to 20 minutes, and should be kept on hand as the base for a quick and nutritious meal.

Rice Dream—This is the brand name of a white, mild-flavored beverage with a consistency similar to skim milk. Made from organic brown rice, safflower oil, and sea salt, Rice Dream is delicious on cereal and may be used in some recipes to replace soymilk or dairy milk; however, it is much lower in protein and tends to curdle when heated.

Rice syrup—This is a thick, sweet syrup made from rice, sometimes with the addition of barley malt. It is made by fermenting the rice with koji, straining it, and then boiling the remaining liquid until it thickens. Rice syrup is less sweet than honey. Like malt, it is metabolized more slowly than other sweeteners. Rice syrup may be used to replace honey in some recipes, but the end result will not be as sweet. I like it in pecan pie, cookies, and breakfast cereal. Rice syrup is often called **yinnie syrup**.

Rye—Rye has a unique taste, somewhat heartier than wheat, yet its nutritional value is quite similar. **Whole rye** may be cooked or sprouted. **Rye flour** is second only to wheat in world popularity for bread baking, and it is the most popular in Scandinavia, Russia, and Germany. Rye flour can be used alone or in conjunction with other flours. However, its gluten content is low, and it does not rise well without the addition of wheat flour (about 30 percent) or wheat gluten.

The distinctive taste and good nutrition of rye can also be enjoyed in the form of **rye flakes.** Dry heat softens the grains so that they can be rolled into flakes. Use rye flakes in granolas or in cookie and bread recipes, or cook them like oatmeal for a breakfast cereal. Cooking time is about the same.

Seitan (*SAY-tan*)—This is cooked wheat gluten, sold in the form of patties, chunks, or slices that have a texture remarkably like that of meat. Dough made from hard wheat is kneaded and rinsed, leaving an elastic mass of gluten, which is then cooked in broth.

Seitan can be used in stews, sandwiches, and stir-fries, or it can be ground in a food processor to be used in chili, burgers, and loaves just like ground meat. It will keep for about one week in the refrigerator, or it can be frozen.

Arrowhead Mills now has a seitan mix that is easy to use and more economical than ready-made seitan (see pages 184–185).

Sesame seeds, hulled—Arrowhead Mills sesame seeds are mechanically hulled and chemical-free: no salt, lyes, bleaches, or chemicals have been applied to these certified organic seeds, nor have they been subjected to high heat. Sesame seeds contain a wealth of nutrition, including protein and calcium. They add a nutty sweetness to baked goods and meatless dishes and are commonly used as a garnish.

Sesame seeds are used to make gomashio, which is a delicious condiment that is used in macrobiotic cooking. To make gomashio, place eight parts sesame seeds to one part sea salt in a dry skillet, stir over medium-high heat until the seeds are toasted, and grind the mixture in a blender. Store in a covered container in the refrigerator, and use to sprinkle over vegetables, salads, and grain or bean dishes. See also **Tahini**.

Shoyu (*SHO-YOU*)—See **Tamari**.

Silken tofu—See **Tofu**.

Soybeans—The soybean is the only legume that offers what is considered a nearly complete protein balance—that is, all of the eight essential amino acids in close-to-ideal proportions. Soybeans must be soaked overnight before cooking, and they take longer than other legumes to cook—at least three hours after soaking.

A wonderful way to use soybeans is in the form of **soymilk**, which is available in unrefrigerated cardboard containers. *The Book of Tofu* by William Shurtleff and Akiko Aoyagi tells how to make soymilk and tofu at home.

Soybeans also make delicious sprouts; however, they must be rinsed more often than other sprouts because they tend to mold. (For information on sprouting, see page 74.)

Sucanat (*SOO-ka-nat*)—This sweetener is made from the juice of organically grown sugar cane that has been dehydrated to form a powder with the taste and consistency of brown sugar. Unlike refined sugar, sucanat is a whole food. It is not quite as sweet as sugar or honey, but is sweeter than malt or date sugar. Sucanat is excellent for making cakes and cookies. Substitute sucanat for brown sugar measure for measure in any recipe.

Sun-dried tomatoes—The sun-dried tomatoes that I call for in this book are not preserved in oil, making them lower in fat and less expensive. Use dried tomato halves that are sold in cellophane bags (I use the Sonoma brand, found in natural foods stores), and tomato bits that come in small jars. If you don't have tomato bits, just cut dried tomato halves with scissors or grind them in a blender.

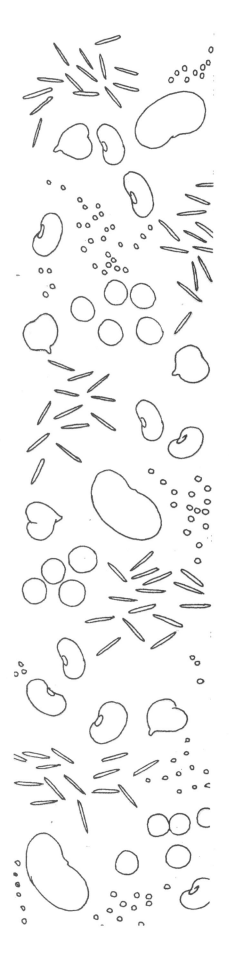

Sun-dried tomatoes and tomato bits add a wonderful richness to soups, stews, dips, and sauces. Their flavor is much more concentrated than that of fresh or canned tomatoes. They also absorb liquid, which makes them a handy thickening agent for some recipes.

Sunflower seeds—Sunflower seeds are perhaps the most versatile of all the nuts and seeds, adding a mild flavor and pleasant crunch to almost any recipe. They are good raw or roasted, whole or ground into a meal or butter. Sunflower seeds may be substituted for nuts in any recipe.

"Sun seeds" are said to be a good survival food because they contain so many important nutrients. They contain about 27 percent protein and 50 percent fat, most of which is unsaturated. They also contain beneficial amounts of calcium, phosphorus, and iron. They are good sources of several B vitamins and vitamins A, D, and E.

Tahini, sesame (*ta-HEE-nee*)—This is a raw purée of hulled sesame seeds. Arrowhead Mills tahini consists of organically grown sesame seeds that are gathered by hand, mechanically hulled, and slowly ground without caustic sodas, salts, chemicals, or additives of any kind. Tahini can be used in Middle Eastern dishes, meatless loaves and burgers, spreads, sauces, and desserts.

Tamari (*ta-MAH-ree*)—Also called wheat-free tamari, this natural Japanese soy sauce has a dark color and rich flavor. **Shoyu** (which is often misnamed tamari) contains wheat but otherwise is similar to tamari. The two can be used interchangeably. Both tamari and shoyu are fermented in wooden kegs for as long as two years. The cheap mass-market soy sauces can in no way compare with the fine flavor of the real thing. Tamari is relatively high in sodium, and should be used in moderation.

Teff—Teff is a tiny brown seed of Ethiopian origin, now grown in North Dakota. The smallest grain, it is high in protein and quite versatile. Uncooked teff can be added to many baked goods or substituted for part of the seeds, nuts, or small grains called for in a recipe. Cooked teff (one part teff in three parts water, simmered for 15 minutes) is gelatinous and adds body to puddings and refrigerator pies. It is an excellent thickener for soups, stews, and gravies. Its mild, slightly molasseslike sweetness makes teff easy to use. Teff pudding, made with cooked whole teff, silken tofu, and sweetener, is deliciously light.

Tempeh (*TEM-pay*)—A traditional food from Indonesia, tempeh is made from partially cooked, split, and hulled soybeans that are inoculated with a special bacterium and incubated for about twenty-four hours. During the incubation, a white, fluffy mold develops around the beans, holding them together in a slab. Tempeh has a firm but tender texture and a very pleasant, somewhat tangy flavor. It is high in protein and easy to digest.

The only drawback to tempeh is that it is very perishable and must be used within a few days after it is made, or it can be frozen. Unlike tofu, tempeh must be cooked before it is eaten. It is not necessary to thaw frozen tempeh before cooking it in most recipes. Cook tempeh by pan-frying, baking, broiling, grilling, or steaming.

Tofu (*TOH-FOO*)—A staple of both Chinese and Japanese cuisines, tofu has become very popular in the West in recent years. It is high in protein, low in calories, rich in calcium, easy to digest, and convenient to use. Tofu can be transformed into an amazing variety of scrumptious dishes, from protein-rich entrées to creamy desserts. If you have tried tofu and found it unappealing, try a few of the recipes found in this book and see if you don't change your mind.

Tofu is made by soaking whole soybeans for eight to ten hours, then grinding them into a purée. This purée is pressed through a cloth to extract the soymilk from the pulp. The milk is cooked and a coagulant (traditionally nigari, which is extracted from sea salt) is added to curdle it. The curds are carefully ladled into a mold, where they are pressed until firm. The resulting tofu is stored in cold water.

It is not necessary to make your own tofu; delicious tofu, in several textures—soft, firm, and extra-firm—is available in the produce section at supermarkets and natural foods stores. When refrigerated, it will keep for a week or more; change the water daily. Old tofu develops an unpleasant, sour odor. Very fresh tofu is especially mild and sweet.

Silken tofu is a very soft and custardlike tofu coagulated with calcium sulfate rather than with nigari. It is sold in cardboard containers and does not have to be refrigerated until it is opened. Silken tofu also comes in three textures. It is milder in flavor than regular tofu and is used in many recipes in this book. However, if a recipe calls for "tofu," use regular tofu; when silken tofu is to be used, I call for it specifically.

Tofu-Parmesan tastes a lot like dairy Parmesan cheese. Use it whenever you would use dairy Parmesan.

T.V.P. (textured vegetable protein)—This high-protein convenience food is made from soybeans. It is quick and easy to use. Added to spaghetti sauces, chili, and sloppy Joe mixes, it gives the texture of ground meat along with its protein boost.

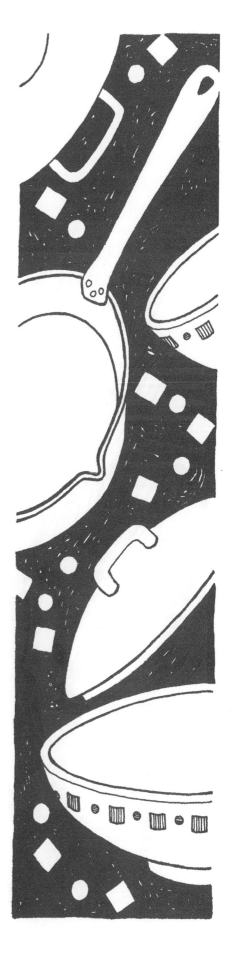

Umeboshi (*oo-meh-BOH-shee*)—This is a salty pickled plum used as a condiment in Japanese cuisine. It is tasty in sauces and salad dressings, and it can be purchased either in the form of whole, unpitted plums or as a paste. It may seem expensive when you buy it, but a little goes a long way.

Vinegar—Some nutrition books say that vinegar is a healthy food; others say that it isn't. I don't know whom to believe, but I'm sure that in moderation it cannot be bad. The word vinegar comes from the French words *vin* (wine) and *aigre* (sour) and it has been used for thousands of years. Rice vinegar is made from fermented rice, cider vinegar from apple juice, wine vinegar from red or white wine, and balsamic vinegar from sweet wine. Although each has its own special flavor and aroma, different vinegars can be used interchangeably in most recipes.

Vital Wheat Gluten—See **Gluten**.

Wakame (*wah-KAH-may*)—This long, thin, green sea vegetable is used in making soups, salads, and vegetable dishes. High in protein, iron, and magnesium, wakame has a sweet taste and a delicate texture. It is perfect in miso soup.

Wheat—Several common varieties of wheat in a number of different forms are available in natural foods stores. **Wheat berries** are the whole grain. They can be ground into flour to use in baking; sprouted or cooked like rice and used in salads, casseroles, croquettes, and vegetable loaves; or added to bread dough for extra texture. See the recipe for Easy Cooked Cereal on page 35. See also **Bulgur**, **Couscous**, and **Gluten**.

Wheat bran, the outer layer or coating on the grain, is generally scraped off during the process of making white flour. It is usually available in bulk at natural foods stores. Wheat bran includes 40 percent dietary fiber and can be substituted for part of the flour in muffins and other baked goods.

Wheat germ is the embryo of the whole wheat grain. It contains major amounts of the B vitamins and vitamin E as well as magnesium, potassium, phosphorus, manganese, copper, zinc, and iodine. Refrigerate raw wheat germ to protect its natural oil from heat and oxidation. Wheat germ, either raw or toasted, can be eaten alone as a breakfast cereal, combined with other grains, or used in a wide variety of recipes, including breads, cookies, and casseroles.

Stone-ground whole wheat flour is relatively coarse, the result of an ancient technique that employs large, granite millstones and retains more nutrients, flavor, and texture than milling with steel blades. Stone-ground wheat is typically a hard red wheat, high in gluten, and therefore best suited for leavened breads. It is sometimes called **bread flour** to distinguish it from **pastry flour,** which is fine-textured, low-gluten flour made from soft wheat. The lighter consistency is preferable for making pastries, cakes, cookies, crackers, and similar baked goods.

Arrowhead Mills **unbleached white flour** is a high-quality all-purpose flour made from choice, hard red winter wheat. Although refined (stripped of the bran and germ), no bleaching, maturing, or preserving agents have been added. Like all white wheat flour, this flour is vitamin-enriched. I do not use unbleached white flour frequently, but it can be useful for the inexperienced cook and for persons on a transitional diet. If you do not like baked goods made from whole grain flour, try the recipes in this book substituting unbleached white flour for half the whole grain flour called for.

Yeast, dry active—Used for leavening, dry active yeast is composed of dormant living microorganisms. Moisture and warmth activate them. Fresh cake yeast may be substituted for dry active yeast tablespoon for tablespoon. Inactive food yeasts, such as torula, brewer's, and nutritional yeasts, have no leavening power.

Yeast, nutritional—An excellent food supplement, nutritional yeast is very rich in B vitamins and protein, but low in calories. Like all other yeasts, nutritional yeast is composed of microorganisms; unlike those of other yeasts, however, they are inactive and safe to eat without cooking. Nutritional yeast has a mild cheeselike or nutty flavor. Don't confuse it with brewer's yeast or torula yeast, both of which taste terrible, or with dry active yeast or fresh cake yeast, which will cause great discomfort if eaten raw.

Used in your daily cooking, nutritional yeast adds flavor and nutrients to soups, sauces, stews, mock meat dishes, and salads. It is surprisingly good sprinkled over green salad.

A NATURAL FOODS SHOPPING LIST

An Introductory Sampler

Starting to cook with natural foods can be intimidating because so many ingredients are unfamiliar. Not all, of course. Anyone who cooks surely has used such natural food basics as olive oil, cornmeal, and dried peas or beans. To give you a start trying these recipes, I have made a list for the first-time natural foods shopper. With these supplies you will be able to make many of the recipes in this book, including those in the introductory sampler at left. They may seem expensive at first, but most of the foods you buy will last a long time. Gradually you can add new flours, grains, beans, seeds, oils, and nuts, as well as try different tofus, seitans, tempehs, and misos. Before long, you'll have a well-stocked natural kitchen.

Brown rice—There are several varieties of brown rice. You may want to start with long grain or brown Basmati and later try the different textures of the shorter grain varieties.

Millet—Millet is light and mild-flavored, a nice alternative to rice. Make sure to buy the hulled kind, because unhulled millet (sold for sprouting) doesn't cook well.

Whole grain pasta—Read the labels; not all the pastas sold in natural foods stores are whole grain. Buy a different kind of pasta each time you shop until you find the ones that you like best.

Whole wheat flour—Get both kinds: bread flour and pastry flour. If you use whole wheat bread flour to make pastries, you will probably be disappointed with how heavy they turn out. Use it to make yeast bread. Later, you may want to try barley and oat flours; both kinds make delicious baked goods.

Oat flakes—This is a basic and inexpensive staple that you will probably use a lot of.

Dried beans—These have a long shelf life and are inexpensive, so start with two or three kinds, such as garbanzos, red lentils, and black beans. Every week, add a new one until you have a nice selection.

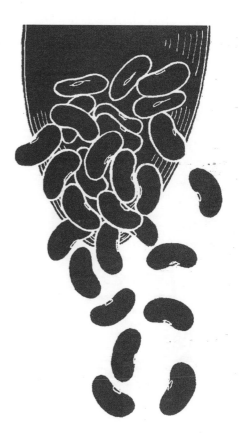

Oil—A good extra-virgin olive oil is not only a healthful oil to use (rich in monounsaturated fats), it adds a wonderful seasoning to many dishes. For general purposes, use a lighter, unrefined safflower, sunflower, or canola oil. I like to buy a different oil every time I need some. Keep all unrefined oils refrigerated.

Tahini and peanut butter—These can be used in many ways. Stir each to blend the separated oil, then refrigerate to keep them from separating again.

Tofu—Don't confuse regular with silken, but do try both in the various textures available. Buy no more than a pound of the regular at a time, keep it refrigerated, and use it within a week. Silken tofu keeps unrefrigerated in its unopened aseptic container. Once you open it, keep any unused tofu, regular or silken, submerged in water and refrigerated. Change the water daily.

Miso—Buy a yellow or white miso that has not been pasteurized. It will contain the "friendly bacteria" that aid in digestion. After you have tried the light misos, buy a darker soy miso and taste the difference.

Soymilk—You can use soymilk any way you use dairy milk. But you can stock up on soymilk because, unlike dairy milk, it has a very long shelf life (stamped on the aseptic container). Refrigerate it after opening. For general purposes, buy an unflavored variety. (If you buy carob or vanilla flavor, your white sauce or cream soup will taste terrible.)

Tamari—I usually use wheat-free tamari because I like the rich flavor. Buy a large bottle; you'll use it often, yet it will last.

Sucanat—Or one of the other natural sweeteners.

Sea salt—A pound of sea salt will last a long time.

A selection of bulk herbs and spices—Most natural foods stores have a wonderful selection of bulk herbs at surprisingly low prices. Basil, bay leaves, thyme, sage, rosemary, oregano, savory, cinnamon, cayenne pepper, curry powder, cumin, and chili powder will get you started. Stock up with small amounts; they go a long way but lose their flavor over time.

Produce—Buy whatever is in season and whatever looks the freshest. Be sure to include onions, garlic, potatoes, and organically grown carrots. To maintain the freshest supply, buy only enough to last until your next shopping trip.

STORING NATURAL FOODS

How you store your natural foods affects how well they retain their nutrients. Listed below are some tips.

- Keep all unrefined oils in the refrigerator. Unrefined oils turn rancid very quickly at warm temperatures. Rancid oils taste and smell terrible and are unhealthy.

- Whole grains naturally contain oil. If the grain is left in unbroken kernels (such as whole grains of wheat, rye, millet, and oats), it may be kept in tightly covered jars in the cupboard. Whole grains that have been cracked, rolled, or ground into flour, meal, grits, or flakes should be refrigerated because the oil, now exposed to oxygen, can easily turn rancid. Brown rice should also be refrigerated because its oils are in the bran layer, near the surface of the grain.

- Nuts, seeds, and nut and seed butters also contain oils and should be kept refrigerated.

- If you buy bulk herbs in small paper bags, transfer them to glass jars with tight-fitting lids when you get home and keep them from light and heat. Otherwise, they'll quickly lose their flavor.

- Bulk tofu should be immersed in water in a covered container and kept in the refrigerator. If you change the water every day or so, tofu will last up to a week or longer if it is really fresh when you buy it. Tofu sold fresh in individually wrapped plastic packages should be refrigerated and then placed in a bowl of water after the package has been opened. Silken tofu that is sold in small cardboard containers may be kept in the cupboard, but after you open the package, store any remaining silken tofu as you do regular tofu.

- Cooked beans and grains will keep in a covered container in the refrigerator for about one week if they are lightly salted (or seasoned with tamari). Cooked beans can also be frozen. Freeze them in 2-cup portions in a freezer bag or plastic container.

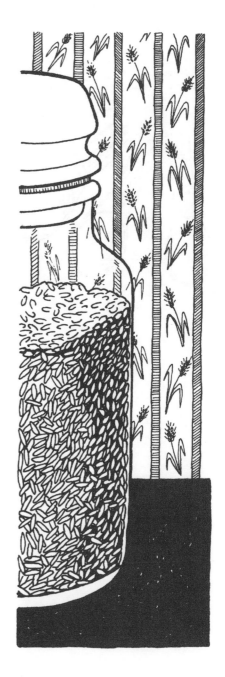

Cooked grains do not freeze well. Having cooked beans and grains on hand will cut down on the time you spend preparing meals.

- Tempeh is usually sold frozen because it is very perishable. Thawed tempeh will keep in the refrigerator three or four days at most.

- Whole grain breads and baked goods that do not contain preservatives also need to be refrigerated, or better yet, frozen, if you are not using them immediately.

- It is almost impossible to keep everything you need in one small refrigerator. Storing natural foods is easier with a large or a second refrigerator.

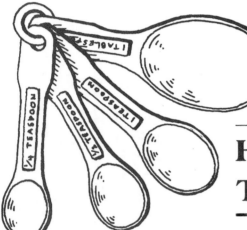

HOW TO FOLLOW THE RECIPES

Here are some tips that will help you successfully follow the recipes found in this book. Best to read them before you start, especially if you are new to natural foods cooking.

- Preheat the oven, except to bake yeast breads.

- If a recipe calls for a cooked grain, and you don't know how to cook it, look up the directions beginning on page 152.

- The cooking times for dried beans can vary according to the age of the beans and the water that you use. Beans take longer to cook in hard water. Other factors that may cause slight variations are the pot that you cook them in and the temperature at which they are cooked. Cook beans until they are tender so that they are easily digestible. There's more about using beans, including approximate times for cooking various kinds, beginning on page 168.

- The cooking time for vegetables can also vary depending on the age of the vegetables, the size you cut them, the exact temperature at which you cook them, and the pan you cook them in. So rather than watching the clock when you cook vegetables, watch the vegetables!

- To save time, cook up a large quantity of beans and grains once or twice a week. When a recipe calls for cooked rice or beans, it will take less time to prepare if these ingredients are already cooked.

- In most recipes, different types of cooked beans can be substituted for each other. It will change the recipe somewhat, but the results will usually be good.

- Except for parsley, garlic, and ginger, and unless otherwise indicated, the herbs used in the recipes are dried; they're more readily available. In substituting fresh herbs for dry, you can sometimes be quite generous. For example, if a recipe calls for 1 teaspoon of dry basil or dill weed, you could use as much as 1/4 cup of chopped, fresh basil or dill weed. Other herbs, such as thyme or rosemary, are stronger flavored and should be used more sparingly. To be safe, try substituting 1 tablespoon of fresh, minced herbs for 1 teaspoon of dried herbs, then taste the recipe and add more if you wish.

- For pancakes, veggie burgers, and sautéed tofu or tempeh dishes, it is possible to reduce the quantity of oil by using nonstick sprays or a nonstick skillet. You may also use nonstick sprays, instead of greasing the pan, for baked goods.

- When a recipe calls for an egg, you can replace it either with a vegetarian egg replacer (available at natural foods stores) or two egg whites.

- As a substitute for soymilk, you may use dairy milk or nut milk in any recipe. Rice beverage can be used in some recipes, but it tends to separate when heated.

- For blending or grinding ingredients, sometimes a blender is best; other times a food processor is better, though often, either will work. I like to use a blender for making nut milks, sauces, and purées that need to be very smooth. A blender seems to yield a finer texture than a food processor, and is handier for blending or grinding small quantities. A food processor blends larger quantities of food, and it grinds and mixes foods, such as dried fruits

or seitan, that a blender cannot grind. A food processor also chops and grates foods, though I rarely use it for this. Where it makes a difference, the recipe will indicate which one to use.

- When a recipe calls for sun-dried tomatoes, do not use those that are preserved in oil and sold in jars. They are expensive and high in fat. Use the dry ones that come in a plastic bag.

- When a recipe calls for barley flour and oat flour, you may substitute whole wheat pastry flour, and vice versa, although baked goods made entirely from barley or oat flour may be crumbly.

- You can make oat flour by grinding steel-cut oats or oat flakes in a blender.

- To make whole grain bread crumbs, just tear up a slice of whole grain bread (stale, toasted, or fresh) and grind it in a blender or food processor. Stale bread may be ground into crumbs and frozen to use later.

- If a recipe calls for sesame oil, do not use toasted sesame oil unless specified. Toasted sesame oil is very strong-flavored and used mainly as a seasoning.

- It is impossible to make dishes that suit everyone's tastes. So feel free to experiment. Add more salt, tamari, or miso if the dish seems bland to you, or decrease the amount to taste; it's healthier to get used to less salt. Also try substituting vegetables for one another, or add or subtract garlic, herbs, and spices.

2. BREAKFAST

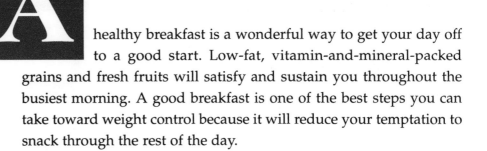

A healthy breakfast is a wonderful way to get your day off to a good start. Low-fat, vitamin-and-mineral-packed grains and fresh fruits will satisfy and sustain you throughout the busiest morning. A good breakfast is one of the best steps you can take toward weight control because it will reduce your temptation to snack through the rest of the day.

A breakfast of whole grains and fruits is quick and easy to prepare, too. Many types of hot porridge will cook in 5 to 10 minutes. If that is too long, try some of the delicious cold cereals made by Arrowhead Mills. Another way to have delicious, quick, whole grain breakfast cereals is to use grains leftover from dinner. Plain, unseasoned rice, millet, quinoa, or buckwheat is delicious served hot or cold, sweetened with some dried fruit, and served with soymilk and fresh seasonal fruit. To heat leftover grains, just place them in a pan with a little water and heat, stirring occasionally, until the water is absorbed. Don't forget about homemade yeast or quick breads, plain or toasted, and spread with nut butter or tahini. Add some fresh juice and you have a quick breakfast that can't be beat. On weekends and special occasions, when you have the time to enjoy a leisurely breakfast, try whole grain pancakes or warm muffins served with fresh fruit and fruit-sweetened jam. Scrambled tofu or a tofu omelet is also nice for a change.

With natural foods there is no reason to get bored. There are so many different varieties of whole grains and ways to prepare them that it is possible to have a different kind of cereal every day of the week. Adding luscious fresh seasonal fruit to your wholesome grains will make your healthy breakfasts as diverse as they are delicious.

Overnight Muesli

This muesli recipe is from my friend Dominique Biscotti, who teaches cooking and is a naturopath in Quebec, Canada.

Serves: 4–6   Time: Soak overnight; 5 minutes to prepare

1. In a glass or ceramic bowl, combine the oats, raisins, almonds, coconut, and water. Cover and let soak overnight.

2. The next morning, add the cinnamon and mix well. Transfer the muesli to individual serving bowls and top each serving with a grated apple, added immediately before serving. Include the peel if the apple is organically grown. (Cut off a small slice of skin to start grating.)

3. Serve as is or with soymilk or yogurt.

This will keep for a few days in the refrigerator.

2 cups oat flakes

1 cup raisins

$1/2$ cup whole almonds

$1/2$ cup unsweetened coconut flakes

2 cups water

$1/2$ teaspoon cinnamon

1 apple per person, grated

Swiss-Style Muesli

Try this for a nutritious breakfast that will keep you going till lunch.

Yield: 5 cups   Time: 20 minutes

1. In a large bowl, combine all the ingredients except the raisins.

2. Place about 1 cup of the mixture in a blender and coarsely grind it. Place the ground cereal in a large bowl. Continue grinding 1 cup at a time until all the mixture is coarsely ground.

3. Add the raisins to the ground cereal and mix well.

4. Transfer the mixture to a glass jar with a tight-fitting lid and store in the refrigerator.

5. To serve, place about $1/3$ cup of muesli in a bowl. Cover with soymilk or skim milk and let soak for 10 minutes or more. Top generously with fresh fruit and a dollop of low-fat yogurt or soy yogurt, if you like.

2 cups oat flakes

$1/2$ cup rye flakes

$1/3$ cup barley flakes

$1/3$ cup hazelnuts

1 cup dried apples

$1/4$ cup malt powder

$1/2$ cup raisins

Maple Nut Granola

Yield: about 5 cups   Time: 40 minutes

3 cups oat flakes

1 cup rye flakes

1 cup raw unsalted nuts
(walnuts, almonds, cashews,
etc., or a mixture of)

1/4 cup sesame seeds

1/4 cup oil

1/2 cup maple syrup

1. In a large bowl, combine the oat flakes, rye flakes, nuts, and sesame seeds. Add the oil and mix well. Add the maple syrup and mix well.

2. Transfer the mixture to a couple of unoiled shallow baking pans and bake at 350°F for 25–30 minutes or until golden brown. Stir 3–4 times during the baking to make sure that the mixture browns evenly.

3. Let the granola cool completely. Store in tightly covered glass jars and refrigerate.

VARIATION: Add 1/2–1 cup of raisins or date pieces to the granola after it is baked.

Apple Granola

Here is a fruit-sweetened granola that is lower in fat than many traditional granolas.

Yield: 6 1/2 cups   Time: 30–35 minutes

4 cups oat flakes

1/4 cup oil

1/2 cup concentrated fruit
sweetener

1 tablespoon cinnamon

1 tablespoon vanilla

1/2 cup sunflower seeds

1 1/2 cups chopped dried apples

1/2 cup raisins

1. In a large bowl, mix together the oats and the oil. In a smaller bowl, combine the fruit sweetener, cinnamon, and vanilla.

2. Pour the liquid mixture over the oats and mix well. Add the sunflower seeds and mix again. Spread the mixture out on a couple of shallow baking pans in a layer no more than 1/2 inch thick. Bake at 350°F for 20–25 minutes or until golden brown. Stir during the baking to keep the mixture from burning around the edges or on the bottom.

3. While the mixture is still hot, transfer it to a large bowl. Add the dried apples and the raisins and mix well.

4. Allow the granola to cool, then store it in tightly covered glass jars and refrigerate.

Sesame Rice Cream

Serves: 2 **Time: 11 minutes**

1. Wash and drain the rice. Place the rice and the sesame seeds in an unoiled skillet or pan and stir over medium-high heat until the seeds begin to brown and give off a nutty aroma and the rice is dry.

2. Transfer the rice–sesame seed mixture to a blender and grind it to a flour. (This flour can be stored in the refrigerator for future quick breakfasts.)

3. Place the ground mixture in a saucepan along with the water and the raisins. Mix well. While stirring constantly, bring the mixture to a boil. Reduce the heat and cook, stirring constantly, for 3–5 minutes or until the mixture thickens.

4. Turn off heat, cover, and let stand for a few minutes before serving. Serve with fresh fruit and soymilk or yogurt.

1/2 cup brown rice

2 tablespoons sesame seeds

2 cups water

1/4 cup raisins or other dried fruit (optional)

Millet Cream

Serves: 2 **Time: 12 minutes**

1. Wash and drain the millet. Place it in an unoiled skillet or pan over medium heat and stir constantly for a few minutes until it is dry.

2. Transfer the millet to a blender and grind it to a flour. (This flour can be stored in the refrigerator for future quick breakfasts.)

3. Place the ground millet in a saucepan along with the water and the dried fruit. Mix well. While stirring constantly, bring the mixture to a boil. Reduce the heat and cook, stirring constantly, for 3–5 minutes or until the mixture thickens.

4. Serve with sliced bananas and soymilk or yogurt.

1/2 cup millet

2 cups water

1/4 cup chopped dried fruit (apricots are especially good)

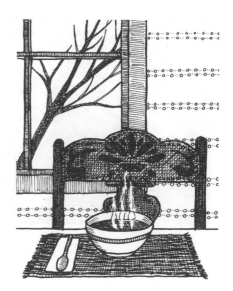

Wheat, Oat, or Rye Porridge

Use any one of these cereals, or mix them in any proportion you like.

1 cup oat flakes, rye flakes, or wheat flakes

2 cups water

1/4 cup raisins or other chopped dried fruit (optional)

Serves: 2–3   Time: 8 minutes

1. Place the cereal, water, and dried fruit in a saucepan. Cover and bring to a boil. Reduce the heat and cook, stirring often, for about 5 minutes or until the mixture thickens.

2. Serve with fresh fruit and soymilk or yogurt.

Peanut Butter Oatmeal

Kids love this one. Grown-ups will, too.

1 cup water

1/3 cup oat flakes

2–3 chopped pitted dates or 2 tablespoons raisins

2 tablespoons crunchy peanut butter

1 apple, grated

Serves: 1–2   Time: 10 minutes

1. Place the water, oat flakes, and dried fruit in a small saucepan. Bring to a boil. Reduce the heat, cover, and cook, stirring occasionally, for about 5 minutes or until the mixture thickens.

2. Add the peanut butter and mix well.

3. Top with a grated apple, added immediately before serving. Include the peel if the apple is organically grown. (Cut off a small slice of skin to start grating.) Serve with some soymilk or a dollop of plain yogurt.

Easy Cooked Cereal

If you would like to have a hearty bowl of hot cereal ready when you wake up in the morning, try this clever strategy.

Yield: About 4 cups; serves 4

Time: 8 hours for first soaking; 8 hours for second soaking

1 cup wheat berries
(soft wheat works better than hard wheat)

3 cups water for first soaking

2½ cups boiling water for second soaking

1. Wash the wheat berries and drain them in a wire mesh strainer. Place the wheat in a medium-sized bowl and cover it with water. Cover the bowl with a cloth or pan lid and let the wheat soak for about 8 hours.

2. At night before going to bed, heat a quart-sized insulated container such as a wide-mouthed Thermos bottle by rinsing it with boiling water. Drain the wheat (save the soaking water to water plants) and place it in the container. Add the boiling water and close the container. Place it on its side and leave overnight.

3. Next morning, the wheat will be cooked and still warm. Serve with soymilk or yogurt and some fresh or dried fruit.

Cooked wheat may be used in place of other cooked grains in meatless loaves and croquettes. It can also be mixed with rice or millet for use in recipes that call for those grains.

Tropicorn Porridge

Plantains are large cooking bananas. As they ripen, they change from being starchy and potatolike to very sweet and delicious; a ripe one will be moderately soft and have lots of black spots on the skin.

Serves: 2–3

Time: 13 minutes

2 cups water

½ cup cornmeal

1 ripe plantain, peeled and sliced

¼ cup date sugar

1. Combine all the ingredients in a heavy saucepan. While stirring constantly, bring to a boil. Reduce the heat and cover. Cook over low heat, stirring occasionally, for 5–10 minutes or until thick.

2. Serve with milk (soy-, rice, or dairy) or yogurt. Top with slices of fresh pineapple.

Golden Porridge

A nutritious way to start a winter morning.

1/4 cup amaranth flour

1/4 cup millet flour

1/4 cup yellow cornmeal

1/3 cup chopped dried apricots

2 1/4 cups water

Serves: 2–3   Time: 12 minutes

1. In a heavy saucepan, mix together the flours and the apricots. Stir in the water and mix until well blended. While stirring constantly, bring the mixture to a boil. Reduce the heat, cover, and cook, stirring occasionally, for about 5 minutes or until thick.

2. Serve hot with fresh fruit and soymilk, dairy milk, or yogurt.

Oatmeal Rice Porridge

This is a good way to use up a cup of leftover rice.

1 cup cooked brown rice (see page 152)

1/2 cup oat flakes

1/4 cup raisins or chopped dried apricots

1 1/2 cups water

Serves: 2   Time: 10 minutes

1. Combine all the ingredients in a saucepan. While stirring constantly, bring the mixture to a boil.

2. Cover, reduce heat to low, and cook, stirring occasionally, for 3–5 minutes, until the cereal is thick.

3. Serve hot with soymilk and fresh fruit.

Breakfast Rice Pudding

Make this pudding when you have some leftover rice on hand.

2 cups cooked brown rice (see page 152)

1/3 cup raisins or other dried fruit

1 teaspoon vanilla

1/8 teaspoon nutmeg

1/2 teaspoon cinnamon

3/4 cup soymilk

Fresh seasonal fruit, sliced

Serves: 2–3   Time: 12 minutes

1. Combine all the ingredients except the fresh fruit in a heavy saucepan. While stirring constantly, bring to a boil. Cover, reduce the heat to low, and simmer, stirring occasionally, for 3–5 minutes or until the raisins are plump and the soymilk has been absorbed.

2. Serve in bowls, topped generously with fresh fruit. At the table, add extra soymilk or a dollop of yogurt, if you like.

Eggless Apple Pancakes

These pancakes are surprisingly good!

Yield: about 12 pancakes; serves: 2–3   Time: 20 minutes

1 package (10$^{1}/_{2}$ ounces) firm silken tofu

$^{1}/_{4}$ cup water or soymilk

1 teaspoon vanilla

1 cup whole wheat pastry flour

2 teaspoons baking powder

1 teaspoon cinnamon

1 cup grated apple

$^{1}/_{2}$ cup raisins (optional)

1. Place the tofu, the water or soymilk, and the vanilla in a food processor or a blender. Blend until smooth and creamy.

2. Combine the flour, baking powder, and cinnamon in a large bowl. Add the blended tofu and mix well. Add the grated apple and the raisins. Mix again. The batter will be thick.

3. Drop the batter, $^{1}/_{4}$ cup at a time, onto a hot, oiled skillet. With the back of a spoon, spread out each pancake as much as you can. Cook about three pancakes at a time over medium heat until they are brown on the bottom. Turn them over and cook the other side.

4. These pancakes are good served plain, with fresh fruit, or with your choice of syrup, honey, or fruit spread.

Buckwheat Pancakes

Yield: 8–10 pancakes; serves: 2–3   Time: 30 minutes

1 cup buckwheat flour

1 teaspoon baking powder

1 egg

1½ cups soymilk

1. In a medium bowl, combine the flour and the baking powder. Mix well. Add the egg and mix well. Stir in the milk and beat until smooth. Let the batter stand for about 10 minutes.

2. Drop the batter, ¼ cup at a time, onto a hot, oiled skillet. Cook over medium heat until bubbles appear on the surface of the pancakes and the batter starts to dry out a little on top. Turn the pancakes over and cook the other side briefly.

3. Serve hot with applesauce and maple syrup.

Whole Wheat Banana Pancakes

Yield: about 6 pancakes; serves: 2–3   Time: 20 minutes

1 cup whole wheat pastry flour

1 teaspoon baking powder

Pinch of nutmeg

1 egg

³⁄₄ –1 cup soymilk

2 bananas, sliced

1. In a medium bowl, combine the flour, baking powder, and nutmeg. Add the egg and mix. Add the soymilk, starting with ³⁄₄ cup and adding more as necessary to make a pourable batter. (It may thicken on standing.) Beat the batter until it is smooth.

2. Drop the batter, ¼ cup at a time, onto a hot, oiled skillet. Top with banana slices. Cook until bubbles appear on the surface around the bananas, then turn the pancake over. Cook until brown on the bottom.

3. Serve with fresh fruit and fruit-sweetened jam, honey, or maple syrup. A spoonful of yogurt is also good.

For plain whole wheat pancakes omit the bananas.

Quinoa Pancakes

A delicious way to use up some leftover quinoa.

Yield: 8–10 pancakes; serves: 3   Time: about 20 minutes

¾ cup whole wheat pastry flour
2 teaspoons baking powder
¾ cup cooked quinoa (see page 152)
1 egg
¾ cup soymilk
½ cup raisins
⅓ cup walnuts

1. In a medium bowl, mix together the flour and the baking powder. Add the quinoa and the egg and mix well. Add the soymilk and beat until the batter is thoroughly mixed. Add the raisins and walnuts and mix well.

2. Drop the batter, ¼ cup at a time, onto a hot, oiled skillet. Cook over medium-high heat until bubbles begin to appear on the surface of the pancakes. Turn them over and cook briefly until the bottoms are golden brown.

3. Serve plain (the rasins add sweetness) or with fresh fruit or unsweetened applesauce. They are also delicious topped with fruit-sweetened jam, fruit sauce, maple syrup, or honey.

Brown Rice and Barley Pancakes

This is a tasty way to use up some leftover brown rice.

Yield: 10 pancakes; serves: 2–3   Time: 20 minutes

1 cup barley flour
1 teaspoon baking powder
1 teaspoon cinnamon
1 cup cooked brown rice (see page 152)
½ cup raisins or date pieces
1 egg
1¼ cups soymilk (approximately)

1. In a medium bowl, mix together the barley flour, baking powder, and cinnamon. Add the rice and the raisins or the date pieces and mix again. Add the egg and mix well. Add the milk and beat until the batter is well mixed.

2. Drop the batter, ¼ cup at a time, onto a hot, oiled skillet and cook over medium-high heat until bubbles appear on the surface of the pancakes and the bottoms are brown. Turn over and cook the other side.

3. Serve with fresh fruit and soy or dairy yogurt, or with your favorite jam, syrup, or honey.

Blueberry Pancakes

These pancakes are a perfect treat for a summer weekend morning.

1 cup barley flour

2 teaspoons baking powder

1/4 teaspoon nutmeg

1 egg

1 teaspoon vanilla

2 tablespoons concentrated fruit sweetener

3/4 cup soymilk

1 1/4 cups blueberries

Yield: about 6 pancakes; serves: 2   Time: about 20 minutes

1. In a medium bowl, combine the flour, baking powder, and nutmeg. Add the egg, vanilla, and fruit sweetener and mix again. Gradually stir in the soymilk and beat until the batter is smooth.

2. Drop the batter, 1/4 cup at a time, onto a hot, oiled skillet and generously sprinkle with blueberries. Cook each pancake over medium-high heat until bubbles appear all over the top and the bottom is golden brown. Turn pancakes over and cook the other side.

3. Serve immediately with fresh fruit and some fruit-sweetened blueberry jam or honey.

Amaranth Pancakes

Amaranth flour produces pancakes with a light texture and a slightly nutty flavor.

1 cup amaranth flour

1 1/2 teaspoons baking powder

1 teaspoon cinnamon

1 egg

2/3 cup soymilk

1/3 cup raisins (optional)

2 tablespoons sunflower seeds (optional)

Yield: 8 pancakes; serves: 2–3   Time: about 20 minutes

1. In a medium bowl, mix together the flour, baking powder, and cinnamon. Add the egg and mix well. Add the soymilk and beat for a few seconds until smooth. Add the raisins and sunflower seeds and mix again.

2. Drop the batter, 1/4 cup at a time, onto a hot, oiled skillet and cook over medium heat until bubbles appear on the surface of the pancakes and the bottoms are brown. Turn the pancakes over and cook the other side.

3. Serve with fresh fruit, fruit-sweetened jams, or your choice of honey or syrup.

Sunday Brunch Tofu Scramble

Serves: 3–4   Time: 15 minutes

1. Heat the oil in a skillet over medium heat. Add the onion and sauté until nearly tender. Add the carrots and the turmeric and sauté for about 2 minutes. Add the tofu, the vegetable broth powder, and the salt.

2. Mix well and continue to cook over low heat for 3–4 minutes, stirring often.

3. Add the parsley, mix well, and serve with whole grain toast or with the Whole Wheat Biscuits (page 132).

1 tablespoon oil

1/3 cup finely chopped onion

1/2 cup grated carrots

1/4 teaspoon turmeric

1 pound tofu, crumbled

1 tablespoon vegetable broth powder

1/2 teaspoon sea salt, or to taste

2 tablespoons minced fresh parsley

Tofu Omelet

Serves: 4   Time: 30 minutes

1. Cut the block of tofu in half. Place one half in a food processor with the flour, miso, turmeric, nutmeg, cayenne pepper, vegetable broth powder, and rosemary. Blend until smooth and creamy. Use a rubber spatula to scrape the sides of the food processor so that all the tofu is well blended.

2. Crumble the remaining tofu into a mixing bowl. Add the pepper, scallions, and blended tofu mixture. Mix well.

3. Heat the oil in a skillet or omelet pan over medium heat. When the oil is hot, spoon in 1/4 of the tofu mixture and press it with a spatula to a 1-inch thickness. If it is too thin, it will not hold together when you turn it. Cook over medium heat until the omelet is brown on the bottom, then turn it over and cook the other side.

4. Repeat Step 3 with the remaining tofu to make four omelets in all.

1 pound tofu

2 tablespoons whole wheat pastry flour

2 tablespoons yellow miso

1/4 teaspoon turmeric

1/4 teaspoon nutmeg

Dash of cayenne pepper, or to taste

1 tablespoon vegetable broth powder

1/2 teaspoon rosemary

1/4 cup finely chopped red bell pepper

3 scallions, chopped

1 tablespoon oil

Breakfast Oat Squares

1 package (10½ ounces) extra-firm silken tofu

¼ cup concentrated fruit sweetener

1 teaspoon vanilla

1 cup oat flakes

½ cup oat flour

2 teaspoons baking powder

1 teaspoon cinnamon

½ cup raisins

Try this as a change from cereal. It is nice to prepare on those mornings when you have a little extra time.

Serves: 4   Time: 15 minutes to prepare; 20–25 minutes to bake

1. Place the tofu, fruit sweetener, and vanilla in a blender or food processor and blend until smooth and creamy. If necessary, scrape the sides so that all the tofu is well blended.

2. In a medium bowl, combine the oat flakes, oat flour, baking powder, cinnamon, and raisins. Add the tofu mixture and mix well.

3. Oil an 8-x-8-inch baking dish and sprinkle with some oat flakes. Spread the batter evenly in the pan. Bake at 350°F for 20–25 minutes, or until a toothpick inserted into the center of the cake comes out clean.

4. Let cool for 10–15 minutes. Cut into squares and serve warm, topped with applesauce, soy or dairy yogurt, or both.

   Leftover oat squares should be stored in a plastic bag in the refrigerator and may be reheated in a toaster oven.

3. SPREADS, DIPS & PATÉS

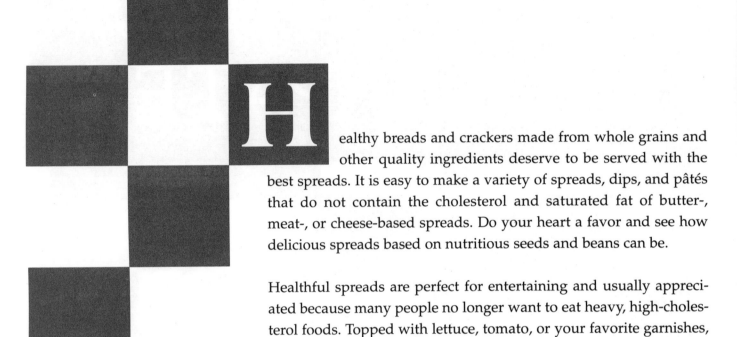

ealthy breads and crackers made from whole grains and other quality ingredients deserve to be served with the best spreads. It is easy to make a variety of spreads, dips, and pâtés that do not contain the cholesterol and saturated fat of butter-, meat-, or cheese-based spreads. Do your heart a favor and see how delicious spreads based on nutritious seeds and beans can be.

Healthful spreads are perfect for entertaining and usually appreciated because many people no longer want to eat heavy, high-cholesterol foods. Topped with lettuce, tomato, or your favorite garnishes, the spreads and pâtés in this section are great in sandwiches. Beware, though: If you take your beautiful homemade sandwiches to school or work, they are sure to become a topic of conversation, and you will probably have to share both samples and recipes.

Tahini Olive Spread

This recipe and the Tahini Carrot Spread (below) are really variations on a theme. But they are both good, and since they taste so different, I decided to include them both to give you an idea of how a basic recipe can be varied.

Yield: 2 cups   Time: 20 minutes

1. Cream together the tahini and the miso until they are well blended. Add the other ingredients and mix well.
2. Use as a sandwich spread. Garnish with sprouts, lettuce, and a thick slice of ripe tomato.

$^1/_2$ cup tahini

2 tablespoons white miso, or to taste

1 cup finely chopped celery (about 2 stalks)

1 cup chopped pitted black olives

$^2/_3$ cup finely grated carrots (about 1 medium carrot)

2 scallions, finely chopped

Tahini Carrot Spread

Yield: about 1$^1/_4$ cups   Time: 10 minutes

1. Cream together the tahini, miso, and water until they are well blended. Add the remaining ingredients and mix well.
2. Use as a spread for sandwiches or crackers with your favorite garnishes.

$^1/_2$ cup tahini

1 tablespoon white or yellow miso

1 tablespoon water

1 cup finely grated carrots (1–2 medium carrots)

1 clove garlic

2 scallions, finely chopped

1 teaspoon tamari

1 tablespoon vinegar (rice or

Sun-Dried Tomato Spread

A versatile spread.

1 package (10½ ounces) extra-firm silken tofu

2 tablespoons olive oil

½ teaspoon sea salt

½ teaspoon basil

1 clove garlic, pressed

12 sun-dried tomato halves, cut into small pieces

Yield: about 1 cup   Time: 15 minutes to prepare, 1 hour to stand

1. Place the tofu, olive oil, salt, basil, and garlic in a blender or food processor. Blend until smooth and creamy. Stop the machine occasionally and scrape the sides with a rubber spatula so that all the tofu gets well blended.

2. Transfer the mixture to a bowl and add the tomatoes. Let stand for at least 1 hour to soften the tomatoes. Mix well.

3. Use as a spread on crackers, bread, or baked potatoes.

This spread will keep in the refrigerator for about a week. For something different try New Potatoes and Green Beans with Sun-Dried Tomato Spread (page 183).

Tofu Sandwich Spread

Yield: about 2½ cups   Time: 15 minutes

1 pound firm tofu

¼ cup mayonnaise or eggless mayonnaise

3 tablespoons nutritional yeast

2 tablespoons tahini

2 tablespoons sweet pickle relish

2 tablespoons minced onion

1 clove garlic, pressed

1 tablespoon Dijon-style mustard

2 tablespoons tamari

Dash of cayenne pepper, or to taste

1. Place the tofu in a mixing bowl. Mash it with a fork. Add the remaining ingredients and mix well.

2. Use as a spread for sandwiches, crackers, and raw vegetables. It's also delicious as a stuffing for tomatoes.

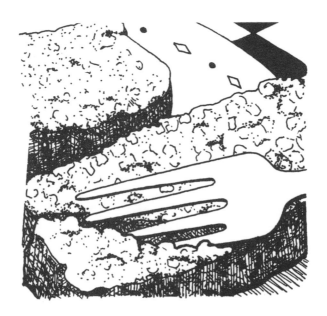

Lentil Pâté

As with many of these pâtés and spreads, preparation time is minimal if you have cooked beans on hand.

Yield: about 2 cups   Time: 30 minutes to prepare; 1 hour to chill

1. Heat the oil in a skillet. Add the onion and the garlic, and sauté slowly over low heat for about 15 minutes. Add the mushrooms, sage, and thyme, and continue to sauté for about 5 minutes longer.

2. Place the lentils in a food processor. Add the sautéed vegetables, the nutritional yeast (if using), the cayenne pepper, and the miso. Blend until smooth.

3. Transfer the pâté to a bowl and chill.

4. Serve with bread. Lentil pâté is a good accompaniment to a simple meal of soup and salad.

1 tablespoon olive oil

1 cup chopped onion (1 medium onion)

6 cloves garlic, minced

1 cup chopped mushrooms (4–5 medium mushrooms)

1 teaspoon sage

1 teaspoon thyme

1½ cups cooked and drained green lentils (see page 169)

2 tablespoons nutritional yeast (optional)

Dash of cayenne pepper, or to taste

1 heaping tablespoon barley miso (or other dark miso)

Sunny Sandwich Spread

Sunflower seeds and sun-dried tomatoes are sensational together in this easy spread.

Yield: about 1 cup   Time: 15 minutes

1. Place the sunflower seeds in a shallow baking pan or on a cookie sheet. Roast them in the oven or a toaster oven at 350°F for about 10 minutes or until they are lightly roasted. Stir occasionally so that they brown evenly and don't burn.

2. Meanwhile, pour the water into a small bowl. Add the tomato halves, wine vinegar, and tamari. Let soak until the sunflower seeds are done.

3. Place the roasted sunflower seeds in a food processor and grind them. With the food processor running, add the garlic, Then slowly add the tomatoes along with the liquid. Stop occasionally and scrape the sides of the container so that all the seeds are ground.

4. Serve on whole grain bread with fresh lettuce or sprouts.

1 cup sunflower seeds

½ cup water

18 sun-dried tomato halves

1 tablespoon wine vinegar

2 tablespoons tamari

2 cloves garlic

Peanut Celery Spread

1/3 cup crunchy peanut butter

1 tablespoon lemon juice

2 teaspoons tamari

1 clove garlic, minced

2 tablespoons water

1 cup finely chopped celery
(2 stalks)

My husband, like many French people, hates peanut butter, but the first time he had a sandwich made with this spread, he asked for seconds.

Yield: about 1 1/2 cups   Time: 10 minutes

1. In a small bowl, mix together the peanut butter, lemon juice, tamari, and garlic. Add the water and beat the mixture with a spoon for a few seconds to give it a nice whipped consistency. Add the celery and mix well.

2. Use this spread on whole grain toast with lettuce or sprouts and a slice of ripe tomato.

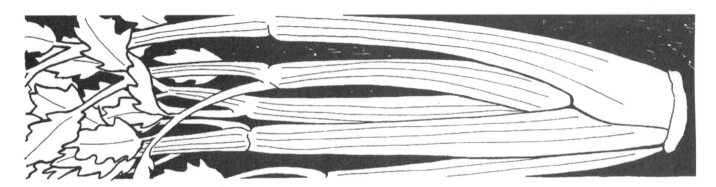

Tofu Peanut Spread

1 cup firm tofu, mashed and lightly packed into cup

1/4 cup crunchy peanut butter

3 tablespoons hot or mild prepared salsa

1/4 cup finely chopped celery
(about 1 small stalk)

2 scallions, finely chopped

2 tablespoons minced fresh cilantro

1 tablespoon tamari, or to taste

Only an American would mix traditional Japanese ingredients with traditional Mexican ingredients and add peanut butter! The fresh cilantro in this spread gives it a surprisingly sassy flavor.

Yield: 1 1/4 cups   Time: 10 minutes

1. Place all the ingredients in a bowl and mix well.

2. Spread on whole grain bread or toast. Top with sprouts, lettuce, or a slice of tomato.

Veggie Pâté

This nutritious pâté is not too rich. It will keep for a week in the refrigerator.

Yield: enough for about 8 sandwiches

Time: 15 minutes to prepare; 30–35 minutes to bake

1. In two or more batches, blend all the ingredients together in a blender or food processor until the mixture is very smooth.

2. Pour the mixture into a well-oiled and lightly floured baking dish. A Pyrex 8½-x-8½-inch dish works well. Bake at 350°F for 30–35 minutes or until set. Chill and cut into squares.

3. To make a great sandwich, spread the veggie pâté generously on a slice of whole grain bread or toast. Spread a second slice with Dijon-style mustard and garnish with lettuce. This pâté also makes nice canapés when spread on crackers or small slices of bread and garnished with thin slices of red pepper and black olives.

1 large potato, scrubbed and cut into cubes (about 2½ cups)

2 cups water

2 tablespoons oil

¼ cup chopped onion

2 cloves garlic

1 teaspoon herbes de Provence (see page 102)

½ teaspoon sage

Dash of cayenne pepper, or to taste

1 cup sunflower seeds

¼ cup tamari

¼ cup nutritional yeast

¼ cup whole wheat or millet flour

Millet Pâté

Make this simple low-fat pâté when you have some leftover cooked millet.

Yield: about 2 cups

Time: 15 minutes

1. Place all the ingredients in a bowl. Mix well.

2. Use this pâté as a sandwich spread on whole grain bread with lettuce or sprouts.

¾ cup cooked millet (see page 152)

½ cup grated carrot (1 medium carrot)

1 cup crumbled firm tofu

2 tablespoons tahini

3 tablespoons white or yellow miso

¼ cup nutritional yeast

¼ teaspoon celery seeds

½ teaspoon savory

Hummus

2 cups cooked and drained chick peas with cooking liquid reserved (see page 169)

$^1/_2$ cup tahini

2 tablespoons olive oil

$^1/_3$ cup lemon juice, or to taste

2–3 cloves garlic

$^1/_2$ teaspoon sea salt

2 tablespoons minced parsley

Hummus is a Middle Eastern specialty that has become a classic of natural foods cuisine. Here is a recipe for traditional hummus as well as sprouted and low-fat versions.

Yield: about 2 cups   Time: 15 minutes

FOOD PROCESSOR METHOD:

1. Place all the ingredients (except the chick pea cooking liquid and the parsley) in a food processor and blend until smooth. If the mixture is too thick, add as much cooking liquid as needed to achieve a spreadable consistency.

2. Add the parsley and mix well. Place in a bowl and chill before serving.

BLENDER METHOD:

1. Place 1 cup of the chick peas and the remaining ingredients (except the chick pea cooking liquid and the parsley) in a blender and blend until smooth.

2. Gradually add the remaining chick peas. If the mixture becomes too thick to blend, add as much cooking liquid as necessary to achieve a spreadable consistency. If your blender is not very powerful, you may have to blend in two batches.

3. Add the parsley and mix well. Place in a bowl and chill before serving.

VARIATIONS:

• *Sprouted hummus:* Use chick peas that have been sprouted for 3 days and then cooked until tender. Follow the recipe as indicated above. Sprouting makes beans easier to digest.

• *Low-fat hummus:* Reduce the tahini to $^1/_4$ cup and omit the olive oil. Follow the recipe as indicated, adding cooking water from the chick peas, if necessary, to achieve the desired spreading consistency.

All variations of hummus are delicious served with warm whole wheat pita bread. As an appetizer, cut the bread in wedges for dipping into the hummus. For a quick lunch, serve hummus with any kind of whole grain bread and a salad.

Hummus is also good as a dip for raw vegetables or crackers.

Split Pea Hummus

Milder than regular hummus, this hummus is pale green and has a hint of mint.

Yield: about 2½ cups   Time: 15 minutes

1. Place all the ingredients in a food processor and blend until smooth and creamy. Add water to achieve the desired consistency.

2. Serve Split Pea Hummus as a sandwich spread or as a dip with crackers or veggies.

If using a blender, the ingredients will have to be prepared in more than one batch. More water or oil will be needed as well. Add the water (or oil) gradually until the mixture is thin enough to blend. Use a rubber spatula to scrape the sides of the blender to make sure all the ingredients are well blended.

2 cups cooked and drained green split peas (see page 169)

½ cup tahini

1 tablespoon olive oil

⅓ cup lemon juice

2 cloves garlic

½ teaspoon sea salt

1½ teaspoons dried mint

2–4 tablespoons water, as needed

Black Bean Hummus

A hummus of a different color.

Yield: about 1½ cups   Time: 15 minutes

1. Place all the ingredients in a food processor and blend until the mixture is smooth and creamy. Stop the machine occasionally and scrape the sides with a spatula to make sure that all the ingredients are well blended.

2. Serve as a dip with tortilla chips or veggies.

If using a blender, the ingredients will have to be prepared in more than one batch.

2 cups cooked and drained black beans (see page 169)

¼ cup tahini

1 tablespoon tamari, or to taste

1 tablespoon balsamic vinegar

1–2 cloves garlic

½ teaspoon cumin

Dash of cayenne pepper, or to taste

Spicy Bean and Pepper Dip

Use this dip with corn chips or as a spread for sandwiches or crackers.

1¹/₂ cups cooked and drained
pinto or kidney beans
(see page 169)

¹/₄ cup chopped onion

1 tablespoon lemon juice

1 tablespoon tamari or shoyu

1 teaspoon chili powder

¹/₂ teaspoon cumin

1 teaspoon basil

Dash of cayenne pepper, or to
taste

¹/₄ cup finely chopped red bell
pepper

¹/₄ cup finely chopped green
bell pepper

Yield: 2 cups   Time 15 minutes

1. Place the beans in a food processor. Add all of the remaining ingredients except the peppers. Blend until smooth and creamy.

2. Transfer the purée from the food processor to a bowl and add the bell pepper. Mix well. Store in the refrigerator.

If using a blender, the beans will have to be prepared in more than one batch.

4. SOUPS

These homemade soups, composed of natural ingredients, are low in fat and packed with vitamins and minerals. The bean- and soymilk-based soups are a good source of protein, too. Add some whole grain bread, some veggie pâté, and a nice big salad, and you've got an easy, hearty meal.

Try these recipes first as written, then feel free to adjust the seasonings, especially the quantity of salt, miso, or tamari. Also, adjust the liquid proportions for a thicker or thinner soup to suit your taste.

A pressure cooker is great for many soups, but don't use it for split pea or red lentil soups—the beans will foam up and clog the vent. If you use a pressure cooker for a soup that was not designed for a pressure cooker, decrease the quantity of liquid in the recipe by about 1 cup, as a pressure cooker uses less water than a regular pot. If the soup becomes too thick, add a little extra liquid after it is cooked.

When you make a bean soup, always cook the beans until they are tender; the exact time will vary with the type and freshness of the bean, the hardness of the water, even the kind of pot you use. So allow ample time; undercooked beans will not make a good soup.

You can add extra flavor and nutrition to soups by using the water that vegetables were steamed in. Keep this liquid in a covered container in the refrigerator (no more than a week) or in the freezer and substitute it for equal quantities of water in your soup.

Greens-and-Rice Soup with Sun-Dried Tomatoes

This soup is really delicious.

Serves: 6   Time: about 1 hour

1. Heat the oil in a large, heavy kettle such as a cast-iron Dutch oven. Add the onion, garlic, and bay leaves. Sauté very slowly over low heat for at least 30 minutes, stirring occasionally.

2. Raise the heat and add the collard greens. Stir over high heat until wilted, then add the remaining ingredients. Bring to a boil, then reduce the heat and simmer, stirring occasionally, for about 30 minutes more or until the collards are nice and tender.

2 tablespoons olive oil

1 large Spanish onion, chopped (about 2 cups)

12 cloves garlic, minced

2 bay leaves

2 cups chopped and firmly packed collard greens

20 sun-dried tomato halves, cut into pieces

1½ teaspoons rosemary

1½ cups cooked brown Basmati rice (see page 152)

5 cups water

¼ cup tamari

Tomato Rice Soup

Serves: 4–6   Time: 30 minutes

1. Heat the oil in a large kettle. Add the onions and sauté for about 10 minutes. Add the bell pepper, basil, and oregano. Continue to sauté for about 5 minutes more.

2. Wash and coarsely chop the tomatoes. Blend them in a blender or food processor in 3–4 batches until you have about 6½ cups purée. Add the tomato purée to the kettle with the sautéed vegetables. Add the salt, rice, and honey.

3. Cover and simmer for about 10 minutes. Add the soymilk and cayenne pepper, and mix well. If the soup is too thick, add a little more soymilk.

2 tablespoons olive oil

2 cups chopped onions (2 medium onions)

1 cup diced green bell pepper

2 teaspoons basil

1 teaspoon oregano

6 medium tomatoes

1 teaspoon sea salt

1½ cups cooked brown rice (see page 152)

1 tablespoon honey

½ cup soymilk

Dash of cayenne pepper, or to taste

Gourmet Mushroom Soup

1 leek

2 tablespoons olive oil

1 large portobello mushroom

8 oyster mushrooms

12 white button mushrooms

1 teaspoon herbes de Provence
(see page 102)

1 sprig fresh rosemary,
or 1 teaspoon dried

1/4 cup whole wheat pastry
flour

1 carton (33.8 fluid ounces)
soymilk

1 teaspoon sea salt

Dash of cayenne pepper, or to
taste

Although this soup can be made with regular white button mushrooms only, portobello and oyster mushrooms make it special.

Serves: 4–6   Time: 40 minutes

1. Cut the root off the leek, then slit the leek from bottom to top and wash thoroughly under running water to remove any sand. Chop all the white part and the tender green part. You can use some of the dark green part but not the toughest outer ends.

2. Heat the olive oil in a large, heavy kettle (a cast-iron Dutch oven works well). Add the chopped leek and sauté until tender, about 15 minutes, stirring occasionally.

3. Meanwhile, wash the mushrooms under running water. The gills of the portobello, must be scraped off and discarded along with the stem. Slice all the mushrooms and add them to the pot with the leeks. Add the herbes de Provence and the rosemary. Sauté until the mushrooms are tender, about 10 minutes, stirring occasionally.

4. Sprinkle the flour into the pot and mix well. While stirring constantly, slowly add about 1 cup of the soymilk. Stir vigorously and cook over medium heat until the soup thickens. Continue to add the remaining milk slowly. Bring to a boil while stirring constantly. Add the salt and the cayenne pepper.

Vegetable Barley Soup

1/4 cup barley

5 cups water

16-ounce can tomato purée

1/4 cup chopped cabbage

1 cup chopped onion
(1 medium onion)

1 medium–large turnip, diced

1 large parsnip, sliced

1 large carrot, sliced

3 bay leaves

1 tablespoon basil

3 tablespoons tamari

Cabbage and root vegetables make this a hearty soup for winter. Scrub the root vegetables, rather than peel them, for more flavor and nutrition.

Serves: 8   Time: about 1 1/2 hours

1. Combine the barley and the water in a large, heavy kettle. Cover and bring to a boil. Reduce the heat and simmer for about 40 minutes.

2. Add the remaining ingredients. Bring to a boil, then reduce the heat and simmer, covered, until all the vegetables are tender (about 40 minutes).

3. If the soup is too thick, add a little water.

Corn and Red Lentil Soup

This thick and hearty soup is a delicious change from regular lentil soup. Red lentils cook much faster than green ones.

Serves: 5   Time: 35 minutes

1. Heat the olive oil in a large, heavy kettle. Add the onion and the cumin. Sauté over medium-low heat until the onion is nearly tender.

2. Add the lentils, water, vinegar, and the sun-dried tomato pieces. Cover and bring to a boil. Reduce the heat and simmer, stirring occasionally, for about 15 minutes or until the lentils disintegrate. Add the zucchini and the corn. Continue to cook until the zucchini is tender.

3. While the soup is simmering, cook the pasta according to the package directions or until tender. Drain the pasta, rinse it, and add it to the soup after the zucchini is cooked.

4. Place the miso in a small bowl. Add about 1/4 cup of the soup and mix well to dissolve the miso. Pour this mixture into the soup. Add the cayenne pepper and tamari.

5. If the soup becomes too thick, thin it with water to the desired consistency.

*The pasta that I use in this soup is wheat-free corn pasta. Not only can it be used by persons allergic to wheat, but it has a unique flavor that is wonderful in this soup.

1 tablespoon olive oil

2 cups chopped onion (preferably a large sweet onion such as Vidalia)

1 teaspoon ground cumin

1 cup red lentils

5 cups water

2 tablespoons wine vinegar

15 sun-dried tomato halves, cut into pieces

1 medium zucchini, sliced

2 cups corn, cut off the cob (2 ears)

*1 cup pasta shells or elbows**

1/4 cup white miso

Dash of cayenne pepper, or to taste

1 tablespoon tamari

Minestrone

Vegetables, beans, and pasta in a rich tomato base.

28-ounce can crushed tomatoes

2 cups cooked pinto beans
or 2 cups cooked chick peas
or 1 cup of each (see page 169)

1 cup green beans, broken into
1-inch pieces

4 cups water (can include
cooking liquid from the beans)

1 cup sliced carrots
(1–2 medium carrots)

1 cup chopped celery (2 stalks)

1 cup chopped onion
(1 medium onion)

3 bay leaves

1 teaspoon basil

1 teaspoon oregano

2 tablespoons tamari,
or to taste

1 medium yellow squash,
quartered and sliced

1 cup uncooked pasta shells
or elbows

Serves: 5–6   Time: 1$\frac{1}{4}$ hours

1. In a large kettle, combine the tomatoes, pinto beans or chick peas, green beans, water, carrots, celery, onion, bay leaves, basil, oregano, and tamari. Cover and bring to a boil. Stir, reduce the heat, and simmer, covered, stirring occasionally until the vegetables are nearly tender (about 35–40 minutes).

2. Add the squash and the pasta, and continue to cook about 10 minutes more or until the pasta is cooked.

Quick Cream of Broccoli Soup

Make this soup in a pressure cooker.

Serves: 4–5   Time: 25 minutes

1. Wash the broccoli and scrub the potatoes. Don't peel the potatoes or the broccoli stems, and include any broccoli leaves. Cut everything into large pieces.

2. Place the potatoes, broccoli, onion, herbes de Provence, tarragon, and water in a pressure cooker. Bring the pressure up, then remove from the heat, and let the pressure fall on its own.

3. Place 1/3 of the cooked vegetables in a food processor with some of the soymilk, miso, and mustard. Blend until smooth and creamy. Transfer the creamy mixture to a large pan. Repeat until all the vegetables have been blended. Add more soymilk if needed to produce the desired consistency and to taste. Reheat the soup if necessary.

If you don't have a pressure cooker, use a large kettle and cook the vegetables in 2 cups of water rather than 1 cup. When they are tender, blend them in a food processor with the remaining ingredients as indicated above.

1 bunch broccoli (about 1 pound)

2 medium potatoes

1 cup chopped onions (1 medium onion)

2 teaspoon herbes de Provence (see page 102)

1/2 teaspoon tarragon

1 cup water

2 cups soymilk (or more, if needed)

1/4 cup white or yellow miso

1 tablespoon Dijon-style mustard

Dash of cayenne pepper, or to taste

Adzuki and Squash Soup

Adzuki beans and winter squash are so good together!

Serves: 4–6   Time: 2½–3 hours

1. Wash and pick over the beans. Place them in a large kettle with the water. Cover, bring to a boil, then reduce the heat and simmer, stirring occasionally, until nearly tender (about 1 hour).

2. Meanwhile, scrape the seeds and strings from the squash cavity, peel the outside with a potato peeler, and cut the flesh into 1/2–1-inch cubes.

3. Add the squash, onion, carrot, vinegar, bay leaves, savory, and rosemary to the pot of beans. Bring to a boil, then reduce the heat and simmer for 1 hour or until the vegetables and beans are tender.

4. Place about 1/4 cup of soup into a small bowl. Add the miso and mix well to dissolve it. Return the mixture to the pot and stir well. Do not boil the soup after adding the miso.

1 cup dry adzuki beans

5½ cups water

1/2 medium butternut squash

1 cup chopped onion (1 medium onion)

1 cup sliced carrot (1 medium carrot)

2 tablespoons balsamic vinegar

2–3 bay leaves

1 teaspoon summer savory

1 sprig fresh rosemary, or 1 teaspoon dried

4 tablespoons barley miso

Potato Kale Soup

Serves: 4   Time: 25 minutes

*1 cup chopped onion
(1 medium onion)*

*5 medium potatoes, scrubbed
and diced (about 5 cups)*

*8 medium kale leaves, chopped
(about 4 cups)*

2 cups water

*1 teaspoon herbes de Provence
(see page 102)*

*2 rounded tablespoons white
miso*

*Dash of cayenne pepper, or to
taste*

2 cups soymilk

1. Place the onion, potatoes, kale, herbs, and water in a pressure cooker. Cook over high heat until the pressure regulator jiggles, then turn down the heat and cook for about 3 minutes. Remove the pressure cooker from the heat and let it cool down on its own.

2. Blend the cooked mixture in a blender or a food processor along with the remaining ingredients. This will have to be done in at least three batches.

3. Reheat and serve.

To make this recipe without a pressure cooker, use a large, covered pot and follow the directions above. Simmer the vegetables until the kale is tender—at least 30 minutes. Add more water if necessary; soups cooked in conventional pots need more water than soups made in pressure cookers.

Cream of Celery Soup

A low-fat soup with a wonderfully creamy texture.

Serves: 4–6   Time: 30 minutes

2 tablespoons olive oil

*1¹/₂ cups chopped onions
(1¹/₂ medium onions)*

4 cups chopped celery (8 stalks)

3 bay leaves

1 teaspoon thyme

¹/₃ cup millet flour

*1 carton (33.8 fluid ounces)
soymilk*

3 tablespoons miso

*Dash of cayenne pepper, or to
taste*

Sea salt to taste (optional)

1. Heat the olive oil in a large, heavy kettle (a cast-iron Dutch oven is perfect). Add the onions, celery, bay leaves, and thyme. Sauté over medium-low heat, stirring often, until the vegetables are tender.

2. Stir the millet flour into the sautéed vegetables, then stir for a minute to heat the flour. Raise the heat to medium-high and slowly add the soymilk, a little at a time, stirring constantly so that it doesn't burn on the bottom. After you have added all the soymilk, keep stirring and bring the soup to a boil.

3. Remove the soup from the heat. Spoon about ¹/₄ cup of soup into a small bowl, add the miso, and mix well. Return this to the soup. Add cayenne pepper and some salt, if you like.

Creamy Corn Chowder

Serves 6   Time: about 1 hour

1. Place the onion, celery, potato, carrot, green pepper, basil, bay leaves, and water in a large, heavy kettle. Cover and bring to a boil. Reduce the heat and simmer, stirring occasionally, until the vegetables are almost tender, about 10 minutes.

2. Add the corn and the vegetable broth powder and simmer another 10 minutes or until the vegetables are tender.

3. In a saucepan, heat the oil. Add the millet flour and mix well. While stirring with a wire whisk, add 2 cups of the soymilk, a little at a time. Let the mixture come to a boil after each addition of soymilk. Continue stirring and cook until thickened.

4. Add this mixture to the cooked vegetables. Mix well. Add the remaining cup of soymilk, the salt, and cayenne pepper. Mix well. If the soup is too thick, add a little more soymilk.

To make this soup faster, you can cook the vegetables in a pressure cooker. Just place all the vegetables except the corn in a pressure cooker with the water. Bring up the pressure until the valve jiggles, then immediately cool the pot down under running water. This will keep the vegetables from becoming overcooked. Add the corn and simmer (in the usual manner, not under pressure) for about 3 minutes more. Make the thickened soymilk sauce as indicated above.

*1¹/₃ cups chopped onion
(1 large onion)*

*1¹/₄ cups chopped celery
(2 large stalks)*

*2¹/₂ cups diced potato
(1 large or 2 medium potatoes)*

*1 cup sliced carrot
(1 medium carrot)*

*¹/₂ cup diced green pepper
(¹/₂ medium pepper)*

1 teaspoon basil

3 bay leaves

2 cups water

*3 cups corn, cut off the cob
(2–3 ears)*

*2 tablespoons vegetable broth
powder*

1 tablespoon oil

¹/₄ cup millet flour

*3 cups soymilk, or more if
needed*

1 teaspoon sea salt, or to taste

*Dash of cayenne pepper, or to
taste*

Vegetable Chili

1 cup red kidney beans

2½ cups water

1 cup chopped onion
(1 medium onion)

2 teaspoons chili powder

1 teaspoon cumin

1 teaspoon basil

2 bay leaves

Dash of cayenne pepper, or to taste

2 tablespoons wine vinegar

1 green pepper, diced

1 yellow squash, sliced

1 zucchini, sliced

1 cup corn, cut off the cob
(1 ear)

12–15 sun-dried tomato halves, cut into small pieces

1½ cups tomato purée (canned or 1 large tomato, blended)

½ cup white wine (optional)

3 tablespoons tamari

My favorite restaurant in Paris is open only for lunch. It is packed with Parisians and run by an American! She makes a chili similar to this one. Sprouting the beans for a day makes them easier to digest.

Serves: 4

Time: overnight to soak beans; 8 hours to sprout beans; about 2 hours to cook

1. Wash the beans and place them in a bowl. Cover them with water and let soak overnight. In the morning, rinse the beans, put them back in the bowl (without water), and let them sit all day to sprout.

2. About 2 hours before you are ready to eat, rinse the beans again. Place them in a large kettle with the water. Cover and bring to a boil. Reduce the heat and let the beans simmer, stirring occasionally, for about 1 hour, or until they are nearly tender.

3. Add the onion, chili powder, cumin, basil, bay leaves, cayenne pepper, and the vinegar. Stir and let simmer for about 30 minutes more.

4. Add the remaining ingredients and continue to simmer, stirring occasionally, until the squash is tender but not overcooked.

5. Serve with cornbread and a salad. If you like, sprinkle each bowl of chili with sharp cheddar cheese or tofu cheese, and chopped scallions or fresh cilantro.

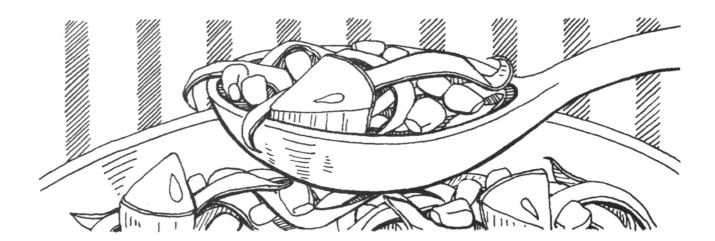

Pinto and Bulgur Chili

Heartier and spicier than the Vegetable Chili (facing page).

Serves: 4

Time: overnight to soak beans; about 1 hour, 10 minutes to cook

1. Wash and pick over the beans. Place them in a bowl with water to cover and let them sit for 8–10 hours. Drain and rinse.

2. Place the beans in a large, heavy kettle with the water. Cover and bring to a boil. Reduce the heat and simmer for about 45 minutes or until the beans are just tender.

3. When the beans are nearly tender, heat the oil in a skillet. Add the onions and garlic. Sauté for about 10 minutes, then add the chili powder, cumin, basil, oregano, and bell pepper. Sauté until the onions and pepper are tender.

4. Add the sautéed onion mixture to the pot with the beans. Add the tomato purée, bulgur, bay leaves, vinegar, and tamari. Simmer for about 15 minutes longer. Taste, then add the cayenne pepper if you want the chili to be spicier.

If the chili becomes too thick, add some water or tomato juice.

1 cup dry pinto beans

2 cups water

2 tablespoons olive oil

2 cups chopped onions (2 medium onions)

4 cloves garlic, minced

1 tablespoon chili powder

1 teaspoon cumin

1 teaspoon basil

1 teaspoon oregano

1 red or green bell pepper, diced

2¹/₂ cups fresh tomato purée (2 large tomatoes, cut into large chunks and blended)

¹/₂ cup bulgur wheat

1–3 bay leaves

2 tablespoons vinegar or lemon juice

3 tablespoons tamari

Dash of cayenne pepper, or to taste

Pinto and Spinach Soup

Pinto beans and spinach often accompany each other in southern country cooking. I use them together in this thick, stewlike soup.

1½ cups pinto beans	
4 cups water	
2 cups chopped onions (2 medium onions)	
1 cup chopped celery (2 stalks)	
2 tablespoons balsamic vinegar	
1½ teaspoons Italian seasoning	
1 teaspoon sea salt	
1 tablespoon tamari	
8 ounces fresh spinach	

Serves: 6   Time: overnight to soak beans; 1½ hours to cook

1. Wash and pick over the beans. Place them in a bowl with water to cover by about 2 inches and let them sit for 8–10 hours.

2. Drain and rinse the beans. Place them in a kettle with the water. Cover and bring to a boil. Reduce the heat and simmer, stirring occasionally, for 45–60 minutes or until the beans are tender. Add the onions, celery, vinegar, Italian seasoning, salt, and tamari. Simmer until tender.

3. Wash, drain, and chop the spinach. Add it to the soup and simmer 2–3 minutes more until the spinach is tender.

If you prefer a thinner soup, add water or vegetable broth to achieve the desired consistency. Adjust the seasonings to taste.

Split Pea Soup

This soup is easy to make, but don't be in a hurry: The secret to any good soup made with beans or peas is to simmer it slowly.

1 cup split peas

4½ cups water

2 cups chopped onions (2 medium onions)

1½ cups sliced carrots (2 medium carrots)

1 cup chopped celery (2 stalks)

3 bay leaves

1½ teaspoons savory

1 tablespoon balsamic vinegar

3 tablespoons white or yellow miso

¼ teaspoon sea salt (optional)

Dash of cayenne pepper, or to taste

Serves: 4–6   Time: 2 hours

1. Wash and pick over the peas. Place them in a large kettle with the water. Cover, bring to a boil, then reduce the heat and simmer for about 1 hour, stirring occasionally.

2. After the peas have simmered for about an hour, add the onions, carrots, celery, bay leaves, savory, and vinegar. Simmer slowly for another hour until the vegetables are tender.

3. When the soup is done, place about ¼ cup in a small bowl. Add the miso and stir until it is dissolved. Pour the miso mixture back into the soup. Taste the soup and add the salt, if desired, and a dash of cayenne pepper.

Delicious with homemade bread and a big green salad.

Leek and Split Pea Soup

Serves: 4–6   Time: about 1 hour, 10 minutes

1. Wash and pick over the peas. Place them in a large kettle with the water. Cover and bring to a boil. Reduce the heat and simmer for about 40 minutes.

2. Add the leeks, onion, and celery. Continue to simmer until the split peas and vegetables are tender (about 30 minutes longer).

3. Add the soymilk and the tarragon to the soup. Place about 1/4 cup of soup in a small bowl, add the miso, and mix well to dissolve. Return the mixture to the soup and mix well. Remove the soup from the heat, add the cayenne pepper, and mix well.

1/4 cup split peas

4 cups water

3 cups chopped leeks (2–3 medium leeks, using the white and light green parts

1 cup chopped onion (1 medium onion)

1 cup chopped celery (2 stalks)

1 cup soymilk

1 teaspoon tarragon

1/4 cup white or yellow miso

Dash of cayenne pepper, or to taste

Country-Style Potato Soup

Sometimes the simplest things are the best.

Serves: 6   Time: 1 hour

1. In a large kettle, combine the potatoes, celery, onions, water, bay leaves, salt, savory, and the vegetable broth powder. Cover and bring the mixture to a boil. Stir, reduce the heat, and simmer for about 30 minutes or until the vegetables are tender, stirring occasionally.

2. Stir in the soymilk. Place about 1/4 cup of soup in a small bowl, add the miso, and mix well to dissolve. Return the mixture to the soup and mix well. Do not boil the soup after adding the miso. Add the cayenne pepper and mix well.

3. Serve with some hearty, whole grain bread.

6 medium potatoes, scrubbed and cut into 1/2-inch cubes (6 cups)

2 cups chopped celery (4 stalks)

2 cups chopped onions (2 medium onions)

2 cups water

4 bay leaves

1/2 teaspoon sea salt

2 teaspoons summer savory

2 tablespoons vegetable broth powder

3 cups soymilk

2 tablespoons white or yellow miso

Dash of cayenne pepper, or to taste

Miso Soup with Wakame and Shiitake Mushrooms

Serves: 4–6   Time: 20 minutes

1/4 cup wakame*

6 cups water

1/4 pound fresh shiitake mushrooms

2 tablespoons toasted sesame oil

3 cloves garlic, minced

1/3 cup chopped scallions (3–4 scallions)

1/4 cup barley miso

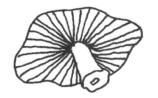

1. Rinse the wakame and place it in a large kettle with the water. Bring to a boil, then reduce the heat, and let it simmer, covered, for about 3 minutes.

2. Rinse the mushrooms under running water and discard the stems. Slice the mushrooms.

3. Heat the sesame oil in a skillet. Add the sliced mushrooms and the garlic. Sauté for 3–5 minutes.

4. Add the sautéed mushrooms and garlic to the wakame and simmer for about 3 minutes. Add the scallions and simmer a minute or two more.

5. Place about 1/4 cup of soup in a small bowl. Add the miso and mix well. Pour the mixture back into the soup. Remove the soup from the heat and mix well. Serve. If you reheat the soup, do not bring it to a boil.

*I have found two types of wakame, a sea vegetable, in the natural foods store where I shop. One kind cooks in about 5 minutes and the other in about 20 minutes. I used the quick-cooking variety, which is already cut into small pieces. If you use the other kind, cut it into small pieces with scissors and then cook it for 20 minutes. Wakame expands about seven times when it is cooked; the 1/4 cup used in this recipe should not be packed tightly into the cup.

Spicy Carrot and Chick Pea Soup

I came up with this unusual soup one day when the only vegetables I had in my refrigerator were carrots and onions.

Serves: 4   Time: 20 minutes

1. Place the water, onion, carrots, curry powder, and nutmeg in a pressure cooker. Cook over high heat until the pressure regulator starts to jiggle. Remove the pressure cooker from the heat and let it cool down on its own. Add the chick peas.

2. Blend 2 cups of the cooked mixture with the cashews, soymilk, and miso in a blender or food processor until very creamy. Do this in two or more batches if necessary. Pour the cashew mixture back into the remaining cooked carrot mixture, stir, and reheat.

3. Serve with some whole grain bread and a green salad for a hearty lunch or an easy dinner.

This soup can be made without a pressure cooker. Cook the vegetables in a covered kettle until they are tender, add the chick peas, then follow Steps 2 and 3. Add enough extra water to make the soup the desired consistency.

2 cups water

*1 cup chopped onion
(1 medium onion)*

*3 cups sliced carrots
(4 medium carrots)*

1 teaspoon curry powder

1/4 teaspoon nutmeg

2 cups cooked and drained chick peas (see page 169)

1/3 cup cashews

1 cup soymilk

2 tablespoons white miso

George's Lentil Soup

George didn't give me this recipe, but I made it to taste like the lentil soup he serves in his Camel's Den Restaurant in Sarasota. Cook it slowly.

Serves: 4   Time: about 1 1/2 hours

1. Heat the olive oil in a large, heavy kettle such as a cast-iron Dutch oven. Add the onion, bay leaves, and cumin. Sauté over medium-low heat until the onion is almost tender. (Cooking the onion slowly brings out its sweetness). Add the garlic and sauté for a minute or two more.

2. Pick over the lentils and wash and drain them. Place the lentils, water, and vinegar in the pan. Cover and bring to a boil. Reduce the heat and simmer, stirring occasionally, for about 40 minutes or until the lentils are tender. This is supposed to be a rather thick soup, but if it becomes too thick, add some more water. Add the tamari and simmer slowly, stirring occasionally, until the broth becomes rich and thick (about 20–30 minutes more).

This soup is good with a dash of hot sauce in it. Place a bottle on the table when you serve it. Serve with whole grain bread and a salad.

2 tablespoons olive oil

*1 large sweet onion
(about 3 cups)*

3 bay leaves

1 teaspoon cumin powder

4 cloves garlic

1 cup dry green lentils

4–5 cups water

2 tablespoons wine vinegar

*2 tablespoons tamari,
or to taste*

Tortilla Soup

An unusual soup with lots of flavor. Serve it before a Mexican meal or with a bean salad for a light lunch.

Serves: 4–6

Time: about 1 hour

2 tablespoons olive oil

1³/₄ cups chopped onion
(1 large onion)

3 cloves garlic, minced

2 bay leaves

¹/₂ teaspoon oregano

1 teaspoon basil*

1 teaspoon cumin

1 green pepper, diced

4 cups water or vegetable stock

1 tomato, chopped

1 tablespoon vegetable broth powder

3 tablespoons tamari

1 cup corn, cut from the cob
(1 ear)

4–5 corn tortillas

Dash of cayenne pepper, or to taste

2 tablespoons minced fresh parsley

1. Heat the oil in a large, heavy kettle. Add the onion, garlic, bay leaves, oregano, basil, and cumin. Sauté very slowly over low heat for about 20 minutes or until the onions are tender. Add the green pepper and sauté for a minute or two more.

2. Add the water, the tomato, the vegetable broth powder, and the tamari. Simmer, covered, for about 30 minutes. Add the corn.

3. Place the tortillas in a toaster oven (or under the broiler of a regular oven) and toast them for a few seconds (about the same time it takes to toast a slice of bread). Cut the tortillas into strips. Cut the strips in half and add them to the soup.

4. Add the cayenne pepper and the parsley. Serve immediately.

*If you have fresh basil, omit the dried basil and add 1–2 tablespoons of fresh basil at the end of the cooking along with the parsley.

Curried Pumpkin Soup in the Shell

This soup always gets rave reviews at parties, from Halloween to Christmas.

Serves: about 12

Time: 1 hour to prepare; about 1 1/2 hours to bake

15–17-pound pumpkin

3 tablespoons sesame oil

4 cups chopped onions
(2 medium–large Spanish onions)

1/4 cup chopped garlic
(about 12 cloves)

2 tablespoons grated fresh ginger

2 tablespoons curry powder

2 tablespoons vegetable broth powder

8 cups soymilk

1 teaspoon sea salt

1/4 cup white or yellow miso

1. Cut the top from the pumpkin as if you were making a Halloween jack-o'-lantern. Save the top for a lid. Using your hands and a big spoon, clean out the inside of the pumpkin, removing all the seeds and the stringy part.

2. Place the pumpkin on a cookie sheet, cut side up, and bake it at 350°F for about 1 hour, or until it just begins to become tender. You must be careful not to let it get too soft to hold the soup. However, if you don't bake it long enough, you won't be able to make the soup. After about 45 minutes of baking, pierce the top of the pumpkin with a sharp knife to test for tenderness. The knife should pierce the pumpkin much more easily than when it was raw, but you should not be able to dent the shell by pressing with your fingertip.

3. While the pumpkin is baking, heat the oil in a large skillet or cast-iron Dutch oven. Add the onions and the garlic. Sauté over low heat for at least 30 minutes. Add the ginger and the curry powder and continue to sauté until the onions are very tender.

4. Remove the pumpkin from the oven. Carefully scrape as much flesh as you can from the inside of the pumpkin without weakening the shell. (If the flesh is too hard to scrape out, it has not baked enough, so return it to the oven until it is just tender.) Place the pumpkin flesh in a blender or food processor with enough of the soymilk to create a smooth, creamy consistency when blended.

5. Place the pumpkin purée in the shell. Add the sautéed onion mixture, any remaining soymilk, the vegetable broth powder, and the sea salt. Place the lid back on the pumpkin and return it to the oven. Bake for about 30 minutes more. Check occasionally to make sure that the shell is not becoming overcooked.

6. Remove about 1/4 cup of soup from the shell to a small bowl, add the miso, and mix well. Add the diluted miso to the soup and mix well.

7. To serve, place the pumpkin shell on a large platter and place a ladle in the shell. Cover with the lid to keep the soup warm.

If you want to take this soup to a party, follow the recipe until the last baking. Finish baking the soup once you are at the party.

Chilled Melon Soup

This easy soup is divinely refreshing.

1 large ripe cantaloupe

1 cup mango, papaya, or orange juice

1 tablespoon honey

1 cup ice cubes

1/2 cup soymilk

Fresh mint for garnish

Serves: 2–4   Time: 10 minutes

1. Have all ingredients well chilled.

2. Cut the cantaloupe in half. Scoop out and discard the seeds. To serve the soup in the shell, cut a thin slice off the bottom of each half to keep the shell from rocking.

3. With a soup spoon or melon baller, scoop out the cantaloupe flesh, leaving enough to keep the shell strong. If you like, you can scoop out the flesh in a way that leaves the edge scalloped.

4. Place the scooped-out flesh in a blender. Add the juice, honey, and ice cubes. Blend until creamy. Add the soymilk and blend again. If your blender is too full, pour the soup into a bowl, then mix in the milk.

5. To serve two persons, pour the soup back into the shells. Refrigerate any leftover soup for later. To serve four persons, pour the soup into four small bowls. Garnish with sprigs of fresh mint.

Shirley's Gazpacho

Light and refreshing.

1 clove garlic

4 ripe tomatoes, coarsely chopped, or a 1-pound can of tomatoes

1/4 cup chopped onion (1/2 small onion)

1 cucumber, peeled and cut into large pieces

2 cups tomato juice

1/2 green pepper, cut into large pieces

1/4 cup wine vinegar

1/2 teaspoon sea salt (if using fresh tomatoes)

Dash of hot sauce (optional)

Serves: 3–5   Time: 15 minutes

1. This soup can be prepared in either a blender or a food processor. If using a food processor, first turn it on and drop the garlic through the feed tube. Add the tomatoes, onion, and half the cucumber. Blend to the desired consistency. Pour the blended mixture into a large bowl.

2. Place the tomato juice, the remaining cucumber, the green pepper, vinegar, and the salt and hot sauce (if you are using them) in the food processor. Blend to the desired consistency. Pour the blended mixture into the bowl with the first mixture. Mix well. Chill for 1 hour or more.

3. If you are using a blender, just blend together all the ingredients, pouring each batch into a large bowl. When all the ingredients have been blended, mix well and chill.

Tasty hummus variations, clockwise from upper left: Traditional Hummus (page 50), Split Pea Hummus (page 51), and Black Bean Hummus (page 51).

Enjoy zesty Tortilla Soup (page 68).

On a cold winter day, flavorful Split Pea Soup (page 64) is a good choice.

5. SALADS

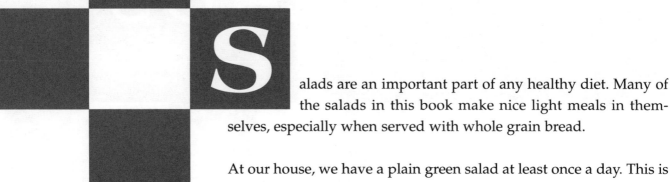

Salads are an important part of any healthy diet. Many of the salads in this book make nice light meals in themselves, especially when served with whole grain bread.

At our house, we have a plain green salad at least once a day. This is the kind of salad we eat the most often. There is no recipe to give for it because it is so simple, but here are a few tips for making salads like a pro:

- More doesn't necessarily mean better. Keep your salad simple. There is no need to add every vegetable or fruit in your refrigerator, especially if the salad is to accompany a meal.

- Mix your greens. Use a variety of lettuces, or add some spinach, arugula, radicchio, watercress, or fresh herbs. Greens such as kale or collards are generally too tough to be good in salads.

- Make sure that your greens are clean, crisp, chilled, and dry. Wash them well and dry them in a salad spinner. When you tear your greens, be careful not to bruise them. Chopping them with a sharp knife is better than tearing them roughly, as bruised leaves will soon lose their crispness.

- Make a fresh dressing to serve with your beautiful greens. It takes only a minute and there are many wonderful recipes in this book. (See pages 89–91.)

- As soon as the dressing is on the salad, serve it. Forget about saving it for later; it will be wilted. If you have made more salad than you think will be eaten, serve the dressing on the side.

Apple Peanut Salad

Kids will like this one.

Serves: 4   Time: 10 minutes

1. In a small bowl cream together the peanut butter, lemon juice, and the apple or pineapple juice.
2. Place the apples in a medium bowl. Add the peanut sauce and the raisins. Mix well and serve.

1/4 cup peanut butter, smooth or crunchy

1 tablespoon lemon juice

1/4 cup apple or pineapple juice

4 apples, diced (peel if not organic)

1/4 cup raisins

Cherry Tomato Salad

This easy salad is both beautiful and delicious.

Serves: 4   Time: 10 minutes to prepare; 1 hour or more to chill

1. In the serving bowl, mix together the basil, garlic, vinegar, and tamari.
2. Slice the tomatoes in two and place them in the serving bowl. Gently mix well. Refrigerate for at least an hour, stirring occasionally.

2 tablespoons finely chopped fresh basil (about 10 leaves)

1 clove garlic, pressed

1 tablespoon balsamic vinegar

1 tablespoon tamari

1 pint cherry tomatoes

Broccoli Salad

Serves: 4   Time: 15 minutes to prepare; 1 hour or more to chill

1. Steam the broccoli until it is tender but still crisp.
2. Place it in a bowl with the remaining ingredients. Mix well, chill, and serve.

5–6 cups broccoli flowerets

1 cup Green Cucumber Dressing (see page 89)

1/2 red bell pepper, finely chopped

2–3 scallions, chopped

1 tablespoon Dijon-style mustard

1/4 teaspoon sea salt

SPROUTING A GARDEN IN YOUR KITCHEN

Sprouting is a great way to enjoy fresh, high-quality produce throughout the year. It requires surprisingly little effort, and it takes up little space in the kitchen. Both children and adults marvel at the miracle of how a few dry seeds can grow into a bouquet of luscious greens in a matter of days. You can't beat the simple satisfaction you derive from growing a portion of your own food. Even the busy city-dweller can practice the art of food cultivation.

When seeds are sprouted, their nutritional content (especially vitamin C) is significantly increased, they become easier to digest, and they require less cooking or none at all. Sprouts are the cleanest food you can eat because while they're growing they must be rinsed two or three times a day. They are also free from pesticides and other additives. Sprouts are crisp and tender; their flavors run from sweet to piquant, depending on the kind of seeds.

WHAT TO SPROUT

Any whole, unbroken seed can be sprouted. Here are some of the more popular ones:

Wheat and rye—These make sweet, delicious sprouts, among the easiest to grow.

Beans—My favorites are chick peas (garbanzos), lentils, kidney beans, pinto beans, adzuki beans, peas, and mung beans.

Alfalfa, clover, radish, and mustard—All of these small seeds make wonderful fine-textured sprouts for salads and sandwiches. They can be mixed and grown together. Clover is mild-flavored and similar to alfalfa. Radish and mustard are very piquant and are best mixed with alfalfa or clover.

Fenugreek—Fenugreek is spicy and aromatic.

Sunflower—Sunflower sprouts are mild.

There are many other kinds of seeds that can be sprouted; look for them in your local natural foods store. Always use seeds that are sold for sprouting or eating; sometimes those sold for gardening have been treated with a fungicide.

HOW TO SPROUT

There are two sprouting methods: one uses a jar, the other a bowl.

Using a Wide-Mouth Glass Jar

Use this method for small seeds such as alfalfa, mustard, clover, fenugreek, and radish. You will need a quart glass jar and a piece of cheesecloth or clean nylon stocking to stretch over the jar opening. Measure two tablespoons of alfalfa seeds or a mixture of alfalfa and other small seeds.

1. Place the seeds in the glass jar. Cover them with room-temperature water, and let them soak for 4–8 hours.

2. Secure the cheesecloth or nylon over the opening of the jar with a string or rubber band.

3. Strain the water out of the jar through the fabric. The seeds will remain in the jar. You may save the soaking water and use it to water your house plants. They will love you for it!

4. Rinse the seeds thoroughly (do not remove the fabric) and immediately pour out the water. Let the seeds drain well.

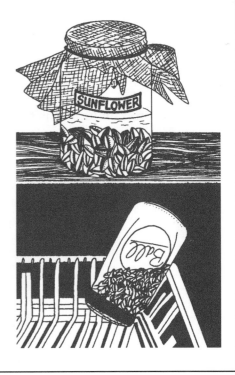

5. Continue rinsing the seeds in this way two or three times a day for 4–5 days (or less in warm climates) until the sprouts have grown to the length you want. The sprouts should nearly fill the jar.

Using a Bowl and Wire Strainer

Use this method for growing large sprouts (beans, grains, and sunflower). It is unbelievably easy!

1. Place the seeds to be sprouted in a bowl that gives them enough room to double without being crowded. About 1 cup is a convenient quantity to sprout; however, you can use more or less, as you wish. If you are using beans, pick them over and remove any broken ones.

2. Cover the seeds with water and let them soak for 8–10 hours.

3. Drain the soaked beans or seeds through a wire strainer (you can save the water for your house plants) and rinse them under running water.

4. Return the drained seeds to their bowl.

5. Rinse and drain them as specified above twice a day for 3–5 days, until the sprouts have grown to the length you want.

SPROUTING TIPS

Follow these guidelines for successful kitchen gardening:

- Your home-grown mung and adzuki sprouts will tend to turn brown before they are as long as the ones you see in stores, which are grown in complete darkness and under pressure. But yours will still be very good; they will just take a little longer to cook.

- Wheat and rye are ready to eat 2–3 days after sprouting (unless you wish to grow wheatgrass, a long, stout sprout that requires a soil medium). If you wait longer, they will become too fibrous to chew.

- The most common mistake that people make in sprouting seeds is not to drain them adequately. Leaving seeds standing in water causes them to rot.

- Mold is a sign of inadequate drainage or too much warmth. If only a few sprouts in a batch have started to mold, pick them out and discard them. Rinse the remaining sprouts well. They will still be good to eat.

- Most books on sprouting recommend growing sprouts in a dark place. This is not necessary. I keep mine on the kitchen counter so that I will

not forget to rinse them, and they do just fine.

- If the sprouts dry up, it is because they were not rinsed frequently enough. Rinse more often in dry environments.

HOW TO USE SPROUTS

Here are some of my favorite ways to use sprouts:

- Use alfalfa or clover sprouts in sandwiches, as a garnish, and in salads. They are also good blended into soups. Add just before serving so they don't cook.

- For a spicier flavor, add a few radish or mustard seeds to alfalfa seeds when you sprout them.

- Wheat or rye sprouts are good as a cold or hot breakfast cereal (or mixed with your favorite cereal). They can also be added to fruit salads, rice or grain dishes, pancake or muffin batters, and bread doughs.

- Fenugreek sprouts are good in curries and grain dishes.

- Lentil sprouts cook very quickly. They may be stir-fried with vegetables for a fast and nourishing entrée.

- If mung sprouts are an inch or longer, they can be stir-fried or added to soups during the last few minutes of cooking. Slightly sprouted mung beans can be cooked like any other beans; they just cook more quickly.

Louise's Red and White Cabbage Salad

This simple salad is surprisingly good.

Serves: 3   Time: 15 minutes

1 cup coarsely shredded red cabbage

1¹/₂ cups coarsely shredded white cabbage

2 tablespoons olive oil

2 tablespoons balsamic vinegar

1 clove garlic, pressed

¹/₄ teaspoon sea salt

1. Mix together all ingredients

2. Serve immediately or chill first.

VARIATIONS:

Add ¹/₄ teaspoon curry powder. You may also add 2 tablespoons currants.

Tofu Salad

Easy and nutritious.

Serves: 4   Time: 20 minutes

1 pound firm tofu

¹/₂ cup tahini

¹/₂ cup finely chopped celery (1 stalk)

³/₄ cup finely chopped scallions (8–9 scallions)

¹/₄ cup finely chopped parsley

2 cloves garlic, pressed

¹/₂ cup nutritional yeast

¹/₄ teaspoon kelp powder or sea salt, or to taste

2 tablespoons lemon juice

2 tablespoons tamari

1. Crumble the tofu in a mixing bowl. Add the tahini and mix well with a wooden spoon. Add the remaining ingredients and mix well with your hands.

2. As a salad, serve on a bed of fresh greens garnished with your choice of raw vegetables. For sandwiches, spread on whole grain bread and garnish with sprouts or lettuce and a slice of tomato. Makes 4 sandwiches.

Sambals

This recipe is from Shirley Knott, who was one of my cooking students. She served it at our end-of-the-session class party. It was a hot summer night, and this dish was very refreshing and well appreciated.

Serves: 6   Time: 20 minutes to prepare; 1 hour to chill

1. In a large bowl, lightly toss together all of the ingredients.

2. Refrigerate 1 hour before serving.

This dish is a wonderful accompaniment to curries or other spicy foods.

1 cucumber, cubed (peel if it has been waxed)

1 tomato, cubed

2 stalks celery, chopped

1 green pepper, diced

2 scallions, chopped

1/2 cup grated fresh coconut

1/4 cup chopped parsley

Marinated Cucumber with Radishes

Cool, crisp, and refreshing.

Serves: 4–6   Time: 15 minutes to prepare; 2–3 hours to marinate

1. Wash and thinly slice the cucumber and radishes. Place them in a shallow serving dish.

2. Pour the sesame oil, tamari, and vinegar over the vegetables and then add cool water to cover. Mix well and allow to marinate in the refrigerator for at least 2 hours before serving.

1 unwaxed cucumber

12 medium–large radishes (1 bunch)

1 tablespoon toasted sesame oil

3 tablespoons tamari

3 tablespoons rice vinegar or cider vinegar

Water

Tropical Mousse with Orange Gel

A pretty jelled salad to serve as a first course at a luncheon.

1/2 cup water

1/2 cup concentrated fruit sweetener

1 slightly rounded tablespoon agar flakes

1 cup mashed avocado (about 1 medium avocado)

1 package (10 1/2 ounces) firm silken tofu

1 tablespoon lemon juice

1 teaspoon grated lemon peel

1 cup finely chopped pineapple (fresh or unsweetened canned)

TOPPING:

2 cups orange juice

2 slightly rounded tablespoons agar flakes

2 tablespoons concentrated fruit sweetener

2 kiwis, peeled and thinly sliced

Serves: 6–9   Time: 40 minutes to prepare; 2–3 hours to set

1. Combine 1/2 cup water, 1/2 cup sweetener, and 1 tablespoon agar flakes in a saucepan. Bring to a boil, then reduce the heat and simmer for 10 minutes, or until the agar is completely dissolved.

2. Place the avocado, tofu, lemon juice, and lemon peel in a food processor. Blend until smooth and creamy. Add the dissolved agar mixture and continue to blend until well mixed.

3. Transfer the mixture to a bowl. Add the pineapple, mix well, and spread the mixture evenly in a lightly oiled 8-x-8-inch cake pan. Refrigerate until set, about 1–2 hours.

4. When the mixture is set, prepare the topping: Combine the orange juice, 2 tablespoons agar flakes, and 2 tablespoons sweetener in a saucepan. Bring the mixture to a boil. Reduce the heat and simmer, stirring occasionally, for 5–10 minutes or until the agar is dissolved.

5. Let the mixture cool for about 10 minutes, then carefully pour it over the avocado cream. Decorate the top with the kiwi slices and refrigerate until set, about 1–2 hours.

6. To serve, cut into squares.

Bunny's Eggplant Salad

This recipe, from Bunny Sarna, a friend, is a traditional Indian recipe that is exquisite despite its simple ingredients.

Serves: 4–6   Time: 1 hour to cook eggplant; 20 minutes to prepare; 1–2 hours to chill

1 medium eggplant (about 12 ounces)

1/3 cup Cashew "Sour Cream" (see page 91)*

1/2 teaspoon sea salt

1–2 tablespoons finely chopped fresh parsley or mint

1. Rub the eggplant lightly with oil and pierce the skin all over at about 1-inch intervals. Place the eggplant on a cookie sheet and bake it at 350°F for about 1 hour or until the eggplant shrivels and is very soft inside.

2. While the eggplant is baking, prepare the Cashew "Sour Cream." Set aside.

3. When the eggplant is done, let it cool for easier handling, then cut it in half lengthwise. Scrape out the flesh with a spoon. Place the flesh in a mixing bowl and mash it with a fork or potato masher. Add the Cashew "Sour Cream" and the salt, and mix well. Chill for 1 hour. Place in a serving bowl and sprinkle with parsley or mint.

4. Serve as a side dish to accompany hot, spicy dishes such as curries.

*Traditionally, this dish is made with real sour cream or a mixture of sour cream and yogurt.

Moroccan Carrot Salad

Simple but unusual, and very tasty.

Serves: 2–4   Time: 10 minutes

2 cups grated carrots (2–3 medium carrots)

1/3 cup fresh-squeezed orange juice

1 teaspoon honey

1/2 teaspoon cumin

1/4 teaspoon sea salt

1 tablespoon grated orange peel (include only if organically grown)

1 tablespoon light sesame oil

1. In a large bowl, combine all of the ingredients and mix well.

2. Let stand about 5 minutes before serving.

VARIATION:
Add 2–4 tablespoons raisins.

Tempeh Salad

Use this salad for sandwiches, or serve it on a bed of fresh greens.

1 package (8 ounces) tempeh

⅓ cup tahini

2 tablespoons water

3 tablespoons lemon juice

2 tablespoons tamari

⅓ cup sunflower seeds

½ cup finely chopped celery
(1 stalk)

½ cup finely chopped onion
(½ medium onion)

1 cup grated carrot
(1 large carrot)

½ teaspoon sage

1 teaspoon herbes de Provence
(see page 102)

Serves: 4   Time: 30 minutes to prepare; 1 hour to chill

1. Cut the tempeh into small cubes and steam for 15–20 minutes.

2. Meanwhile, place the tahini, water, lemon juice, and tamari in a medium bowl and mix well.

3. Coarsely grind the sunflower seeds in a blender. Add the seeds to the tahini mixture. Add the remaining ingredients. Then add the steamed tempeh and mix well. Chill 1 hour before serving.

Tempeh salad, spread on whole grain bread, makes a hearty and satisfying sandwich. Garnish with a slice of tomato and some lettuce or sprouts.

Springtime Tempeh Salad

This salad makes a high-protein light lunch.

1 package (8 ounces) tempeh

1 pound fresh asparagus

⅔ of a 10½-ounce package of extra-firm silken tofu

2 tablespoons olive oil

1 tablespoon umeboshi paste

1 tablespoon Dijon-style mustard

1 teaspoon tarragon

1 cup frozen peas (or lightly steamed fresh)

3 scallions, chopped

1 stalk celery, finely chopped

Serves: 3–4   Time: 30 minutes to prepare; 1 hour to chill

1. Cut the tempeh into small cubes and steam for 15–20 minutes.

2. Wash the asparagus and snap off the tough bottom part of the stems. Cut the remaining asparagus into 1-inch pieces and steam them for about 4 minutes or until they are tender but still crisp.

3. Place the tofu, oil, umeboshi paste, mustard, and tarragon in a food processor. Blend until very smooth and creamy. Scrape the sides of the food processor occasionally to make sure that all the tofu is blended.

4. Mix the steamed tempeh with the tofu dressing. Add the steamed asparagus, frozen peas (no need to cook them first), scallions, and celery. Mix well and chill for 1 hour.

5. Serve on a bed of fresh salad greens.

Orient Express Pasta Salad

The sea vegetable arame and Oriental seasonings make this pasta salad refreshingly exotic.

Serves: 3–4   Time: 30 minutes to prepare; 30 minutes to chill

1. Rinse the arame through a wire strainer. Put it in a small bowl and cover it with water. Let soak for about 5 minutes, then drain the arame and place it in a small saucepan with the water, tamari, and toasted sesame oil. Bring the mixture to a boil, then lower the heat and simmer for about 10 minutes or until most of the liquid has been absorbed. Set aside.

2. While the arame is cooking, steam the carrots until they are tender but still crisp.

3. Bring a large kettle of water to a boil and cook the pasta al dente. Drain the cooked pasta and rinse briefly in cool water.

4. Place the sesame seeds in a small oven-proof dish and bake them at 350°F for about 10 minutes or until they are lightly toasted. (A toaster oven may be used.)

5. Place the arame with any remaining liquid, the steamed carrots, the cooked pasta, and the toasted sesame seeds in a large bowl. Add the frozen peas (no need to cook or thaw them first) and the scallions.

6. In a cup or small bowl make the dressing: Mix together the sesame oil, tamari, vinegar, and ginger.

7. Pour this dressing over the salad. Toss and chill for 1 hour. Toss again before serving.

$^1/_2$ cup arame

2 tablespoons water

1 tablespoon tamari

1 teaspoon toasted sesame oil

$1^1/_3$ cups diagonally sliced carrots (about 2 medium carrots)

6 ounces (about 2 cups) whole grain pasta spirals

2 tablespoons sesame seeds

$^1/_2$ cup frozen peas

2–3 scallions, finely chopped

DRESSING:

2 tablespoons light (not toasted) sesame oil

1 tablespoon tamari

2 tablespoons rice or cider vinegar

1 teaspoon finely grated fresh ginger

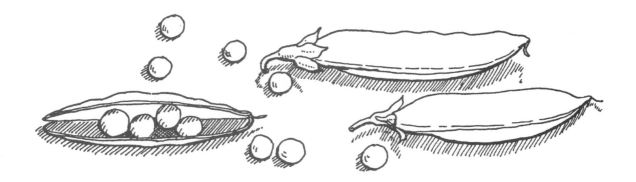

Pasta Salad with Fennel

1 bulb fennel

1 ear corn

6 ounces (about 2 cups) whole wheat pasta spirals

1/2 cup Sweet Red Pepper Dressing (page 90), or to taste

1 red bell pepper, diced

2–3 scallions, chopped

1/3 cup fennel leaves, finely chopped

1 small head Boston lettuce

1 recipe Umeboshi Cream (page 91) (optional)

The mild anise flavor of the fennel makes this pasta salad especially refreshing.

Serves: 3–4   Time: 40 minutes to prepare; 1 hour to chill

1. Wash the fennel, slice it, and separate the slices. Steam until it is barely tender, about 5 minutes. Place the steamed fennel in a large bowl.

2. Cut the corn off the cob and steam it for 2–3 minutes, then place it in the bowl with the fennel. Refrigerate while you prepare the other ingredients.

3. Cook the pasta according to the directions on the package. Some whole wheat pasta takes 12–18 minutes to cook. Test it by tasting. Do not overcook. When the pasta is done, drain it and rinse it well in cool water. Add the pasta to the steamed vegetables. Mix in the salad dressing and refrigerate while you prepare the remaining vegetables.

4. Mix in the red pepper, scallions, and fennel leaves, and return the salad to the refrigerator to chill for 1 hour.

5. Serve on a bed of Boston lettuce. Top with a dollop of Umeboshi Cream, if you like.

Quinoa Tabouli

1 cup quinoa

2 cups water

2 tablespoons olive oil

2 tablespoons minced fresh mint, or 1 teaspoon dried

1/2 teaspoon sea salt

1/4 cup lemon juice

3 cloves garlic, pressed

1/2 cup finely chopped scallions (6 scallions)

3/4 cup finely chopped fresh parsley

I like this dish even better than traditional tabouli made with bulgur wheat.

Serves: 4–6   Time: 25 minutes to prepare; 1 hour or more to chill

1. Place the quinoa in a medium saucepan, cover it with water, and swish it around with your hand to wash it. Drain the quinoa through a wire strainer and return it to the pan. Add 2 cups water, cover, and bring to a boil. Reduce the heat and simmer for 15–20 minutes or until the water has been absorbed.

2. Place the cooked quinoa in a medium bowl. Add the olive oil, mint, salt, lemon juice, and garlic. Mix well and refrigerate for about 1 hour or until chilled. Add the scallions and parsley. Mix well.

Walnut Rice Salad

Easy to prepare, this is a nice dish to take to a potluck dinner or picnic. It's best with freshly made rather than leftover rice.

Serves: 4–6   Time: 50 minutes to prepare; 1–2 hours to chill

1. Wash and drain the rice. Place it in a pan with the water. Cover and bring to a boil. Reduce the heat and simmer for about 45 minutes or until the water is absorbed.

2. Meanwhile, place the walnuts in an oven-proof dish and bake at 350°F until they are lightly toasted, about 10 minutes; check them and stir occasionally to make sure they do not burn.

3. Transfer the rice to a medium bowl. Add the walnuts, oil, vinegar, salt, and garlic. Mix well and chill for at least 30 minutes. Add the remaining ingredients. Mix well and refrigerate until chilled, about 1–2 hours.

1 cup long grain brown or brown Basmati rice

2 cups water

1 cup walnut pieces

2–3 tablespoons walnut or hazelnut oil

2 tablespoons rice vinegar

$1/2$ teaspoon sea salt

2 cloves garlic, pressed

$1/2$ cup chopped scallions

$1/2$ cup minced fresh parsley

1 red bell pepper, finely diced

Greek Rice Salad

As with Walnut Rice Salad (above), this delicious salad is best when you cook and chill the rice fresh, instead of using leftover rice.

Serves: 3–4   Time: 1 hour to prepare; 1 hour or more to chill

1. Wash and drain the rice. Place it in a pan with the water. Cover and bring to a boil. Reduce the heat and simmer for about 45 minutes or until the water is absorbed.

2. While the rice is cooking, steam the green beans until they are tender but still crisp. Transfer them to another container and place, uncovered, in the refrigerator to cool while you prepare the remaining ingredients.

3. Rinse the cooked rice briefly in cool water and drain well through a wire strainer. Place the rice, green beans, bell pepper, olives, scallions, and feta cheese in a large bowl. Pour the oil and the lemon juice over the mixture. Add the basil and the oregano and mix well. Refrigerate until chilled.

4. To serve, place a curly lettuce leaf on the side of each plate. Place a mound of the rice salad in the middle of the plate, covering part of the lettuce, then garnish with the chopped tomato.

1 cup brown rice

2 cups water

2 cups cut green beans (1-inch pieces)

$1/2$ green bell pepper, finely chopped

$2/3$ cup halved pitted black olives

3 scallions, chopped

$1^1/3$ cups crumbled feta cheese

$1/4$ cup olive oil

2 tablespoons lemon juice

2 tablespoons fresh basil, or 1 teaspoon dried

1 tablespoon fresh oregano, or $1/2$ teaspoon dried

1 large ripe tomatoes, chopped

Greek New Potato and Green Bean Salad

Served on lettuce leaves, this salad makes a scrumptious light meal.

1³/₄ pounds new potatoes, scrubbed and quartered

3 cups cut green beans (1-inch pieces)

¹/₄ cup olive oil

¹/₄ cup balsamic vinegar

2 tablespoons tamari

¹/₃ cup finely chopped onion (¹/₂ small onion)

1 cup sliced pitted black olives

1 cup crumbled feta cheese (optional)*

¹/₄ cup chopped fresh basil (or ¹/₄ cup parsley and 1 teaspoon dried basil)

Serves: 4 as a main dish, 8 as a side dish

Time: 30 minutes to prepare; 2 hours to chill

1. Place the potato chunks in a large pot. (I use my pressure cooker for this). Place the green beans on top. Add about an inch of water (less if using a pressure cooker), cover, and bring to a boil. Lower the heat and simmer until the potatoes are tender but still firm. Stir occasionally and add more water if necessary to keep the potatoes from sticking. If you are using a pressure cooker, bring the pressure up, let the valve jiggle for a few seconds, then immediately cool the pot down under running water.

2. With a slotted spoon, transfer the cooked vegetables to a large bowl. In a small bowl, mix together the olive oil, vinegar, and tamari, and pour this mixture over the cooked vegetables. Add the chopped onion and mix well. Place the salad in the refrigerator for about 30 minutes to cool.

3. Add the olives, feta, and basil to the cooled salad. Mix well and chill. Mix again before serving on a bed of Boston lettuce. A garnish of cherry tomatoes would be nice.

*This salad is good without feta, but you may want to add more olives.

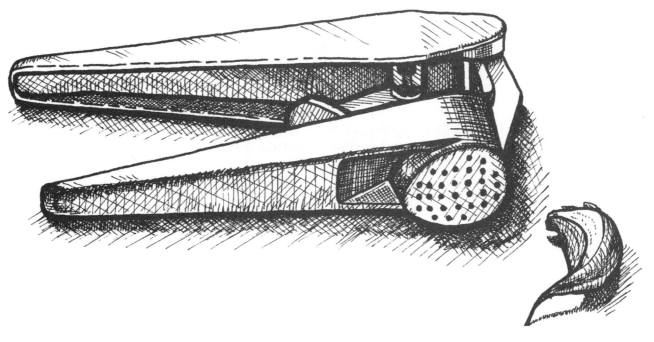

Green Beans and Hazelnut Salad

This luscious salad is elegant in its simplicity.

Serves: 4–6   Time: 20 minutes to prepare; 1–2 hours to chill

1. Steam the green beans until they are tender but still firm.

2. Place the nuts in a small bowl. Add 1 tablespoon oil and stir to coat them. Place the oiled hazelnuts in an oven-proof pan and roast them in an oven or toaster oven at 350°F until they are roasted, about 10 minutes. Stir them occasionally so they don't burn. When done, they will be very dark and give off an aroma.

3. In a small bowl, mix together the remaining oil, vinegar, tarragon, salt, and garlic. Place the cooked beans and the roasted nuts in a medium bowl. Pour the dressing over them, mix well, and chill for about 1 hour. Mix again before serving.

Note: For best results, use perfectly fresh green beans and don't over- or understeam them.

3 cups (about 12 ounces) cut fresh green beans (1-inch pieces)

1 cup whole raw hazelnuts

1 tablespoon oil (preferably, hazelnut oil)

DRESSING:

1 tablespoon oil (preferably, hazelnut oil)

2 tablespoons balsamic vinegar

1 teaspoon tarragon

1/2 teaspoon sea salt

1 clove garlic, pressed

Pinto Salad

Serve this oilless salad with some homemade corn bread for a light meal.

Serves: 2–4   Time: 20 minutes

1. In a medium bowl, combine the beans, scallions, celery, and tomato. In a small bowl combine the garlic, tamari, vinegar, tomato paste, basil, cumin, and cayenne pepper. Mix well.

2. Pour the tamari mixture over the beans and vegetables and mix well. Chill for about 1 hour, if the beans are hot. Marinate, if desired, or serve immediately on a bed of fresh lettuce.

2 cups cooked and drained pinto beans (see page 169)

3 scallions, chopped

2 stalks celery, finely chopped

1 ripe tomato, chopped

1 clove garlic, pressed

2 tablespoons tamari

2 tablespoons balsamic vinegar

2 tablespoons tomato paste

2 tablespoons fresh, or 1 teaspoon dried basil

1 teaspoon cumin

Dash of cayenne pepper, or to taste

Lentil Salad

1 cup dried green lentils

2¹/₂ cups water

2 tablespoons olive oil

2 tablespoons tamari

2 tablespoons balsamic vinegar

2 teaspoons Dijon-style mustard

¹/₃ cup chopped onion
(1 small onion) or scallions
(3–4 scallions)

¹/₃ cup minced fresh parsley

¹/₂ red bell pepper, finely chopped

¹/₃ cup finely chopped unsweetened dill pickle

1 teaspoon summer savory

1. Wash and pick over the lentils. Place them in a medium pot with the water. Cover and bring the water to a boil. Reduce the heat and simmer, stirring occasionally, until the water is absorbed and the lentils are tender but not too soft, about 40–45 minutes.

2. Drain the cooked lentils and rinse them briefly under cool water. Drain again, then place them in a medium bowl. Add the remaining ingredients and mix well. Chill for at least 1 hour before serving.

3. Serve on a bed of fresh greens accompanied by some whole grain bread. This salad makes a nice light lunch.

6. SAUCES, CONDIMENTS & DRESSINGS

A sauce can greatly enhance a meal, not only in taste and appearance, but nutritionally as well. You won't have to feel guilty about serving and enjoying the sauces in this book. They are lower in fat than many sauces, and they contain neither cholesterol nor saturated fat. They do contain nutritious ingredients such as tofu, tomatoes, nuts, and soymilk, and they are flavored with tamari, miso, herbs, and spices.

These sauces are easy as well as quick to make. A sauce, along with some vegetables, can turn a plate of cooked rice, millet, or other grain (see page 152) into a delicious, well-balanced meal. Try these examples for starters:

- Millet with steamed green beans, topped with the Creamy Tomato Sauce (page 95).

- Buckwheat with sautéed onions and mushrooms, topped with Tahini Milk Gravy (page 98) and accompanied by a salad.

- Quinoa with stir-fried snow peas, red bell pepper, and scallions, topped with a dollop of Umeboshi Cream (page 91).

- Bulgur with broccoli and carrots, topped with Hummus Sauce (page 100).

- Bulgur with steamed mixed vegetables and Spicy Peanut Sauce (page 101).

- Brown rice with steamed cauliflower or broccoli, topped with Soy Cheese Sauce (page 100), Golden Cashew Sauce (page 99), or Creamy Dill Sauce (page 102). Add a salad.

- Brown rice or millet with Spinach in Cream Sauce (page 231).

Lemon Scallion Dressing

A low-fat dressing with a pale green color and a tangy lemon flavor.

Yield: about 1 cup   Time: 5–10 minutes

1. Place all the ingredients in a blender or food processor and blend until smooth and creamy.

2. Serve on any green salad or mixed vegetable salad.

This dressing is best fresh but will keep about three days refrigerated in a tightly covered jar.

$1/4$ cup lemon juice

$1/3$ cup water

3 scallions, chopped

2 tablespoons olive oil

2 tablespoons yellow miso

1 tablespoon chopped fresh basil, or $1/2$ teaspoon dried

$1/4$ of a $10^1/2$-ounce package of extra-firm silken tofu

Green Cucumber Dressing

This is another low-fat dressing that you can use generously.

Yield: about 2 cups   Time: 30 minutes

1. Blend the ingredients in a blender or food processor until smooth and creamy. If using a blender, start with the cucumber, oil, and lemon juice. When they are blended, add the remaining ingredients and blend until smooth.

2. Serve on any green salad or mixed vegetable salad.

This dressing is best fresh but will keep about three days refrigerated in a tightly covered jar.

1 cucumber, cut into chunks (peel if the skin has been waxed)

2 tablespoons olive oil

2 tablespoons lemon juice

2 tablespoons white miso

$1/3$ of a $10^1/2$-ounce package of extra-firm silken tofu

1 scallion, chopped

2 tablespoons chopped fresh parsley or dill weed

Sea salt to taste (optional)

Sweet Red Pepper Dressing

This dressing is rich in flavor but not in fat.

1 red bell pepper, cut into chunks

1/4 cup olive oil

1 teaspoon honey

2 tablespoons white miso

1 teaspoon basil

Yield: about 1 cup   Time: 10 minutes

1. Place all the ingredients in a blender or food processor. Blend until very smooth, scraping the sides of the blender or food processor with a spatula if necessary.

2. Serve on any green salad or mixed vegetable salad.

VARIATION:

For a tangy dressing, substitute umeboshi paste for the honey.

Peanut Salad Dressing

Exotic, easy, and nutritious.

1/2 cup peanut butter, smooth or crunchy

1 tablespoon tamari

1 tablespoon rice vinegar

1 teaspoon toasted sesame oil

1/4 cup water

1 clove garlic, pressed

Yield: 3/4 cup   Time: 5 minutes

1. In a small bowl, cream together the peanut butter, tamari, vinegar, and sesame oil. Gradually add the water while stirring briskly. Add the garlic and mix well.

2. Serve on any green salad.

This dressing will keep a week or more in the refrigerator.

Tarragon Mustard Vinaigrette

I make this dressing often.

1/2 cup olive oil

2 tablespoons wine vinegar

2 tablespoons tamari

1 tablespoon Dijon-style mustard

1 teaspoon tarragon

2 cloves garlic, pressed

Yield: 3/4 cup   Time: 5 minutes

1. Place all the ingredients in a small glass jar and shake to blend. It's best after standing 1–2 hours and will keep for weeks in the refrigerator.

2. Serve on green salad or as a dip for artichokes.

Tahini Dressing

Yield: ³/₄ cup   Time: 5–10 minutes

1. In a small bowl, mix together the tahini, tamari, lemon juice, and garlic. While stirring vigorously, slowly add the water. Continue to stir until the mixture is well blended. Add the parsley and mix again. This dressing will keep about a week in the refrigerator.

2. Serve on a green salad or over steamed vegetables, rice, or tofu.

VARIATION:

For a dipping sauce to use with raw vegetables or crackers, add less water.

¹/₃ cup tahini

1 tablespoon tamari

1 tablespoon lemon juice

1 clove garlic, pressed

¹/₄ cup water

1 tablespoon finely minced fresh parsley

Cashew "Sour Cream"

Rich and yummy without the saturated fat of real sour cream.

Yield: 1 cup   Time: 5–10 minutes

1. Place all the ingredients in a blender and blend for about 2 minutes or until very smooth and creamy. To be successful, this recipe must be well blended.

2. Use in the Hot Eggplant Mash with Rice (page 163) and Bunny's Eggplant Salad (page 79). This dressing is also a good substitute for sour cream in fruit salads or on potatoes.

Cashew "Sour Cream" thickens a little on standing and will keep about three days in the refrigerator.

¹/₂ cup raw cashews

¹/₂ cup soymilk

2 tablespoons lemon juice

Umeboshi Cream

Use Umeboshi Cream wherever you would use mayonnaise.

Yield: about 1 cup   Time: 5 minutes

1. Blend together all ingredients in a blender or food processor until very smooth and creamy. Use a rubber spatula to scrape the sides of the blender or food processor occasionally to make sure that all the tofu is well blended.

2. Use on artichokes, new potatoes, Asparagus Orientale (page 219) or Barley with Mushrooms and Walnuts (page 156).

Umeboshi Cream will keep for three or four days in the refrigerator in a covered container.

1 package (10¹/₂ ounces) extra-firm silken tofu

1 tablespoon umeboshi paste (pickled salted plum paste)

2 tablespoons olive oil

1 clove garlic

Carrot Sauce

A colorful sauce to serve over a dinner loaf.

1 tablespoon oil

3 tablespoons whole wheat pastry flour

1½ cups fresh carrot juice

1 tablespoon Dijon-style mustard

¼ teaspoon sea salt

1 tablespoon fresh dill weed

Yield: about 1½ cups   Time: 15 minutes

1. Heat the oil in a small saucepan. Add the flour and mix well.

2. While stirring constantly over medium-high heat, slowly pour in the carrot juice. Continue to stir and cook until the sauce is thick.

3. Add the mustard, salt, and dill. Serve immediately.

This sauce is especially good over Almond Rice Loaf (page 191).

Fresh Mango Chutney

Make this easy chutney to add an exotic touch to curries and grain dishes.

1 large mango

2 tablespoons balsamic vinegar

½ cup raisins

1 tablespoon honey

2 teaspoons grated fresh ginger

½ teaspoon cinnamon

Dash of cayenne pepper, or to taste

Yield: about 1⅔ cups   Time: 15–20 minutes

1. The mango must be good and ripe so that it will be sweet enough. The skin should be orange-red with black spots, and give slightly to pressure. With a sharp paring knife, peel the mango: Insert the knife at the stem end, going deep enough to cut through the skin but not the fruit. Cut all the way around the widest part of the fruit. Then cut the skin lengthwise three or four times on each side. Now remove the skin: Starting at one end or the other, just peel off the strips of skin that you have cut. If the mango is fully ripe, the skin will peel off easily.

2. Slice the flesh away from the large, flat pit in the center of the fruit, and dice the flesh. Measure 1½ cups of fruit and combine it in a heavy saucepan with the remaining ingredients. Stirring constantly, bring the mixture to a boil. Reduce the heat and simmer over low heat, uncovered, for 5–10 minutes or until the raisins are plump.

3. Place the mixture in a blender or a food processor. Blend briefly; the chutney is better if it is not too smooth. Chill before serving. Mango chutney will keep several days in the refrigerator.

Serve with curries or grain dishes. For a real Indian treat, make the recipes for Whole Wheat Dosas (page 134) and Vegetable Dal Curry (page 173). Stuff the dosas with the curry and serve the chutney on the side.

Apple Chutney

An easy-to-make condiment to spice up any curry.

Yield: about 2 cups   Time: 15–20 minutes

1. Peel the apples if they are not organically grown. Otherwise, just wash them and cut them into small cubes. Place them in a small, heavy saucepan. Add the remaining ingredients. Bring the mixture to a boil. Cover, reduce the heat, and simmer for 3–5 minutes.

2. Place the mixture in a blender and blend briefly to grind the ingredients coarsely. Do not blend till smooth; it is better with a little texture.

3. Serve chilled as a condiment to accompany curries. Apple Chutney will keep at least a week in the refrigerator.

2 medium apples, diced

$^1/_3$ cup raisins

3 tablespoons concentrated fruit sweetener

$^1/_4$ cup water

2 tablespoons vinegar

$^1/_8$ teaspoon cayenne pepper, or to taste

1 tablespoon minced fresh ginger

2 teaspoons cinnamon

$^1/_2$ teaspoon coriander

Cranberry Sauce

A sweet and tangy complement to a healthy holiday dinner.

Yield: about 3$^1/_2$ cups   Time: 30 minutes

1. Rinse the cranberries and place them in a saucepan with the other ingredients. Bring to a boil, reduce the heat, and simmer, stirring occasionally until all the cranberries have burst and the sauce begins to thicken, about 20–25 minutes. Chill before serving.

2. Serve with Holiday Dinner Loaf (page 214).

12-ounce package fresh cranberries

1$^1/_4$ cups fresh-squeezed orange juice

1 tablespoon grated orange peel from organically grown orange

$^1/_4$ cup fruit-sweetened plum jam

$^1/_4$ cup honey

Fresh Salsa

Fresh salsa takes only a few minutes to make. It is so much better than the bottled kind.

Yield: about 2 cups — Time: 20 minutes

1–2 fresh jalapeño peppers, or to taste

1½ cups fresh tomato purée (2 small tomatoes blended in a blender)

¼ cup minced onion

⅓ cup minced yellow bell pepper

½ teaspoon sea salt

1 tablespoon balsamic vinegar

½ teaspoon basil

½ teaspoon oregano

2 tablespoons finely chopped fresh cilantro

1. Place the jalapeño peppers under the broiler or on a grill for about 5 minutes, turning often until they become blistered all over. Place them in a paper bag for about 10 minutes or until they are cool enough to handle. Peel the skin from the peppers, then cut them in half and remove their seeds and stems. Chop the peppers very finely and place them in a bowl.

2. Add the remaining ingredients and mix well. Store in a covered container in the refrigerator. Fresh salsa will keep for about a week.

3. Serve with bean dishes, Tex-Mex Corn Cakes (page 205), or corn chips.

Barbecue Sauce

Yield: 1½ cups — Time: 10 minutes

6-ounce can tomato paste

¼ cup molasses

1 teaspoon liquid smoke flavor*

½ teaspoon cinnamon

½ teaspoon allspice

2 cloves garlic, pressed

2 tablespoons tamari

½ cup water

1 tablespoon vinegar (wine, balsamic, or cider)

⅛ teaspoon cayenne pepper, or to taste

1. Combine all the ingredients and mix well. Store in a covered container in the refrigerator. It will keep for a week or more.

2. Brush over grilled tofu, tempeh, or seitan, or over veggie burgers.

*Liquid smoke flavor can be purchased in most supermarkets.

Worcestershire Sauce

A version of the traditional sauce, minus the anchovies, to spice up tofu and tempeh dishes.

Yield: about 1/2 cup sauce   Time: 10 minutes

1. Mix together all the ingredients.

2. Serve over stir-fried, pan-fried, baked, or grilled tofu or tempeh. You may also serve with veggie burgers and meatless loaves.

Worcestershire sauce will keep for several weeks in the refrigerator stored in a closed glass jar.

*Liquid smoke flavor can be purchased in most supermarkets.

1/3 cup tamari

1/4 cup honey

1 tablespoon balsamic vinegar

1/2 teaspoon dry mustard

1/8 teaspoon cayenne pepper, or to taste

1/2 teaspoon liquid smoke flavor*

1/2 teaspoon cinnamon

1/4 teaspoon allspice

Creamy Tomato Sauce

This nutritious sauce tastes very rich, but it is low in fat.

Yield: about 2 1/2 cups   Time: 20 minutes

1. Heat the olive oil in a large skillet. Add the onion, garlic, and herbs. Sauté over medium-low heat until the onions are tender. Add the tomato bits and the water. Stir and cover.

2. Place the tofu and the miso in a blender or food processor and blend until creamy. Add the tofu mixture to the onion mixture and stir. Add the fresh tomato and cook until just heated. It will separate a little, so stir before serving.

3. Serve the sauce over your favorite whole grain pasta. Sprinkle with Parmesan cheese or tofu-Parmesan, if desired, and garnish with fresh chopped parsley or basil. Accompany with a big green salad for a nice simple meal.

2 tablespoons olive oil

1 cup chopped onion (1 medium onion)

2 cloves garlic (or more to taste), minced

1 teaspoon herbes de Provence (see page 102)

1/4 cup sun-dried tomato bits

1/4 cup water

1 package (10 1/2 ounces) soft silken tofu

2 tablespoons white miso

1 fresh ripe tomato, chopped (optional)

Quick and Light Fresh Tomato Sauce

3 small ripe tomatoes

1/4 cup sun-dried tomato bits

2 tablespoons fresh basil, or
1 teaspoon dried

1 teaspoon honey

1 tablespoon arrowroot

2 tablespoons water

1 tablespoon white miso

Who says a good tomato sauce has to contain lots of olive oil and simmer for hours?

Yield: about 2 cups   Time: 15 minutes

1. Cut the tomatoes into large chunks. Blend them in a blender or food processor. You should have 2 cups of purée.

2. Place the tomato purée in a saucepan, and add the sun-dried tomato bits and the basil. Cover and bring to a simmer. Cook for about three minutes, or until the red color of the tomatoes darkens. Add the honey.

3. Dilute the arrowroot in the water and add it to the tomato mixture. Stir the mixture and continue to cook for about 1 minute or until the sauce thickens.

4. Spoon about 1/4 cup of the sauce from the pan into a small bowl. Add the miso and stir to dissolve. Add the mixture to the sauce. Mix well and serve.

Almost-Instant Tomato Sauce

1 large or 2 small, ripe tomatoes

1 tablespoon arrowroot

1/4 teaspoon sea salt

1 tablespoon fresh basil, or
1/2 teaspoon dried

This is an even simpler version of the Quick and Light Fresh Tomato Sauce (above).

Yield: about 1 1/3 cups   Time: 10 minutes

1. Cut the tomato into large chunks. Place them in a blender and blend with the other ingredients. You should have about 1 1/3 cups tomato purée.

2. Place the mixture in a saucepan and bring it to a boil. Simmer for 2–3 minutes.

This simple sauce is good over veggie burgers or loaves.

VARIATIONS:

• Sauté some garlic, onions, green pepper, and mushrooms in about 1 tablespoon of olive oil before adding the tomatoes in this recipe or the Quick and Light Fresh Tomato Sauce (above).

• Omit the arrowroot and thicken the sauce with tomato paste to the desired consistency.

Green Sauce

A creamy spinach sauce that is good over meatless loaves, grains, and vegetables.

Yield: about 1¹/₃ cups   Time: 15 minutes

1. Heat the oil in a medium saucepan. Add the flour and mix well.

2. Add the spinach and stir over medium-high heat until the spinach is wilted.

3. While stirring constantly, slowly pour in the soymilk. Cook over medium-high heat, stirring constantly, until the sauce is thick. Add the salt, nutmeg, and mustard.

4. Place the sauce in a blender and blend until smooth. If the sauce is not served immediately, return it to the saucepan to reheat. When the sauce cools it will thicken, so add more soymilk as necessary to achieve the desired consistency when you reheat.

This sauce is especially good over Quinoa Loaf (page 191).

1 tablespoon oil

3 tablespoons whole wheat pastry flour

2 cups spinach, washed, chopped, and packed to measure

1 cup soymilk (approximately)

¹/₄ teaspoon sea salt

¹/₈ teaspoon nutmeg

¹/₂ teaspoon dry mustard

Tahini Brown Sauce

This flavorful tahini sauce contains no added oil.

Yield: about 1¹/₃ cups   Time: 10–15 minutes

1. In a small saucepan mix the tahini and flour into a paste; it will separate into crumbs like a roux as it is heated. Cook over high heat, stirring constantly, until the flour starts to brown and emit a roasted aroma.

2. Remove the pan from the heat and stir in some of the water. Stir vigorously and return the pan to the heat. Continue to stir and add the remaining water. Cook over medium-high heat, stirring vigorously, until the sauce is thick and smooth. Add the tamari and the cayenne pepper.

This sauce is delicious over grain dishes.

3 tablespoons tahini

2 tablespoons whole wheat pastry flour

1¹/₄ cups water

1 tablespoon tamari, or to taste

Dash of cayenne pepper, or to taste

Mushroom Wine Sauce

Yield: about 3½ cups   Time: 35 minutes

2 tablespoons olive oil

1½ cups chopped onions
(2 medium onions or ½ large
Spanish onion)

2½ cups sliced mushrooms
(about 10–12 medium
mushrooms)*

1 teaspoon herbes de Provence
(see page 102)

¼ cup whole wheat pastry
flour

1 cup dry red wine

1 cup water

3 tablespoons tamari

1. Heat the oil in a large, heavy saucepan or kettle (I use my cast-iron Dutch oven). Add the onions and sauté over low heat, stirring occasionally, for about 20 minutes. Add the mushrooms and the herbs. Continue to sauté, stirring, until the mushrooms are tender.

2. Stir in the flour and mix well. Add about ¼ cup of the wine and mix well. Raise the heat to high and add the remaining wine and the water, about ¼ cup at a time, while stirring vigorously. Let the mixture come to a boil between each addition.

3. Add the tamari and simmer for about 5 minutes, stirring often until the sauce has reached the thickness you prefer.

This sauce is delicious with Holiday Dinner Loaf (page 214), or over any grain dish or meatless loaf. It is also good with baked marinated tofu or tempeh.

*You may use all white button mushrooms, or add some shiitake, portobello, or oyster mushrooms, if you like.

Tahini Milk Gravy

Rich, creamy, and very nutritious with the nutty taste of sesame.

Yield: about 1½ cups   Time: 10 minutes

1 tablespoon oil

2 tablespoons whole wheat
pastry flour

¼ cup tahini

1¼ cups soymilk

¼ teaspoon sea salt, or to taste

Dash of cayenne pepper, or to
taste

1. Heat the oil in a small, heavy saucepan. Add the flour and stir over high heat until the flour begins to emit a nutty aroma. Lower the heat to medium, add the tahini, and stir for a minute or two.

2. Remove the pan from the heat, stir in a little of the soymilk, and mix well. Return the pan to medium-high heat. Stirring vigorously with a wire whisk, slowly pour in the remaining soymilk. Bring to a boil and cook, stirring constantly, until the sauce has thickened. Add the salt and the cayenne. Taste the sauce and adjust the seasoning if necessary.

3. This sauce will thicken on standing. When ready to serve it, stir in enough soymilk or water to achieve the desired consistency.

Serve this sauce over simple grain and vegetable dishes. For example, brown rice or buckwheat with broccoli, carrots, and onions topped with this sauce would make an easy, well-balanced meal.

Red Pepper Sauce

A mild sauce with a pretty color.

Yield: about 1½ cups   Time: 10 minutes

1. Place the pepper, soymilk, tahini or cashew butter, and arrowroot in a blender. Blend until very smooth and creamy.

2. Pour the mixture into a saucepan. While stirring constantly with a wire whisk, bring the mixture to a boil. Reduce the heat and add the remaining ingredients. Mix well.

3. Sprinkle with basil just before serving.

1 red bell pepper, cut into chunks

½ cup soymilk

2 tablespoons tahini or cashew butter

1 tablespoon plus 1 teaspoon arrowroot

¼ teaspoon sea salt, or to taste

2 teaspoons Dijon-style mustard

Dash of cayenne pepper, or to taste

1 tablespoon minced fresh basil, or ½ teaspoon dried

Golden Cashew Sauce

This sauce has the appearance and richness of a cheese sauce, but its delicious flavor is all its own.

Yield: about 2 cups   Time: 10 minutes

1. Place all the ingredients in a blender. Blend until smooth and creamy, about 2–3 minutes.

2. Pour the blended mixture into a saucepan. Bring to a boil, stirring constantly. Reduce the heat and cook for a few seconds, stirring constantly, until the sauce has thickened. If the sauce becomes too thick, just add more water.

The sauce thickens further on standing. If you reheat it, you may want to thin it with water. On the other hand, the sauce is delicious thick and chilled. Serve over steamed broccoli or asparagus, or with hot grilled polenta.

⅔ cup raw cashews

1¼ cups water

1 tablespoon Dijon-style mustard

2 tablespoons nutritional yeast

2 tablespoons yellow or white miso

½ teaspoon turmeric

Dash of cayenne pepper, or to taste

Soy Cheese Sauce

Use this sauce wherever you would use a cheese sauce.

1 cup soymilk (approximately)

1/2 cup grated soy cheese (cheddar-flavor)

2 tablespoons whole wheat pastry flour

1 tablespoon vegetable broth powder

2 teaspoons Dijon-style mustard

1/2 teaspoon sea salt, or to taste

Dash of cayenne pepper, or to taste

Yield: about 1 1/4 cups   Time: 10 minutes

1. Place 1 cup of soymilk in a small, heavy saucepan. Place the soy cheese in a small bowl and add the flour. Mix well and add to the soymilk. While stirring constantly, bring the soymilk to a boil. Cook for a few seconds, stirring constantly, until thickened. Add the remaining ingredients and mix well.

2. If the sauce becomes too thick, thin it to the desired consistency with a little more soymilk.

This sauce is good over grain dishes such as Bulgur and Leeks with Soy Cheese Sauce (page 227) or over steamed broccoli or cauliflower.

Hummus Sauce

This is a different way to enjoy an old favorite.

1 cup cooked and drained chick peas (see page 169)

1/4 cup tahini

1 cup water

1 clove garlic

1/2 teaspoon sea salt

1 teaspoon tamari

Dash of cayenne pepper, or to taste

Yield: about 1 3/4 cups   Time: 15 minutes

1. Blend together all the ingredients in a blender until smooth.

2. Pour the mixture into a saucepan. While stirring constantly, bring the mixture to a boil. Continue to stir and cook for a few seconds more or until the sauce is thick.

If you have both leftover rice and leftover chick peas, you can have a tasty, nourishing meal almost instantly. Heat the rice while you make the sauce. Steam or pressure-cook a vegetable, such as broccoli flowerets. Top the rice with the vegetable and then the sauce.

Spicy Peanut Sauce

Use this sauce to lend an Indonesian note to grain and vegetable dishes.

Yield: about 1¼ cups   Time: 10 minutes

¼ cup peanut butter (preferably, crunchy)
1 tablespoon tamari
1 tablespoon lemon juice
⅔ cup water
1–2 cloves garlic, pressed
Dash of cayenne pepper, or to taste

1. Place the peanut butter in a small saucepan. Add the tamari and the lemon juice and mix well. Add about ⅓ cup of the water and mix well until smooth. Add the garlic and cayenne papper.

2. Heat over high heat, stirring constantly, until the mixture starts to thicken. Slowly add the remaining water, continuing to stir and cook until the sauce has reached the consistency you prefer.

Walnut Onion Gravy

Yield: about 1¼ cups   Time: 15 minutes

1 tablespoon oil
1 cup chopped sweet onion (½ medium–large onion)
½ teaspoon tarragon
½ cup chopped walnuts
3 tablespoons whole wheat pastry flour
1 cup water
1 tablespoon tamari

1. Heat the oil in a skillet. Add the onions and the tarragon. Sauté over medium-low heat until the onions are nearly tender.

2. Add the walnuts and raise the heat to medium-high. Stir until the walnuts begin to brown. Add the flour and continue to stir until the flour is browned.

3. Remove the skillet from the heat. Slowly pour the water into the skillet while stirring vigorously. Return the skillet to the heat and cook, stirring constantly, for a minute or two until the mixture has thickened.

4. Add the tamari, mix, and serve.

Walnut gravy is delicious with Simple Millet Croquettes (page 188) or any other plain or mild grain dish. It is also good with potatoes or cauliflower.

Creamy Dill Sauce

This sauce is good either hot or cold.

1 package (10½ ounces) soft silken tofu

2 tablespoons yellow miso

¼ cup chopped fresh dill weed

2 scallions, chopped

Dash of cayenne pepper, or to taste

Yield: about 1½ cups   Time: 10 minutes

1. Place all the ingredients in a blender or food processor and blend until smooth and creamy.

2. To serve the sauce warm, transfer it to a saucepan and heat over medium heat, stirring often, until it is hot. Do not boil.

This sauce is delicious over steamed vegetables such as broccoli or cauliflower. It is also good over mixed vegetables with pasta.

VARIATION:
Turn this sauce into a dip by substituting firm silken tofu for soft.

Herbes de Provence

3 tablespoons thyme

3 tablespoons marjoram

3 tablespoons summer savory

1 tablespoon basil

2 teaspoons rosemary

½ teaspoon rubbed sage

½ teaspoon fennel seeds

A beautiful mixture of herbs that grow plentifully in the South of France, herbes de Provence can be purchased in gourmet stores. Better yet, make your own with dried bulk herbs from the natural foods store, or best, with herbs grown in your own garden.

Yield: about ¾ cup   Time: 5 minutes

1. Mix the ingredients together well and store in a tightly covered glass jar.

2. Use in any recipe that calls for herbes de Provence.

7. BREADS

You can't buy anything that smells and tastes as good as home-baked bread. Baking breads at home not only assures you of freshness, it puts you in control of everything that goes into a very important part of your diet. Even breads sold in natural foods stores and bakeries often contain much more fat, sweetener, and salt than necessary. When you make your own, you can keep these ingredients to a healthy minimum. You can also choose the highest-quality organically grown whole grain flours, oils, and sweeteners.

Making yeast breads and quick breads is easier than you might think. It can become a relaxing and rewarding hobby that is sure to be appreciated by all your friends and family.

Bread-making, like other aspects of healthy cooking, has improved over the years. No longer does a healthy loaf have to be a macrobiotic brick. The addition of Vital Wheat Gluten to yeast breads and the supplemental use of whole grain flours other than wheat in quick breads, as well as improved techniques, make loaves that are not just good for people concerned about health, but just plain good.

Sourdough Rye

One of the easiest, most healthful, and delicious breads you can make, this bread is rich and satisfying.

Yield: 1 loaf

Time: 20–30 minutes to prepare; 8 hours to rise; 1 hour to bake.

1. In a large bowl, mix together the Sourdough Starter, water, molasses, salt, oil, and wheat flour. Slowly stir in enough of the rye flour to make a kneadable dough.

2. Turn the dough out onto a tabletop or countertop that has been generously sprinkled with some of the remaining rye flour. Knead in enough of the remaining rye flour to make a dough that is smooth, firm, and not sticky. Take your time, because this bread really profits from a long and thorough kneading.

3. Shape the dough into a loaf and place it in a well-oiled loaf pan, $4^1/_2$ x $8^1/_2$ x $2^1/_2$ inches. To keep the bread from sticking, sprinkle the oiled pan with cornmeal or oat flakes. Sprinkle the top of the loaf with a light coat of additional cornmeal or oat flakes.

4. Place the loaf in a warm place. Cover it lightly with a damp cloth and let it rise for about 8 hours. When the dough has risen enough, it will be almost double in bulk.

5. Bake at 350°F for 1 hour. Remove the bread from the pan and let it cool on a rack before storing.

VARIATIONS:
- *Caraway Rye:* Knead 1 tablespoon of caraway seeds into the dough.
- *Wheatless Rye:* Omit the whole wheat flour and use only rye flour. A heavier but very flavorful bread will result.

1 cup Sourdough Starter (see page 106)

1 cup warm water

2 tablespoons molasses (or other sweetener)

1 teaspoon sea salt

2 tablespoons oil (optional)

2 cups whole wheat bread flour

2 cups whole rye flour (approximately)

Cornmeal or oat flakes

Sourdough Starter

2 cups whole wheat or rye flour

2 cups warm water

1 tablespoon dry active yeast

1 clove garlic

The hearty Old World flavor of dark and pungent sourdough surpasses that of even the fanciest pastries or croissants. Here's the starter for the Sourdough Rye on page 105. Use it for other sourdough breads, too.

Yield: 3 cups   Time: 3 minutes to prepare; 3–4 days to ferment

1. Mix together all the ingredients in a clean glass, ceramic, or plastic container that is large enough to allow the mixture to double without overflowing. Cover the container with a cloth or a piece of plastic that has a hole punched in it.

2. Let the mixture sit in a warm place for three or four days. A good place is on top of a hot water heater or refrigerator. It should bubble up and fall several times and should begin to emit a sour but pleasant aroma. If the starter turns pink or orange or develops an unpleasant odor, throw it away and start again.

3. After three or four days of fermentation, discard the garlic and use the starter according to your chosen recipe. If you are unable to use it immediately, store it in the refrigerator. After one week of storage, the starter should either be used or "fed" to keep it active.

   To feed the starter, just mix in a little flour and water (about $1/2$ cup of each). Let the starter sit at room temperature for a few hours, or until it has bubbled up and fallen again. The older a starter gets, the better it becomes, so it is worthwhile keeping it going.

4. Each time that you use some of your starter, replace it with more flour and water. For example, if you use 1 cup of starter, add about $1/2$ cup of flour and $1/2$ cup of water. Let the starter sit in a warm place for 3–4 hours or until it has bubbled up and fallen again before returning the container to the refrigerator.

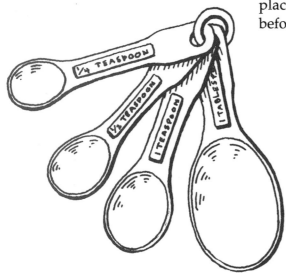

BASIC BREAD, ANALYZED

To the novice, most bread recipes are rather vague. Therefore, I have broken down the basic bread recipe and explained the function of each ingredient and the purpose of each step. I've included some tricks and tips that even the more experienced baker may find helpful.

BASIC BREAD

Yield: 2 loaves　　　　　　　Time: 3 1/2 hours

1/2 cup warm water

Drop of honey

---

2 tablespoons dry active yeast

---

2 cups warm water

1/4 cup oil

1/4 cup honey

---

2 teaspoons sea salt

1/4 cup gluten flour or 3 tablespoons Vital Wheat Gluten

---

7 cups whole wheat bread flour (approximately)

---

1. Place the 1/2 cup of water, the drop of honey, and the yeast in a small bowl. Let sit for 10 minutes to dissolve the yeast.

2. In a large bowl, mix together the remaining water, the oil, honey, salt, and the dissolved yeast mixture. Add the gluten flour or Vital Wheat Gluten and about 3 cups of the whole wheat flour. Beat with a wooden spoon for about 100 strokes. Add as much of the remaining flour as necessary to make a kneadable dough.

3. Turn the dough out onto a well-floured surface and knead in enough flour to make a smooth dough that is not sticky.

4. Place the kneaded dough in a large, oiled bowl. Oil the top of the dough. Cover the bowl with a clean, damp cloth and let it sit in a warm place until the dough has doubled in bulk. Punch down.

5. Shape the dough into two loaves and place them in two well-oiled loaf pans, 4 1/2 x 8 1/2 x 2 1/2 inches. Bake at 350°F for 45 minutes.

THE INGREDIENTS

1/2 cup warm water: To dissolve the yeast. The water temperature should be about 100°F. Water that is too hot (over 120°F) will kill the yeast; if it is too cold, the yeast will work very slowly.

Drop of honey: Food for the yeast. Malt, maple syrup, molasses, rice syrup (yinnie syrup), or sorghum may be substituted for the honey.

2 tablespoons dry active yeast: The leavening agent. Yeast is a microorganism of vegetable origin. Dry active yeast is alive but dormant. When provided with moisture, food, and warmth, it "awakens" and rapidly begins to grow. As the yeast multiplies, it gives off carbon dioxide. It is this gas that makes the bread rise.

Two tablespoons of yeast is the equivalent of two packages. If you bake bread often, the least expensive way to buy yeast is in bulk at a natural foods store. Dry active yeast may be stored in the refrigerator for several months.

Fresh cake yeast may also be used in any bread recipe; in fact, most bakers prefer it. Some bakeries will sell fresh yeast if you ask for it. Its only disadvantage is that it doesn't store as well as dry active yeast. Fresh yeast may be kept in the refrigerator for two weeks, or in the freezer for two months. For 1 tablespoon of dry active yeast, substitute 1 small cake or 1 tablespoon of fresh yeast.

Do not try to substitute nutritional yeast, torula yeast, or brewer's yeast for bread yeast, because these yeasts are inactive.

2 cups warm water: Bread is basically flour and water. The water holds the flour together. The water should be lukewarm (about 100°F).

1/4 cup oil: Oil makes a more tender bread. If you prefer, however, you may decrease the oil or leave it out completely. The bread will be slightly drier and get stale faster, but it will still be good.

1/4 cup honey: This is more food for the yeast so it will continue leavening the dough, and it adds flavor to the bread. If you prefer, you may decrease the amount of honey (or other sweetener) in this recipe to as little as 1 table-spoon, or increase it to as much as 1/3 cup, and still make a good loaf of bread.

2 teaspoons sea salt: Without salt, bread tastes bland and seems to be missing something. However, if you are on a low-sodium diet and wish to decrease or leave out the salt, you may.

1/4 cup gluten flour or 3 tablespoons Vital Wheat Gluten: Gluten is the protein of the wheat. It is a sticky, elastic substance that helps you to make a light-textured, spongier bread that does not crumble when sliced. If you do not care for such a bread, you may leave out the gluten flour and still get excellent results. There is, after all, gluten in regular whole wheat flour.

7 cups whole wheat bread flour: Bread flour is a high-gluten flour (pastry flour is a low-gluten flour). The quantity of flour can never be exact in a bread recipe because of such variables as the humidity of your kitchen and the moisture content of the flour. Add the flour gradually during mixing and kneading. You will know you have added enough when the dough no longer sticks to your hands or the board. For the best bread, use flour that is freshly ground from organically grown wheat.

If you want your bread to rise as quickly as possible, have all ingredients (except for the warm water) at room temperature.

THE METHOD

Step 1

Place the 1/2 cup of water, the drop of honey, and the yeast in a small bowl. Let sit for 10 minutes to dissolve the yeast.

This step is called proofing the yeast. Yeast becomes inactive when it gets old. If you mix up a large batch of dough with inactive yeast, the result will be disappointing, to say the least. Therefore, it's a good idea to check, or proof, the yeast before adding the other ingredients. If the yeast is active, it will foam up and begin to bubble after a few minutes. If it is inactive, it will just sit there. If this happens, throw it out and get some new yeast.

If you make bread regularly and you are sure that your yeast is active, you can omit this step. In fact, I have omitted it in most of my recipes. However, to play it safe, you may proof the yeast. Just use 1/4–1/2 cup of the water from the recipe along with a drop of honey. When the yeast has bubbled up, add it back to the recipe.

Step 2

In a large bowl, mix together the remaining water, the oil, honey, salt, and the dissolved yeast mixture.

This combines the liquid ingredients and ensures that the salt is evenly distributed.

Add the gluten flour or Vital Wheat Gluten and about 3 cups of the whole wheat flour. Beat with a wooden spoon for about 100 strokes.

This activates the gluten. It will make the batter smoother and more elastic and help to make a lighter bread.

Add as much of the remaining flour as necessary to make a kneadable dough.

This will take about 2 cups of flour. When the dough is too stiff to stir and begins to pull away from the sides of the bowl, it is ready to knead. During kneading, you will add enough of the the remaining flour to make a dough that is not sticky.

Step 3

Turn the dough out onto a well-floured surface and knead in enough flour to make a smooth dough that is not sticky.

Sprinkle your work surface generously with flour (use at least 1/2 cup). Place the dough on the floured surface, then sprinkle the top of the dough very generously with more flour.

Now to work! Kneading should be done vigorously and rhythmically. Fold the dough toward you, then push it away. Repeat these motions several times until the dough becomes wider than it is long, then give it a quarter turn, and fold and push some more. Fold, push, fold, push, then turn. Use your body weight to push into the dough. As you work, add as much flour as necessary to keep the dough from sticking.

Kneading elasticizes the gluten in the dough and makes a light-textured bread that does not crumble when you slice it. When the dough can be kneaded without adding more flour to keep it from sticking, it is almost ready. Continue kneading until the dough becomes very smooth and feels satiny (some people say that it feels like an ear lobe). A good bread usually requires about 20 minutes of kneading. You can get by with 5–10 minutes of kneading, but the results will be heavier. Overkneading is highly unlikely; it's practically impossible to overknead by hand.

Kneading can be fun. Sometimes I put on lively music and knead to the music. If you knead really vigorously, you can raise your heart and respiratory rate high enough to give yourself an aerobic workout!

Step 4

Place the kneaded dough in a large, oiled bowl. Oil the top of the dough. Cover the bowl with a clean, damp cloth and let it sit in a warm place until the dough has doubled in bulk.

Use the same bowl in which you mixed the dough; it's not necessary to wash the bowl. You oil the bowl to keep the dough from sticking to it, and you oil the top of the dough to keep it

KNEADING THE BREAD

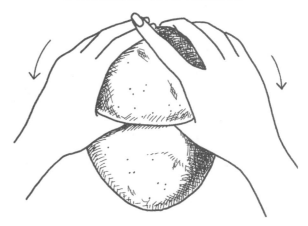

a. Fold the dough toward you.

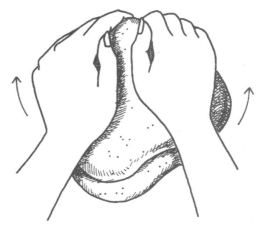

b. Push the folded dough away from you.

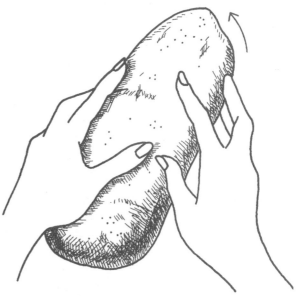

c. When the dough becomes wider than it is long, turn it and repeat Steps a and b.

from drying out. Covering the bowl with a damp cloth also keeps the dough moist.

The ideal temperature for rising is about 85°F. Therefore, on a warm summer day, room temperature is perfect. However, if your house is cool, you might wish to place your dough over a hot water heater, on top of your refrigerator, in front of a warm, sunny window, or under a wood stove. If you are careful not to overheat the dough, you can even let it rise in the oven. To do this, turn the oven on as low as it will go for just a couple of minutes. Then turn the oven off and place the dough in it. A bowl of hot water in the oven will help to keep it warm without overheating. Another alternative is a styrofoam-lined cooler chest with a half-gallon bottle of hot water in it. Avoid putting the dough in a place that is warmer than 120°F, because the heat will kill the yeast.

The time required for dough to double in bulk depends on the temperature of the place where it is rising and the temperature of the ingredients. If your ingredients were at room temperature when you started to mix the dough, and the kneaded dough is in an 85°F environment, rising should take about 1 hour. (Sourdough will take much longer.) However, if the ingredients were cold (just out of the freezer or refrigerator), rising can take 3 hours or longer. If you place the dough in a cold room or in the refrigerator, it can take 8 hours or longer to double. This can be used to your advantage (see "Bread-Making for the Busy Cook" on page 112).

Punch down.

This means just what it says. Hit your big, beautiful dough right in its middle with your fist and watch it fall.

After you have punched down the dough, you may let it rise in the bowl a second time. I don't knead it a second time because this makes the dough less pliable for shaping into a loaf. The second rising is not absolutely necessary, but it does seem to make a lighter bread. The dough should double in size in this second rising, taking less time then the first, 45 minutes or less.

Step 5

Shape the dough into two loaves and place them in two well-oiled loaf pans, 4½ x 8½ x 2½ inches.

When you shape the loaves, it is important to get out all the air. Air bubbles left in the dough will make big holes in the bread. There are several ways to shape the dough into loaves. Here are two of my favorites:

Method 1: Cut the dough into two portions of equal size. Flatten out each piece into a rectangle. Roll up the dough very tightly, like a jelly roll. Pinch the outer edge of the roll to dough underneath it (this will be the bottom of the loaf), then pinch together at each end to seal.

Method 2: Knead the dough for a couple of minutes to eliminate the air bubbles, then cut the dough into two portions of equal size. The cut side of the dough will make the bottom of the loaf, and the rounded side will be the top. Hold the dough with the cut side facing down. Using both hands, stretch the sides of the dough to form a smooth and round top surface. Then tuck the stretched ends of the dough tightly under at the bottom of the loaf. Pinch together the bottom of the loaf to seal it.

Oil the loaf pans very generously with a

SHAPING THE DOUGH INTO A LOAF: METHOD 1

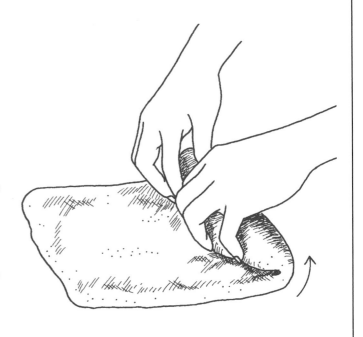

good-quality vegetable oil. If you like, you can sprinkle the oiled pans with cornmeal or oat flakes. This makes the bread look nice and taste good, and helps to keep the loaves from sticking. Place the loaves in the pans. You can lightly cover the loaves with a damp towel so that they won't dry out as they rise. To keep the towel from sticking to the dough, you can sprinkle the loaves with oat flakes or occasionally lift the towel.

Bake at 350°F for 45 minutes.

Bake the bread on the middle rack of the oven. Don't preheat the oven; the dough will rise more before beginning to bake. After 45 minutes, remove one of the loaves from the pan and tap it on the bottom with your knuckles. If the bread sounds hollow, it is done. If you are still not sure, you may carefully take a slice from the loaf and examine it. If the bread is not done, place the loaf and the slice back in the pan, and bake for a few minutes more. As you gain experience, you will be able to tell when your bread is done by its smell.

Remove the hot bread from the loaf pans and let it cool on a wire rack for 10–15 minutes before slicing. Let it cool completely before wrapping it.

SHAPING THE DOUGH INTO A LOAF: METHOD 2

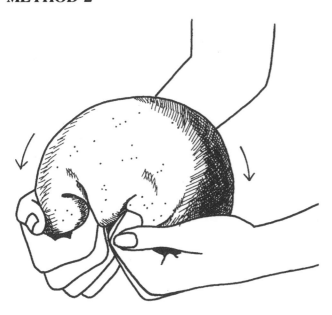

TROUBLESHOOTING

Every beginning baker will occasionally have a less-than-perfect batch of bread. Don't be discouraged; this is how we learn. It is important, however, to know what went wrong in order to keep it from recurring. Listed below are some of the most common complaints of novice bakers and what causes them.

• *The bread is crumbly and falls apart when sliced.*
—You did not knead the dough enough.
—You used pastry flour instead of bread flour.
—In improvising, you added too much low-gluten flour (such as barley flour, rice flour, or cornmeal) to your dough.

• *The bread is heavy.*
—Any bread that contains grains other than wheat will be heavier than a wheat bread. Sourdough breads are also relatively heavy. This does not mean that the bread is unsuccessful; some breads are just heavy by nature. In my opinion, the best bread you can eat is a hearty sourdough rye. The Basic Bread recipe on page 107 yields a very light whole wheat bread. If you have followed each step carefully, kneaded the dough well, and are still not satisfied with the results, try substituting unbleached white flour for half of the whole wheat flour.

• *The bread is dry.*
—You kneaded too much flour into the dough.
—You baked the bread too long, at too low a temperature.

• *The bread is sticky and too moist.*
—You did not bake the bread long enough.
—You left the bread in the pans too long after baking.
—You stored the bread in plastic bags while it was still hot.

• *The bread did not rise.*
—You forgot the yeast.
—The yeast was inactive.
—You killed the yeast by placing the dough in an environment that was too hot.
—You killed the yeast by mixing it with water that was too hot.

—You used cold ingredients and did not wait long enough before mixing them.

• *The bread rose well, but then fell during baking.*
—You let the dough rise too much before baking. It should rise no more than double its bulk.

• *The bread rose and then fell over the sides of the pan like an enormous mushroom.*
—You made the dough too soft. Add more flour the next time.

WHAT TO DO WITH A DOUGH THAT WILL NOT RISE

More than once, I have made up a big batch of bread dough, kneaded it for 20 minutes, and then realized that I had forgotten to add the yeast. If this ever happens to you, there are two ways to keep from wasting all that dough:

• *Make chapati:* Follow the recipe for rolling and cooking Chapati (page 135). They are delicious, and they can be used in hundreds of ways. Chapati may be frozen.

• *Make pasta:* This works with any 100 percent wheat dough but may not work with rye or multigrain doughs.

BREAD-MAKING FOR THE BUSY COOK

The Refrigerator Method

If you are too busy to stay around the house waiting for dough to rise, but would still like to enjoy the pleasures of bread-making, the refrigerator method for raising the dough can come in very handy. It allows you to make a batch of bread dough, let it rise once, and then leave it unattended for several hours until you have the time to bake it.

Here are two schedules for making bread by this method; maybe one of them will work for you.

Morning Schedule

Mix the bread dough the first thing in the morning. Let it rise once and then punch it down. Shape the dough into loaves. Oil the loaf pans well, then sprinkle them with cornmeal or oat flakes. Place the loaves in the pans and sprinkle the top of the loaves with additional cornmeal or oat flakes (this will keep the dough from sticking). Place the loaves in plastic bags that are large enough to allow for expansion of the dough; close them with twist-ties, and place the loaves in the refrigerator. Arrange the bags so that they are loose around the top of the loaves.

Now you may go about your business and forget about the dough for 8–10 hours. As you are preparing dinner, remove the dough from the refrigerator and take it out of the plastic bags. The dough should have doubled in bulk. Place the loaves in the oven without preheating it and bake at 350°F for 45 minutes as usual. You will have fresh bread for dinner!

Evening Schedule

Mix the bread dough a couple of hours before going to bed. Let it rise once and punch it down. Shape the dough into loaves. Prepare the loaves for rising as indicated above, and let them rise in the refrigerator all night while you sleep. When you wake up, place the loaves in the oven without preheating it and bake at 350°F for 45 minutes. You will have fresh bread for breakfast!

Orange Sesame Bread

I love this bread!

Yield: 1 large loaf   Time: 3–4 hours

1 cup orange juice

1/2 cup water

1 1/2 tablespoons grated orange peel from an organically grown orange

2 tablespoons oil

1/4 cup molasses

1 tablespoon dry active yeast

1 teaspoon sea salt

1/2 cup gluten flour or 2 tablespoons Vital Wheat Gluten

3 1/4–3 1/3 cups whole wheat bread flour

2 tablespoons sesame seeds

1. Combine the orange juice and water in a small saucepan. Heat until warm but not hot. Pour the mixture into a large mixing bowl. Add the orange peel, oil, molasses, and yeast. Let sit for about 10 minutes to dissolve the yeast.

2. In a medium bowl, mix together the salt, gluten flour or Vital Wheat Gluten, and 2 cups of the bread flour. Add this mixture to the juice/yeast mixture in the large bowl. Beat and let sit for 20–30 minutes, or until the sponge has risen. Stir down and add enough of the remaining flour to make a kneadable dough.

3. Knead in only as much of the remaining flour as necessary to make a dough that is smooth and not too sticky. Knead for at least 10 minutes. Oil the bowl in which you mixed the dough and return the dough to the bowl. Turn it over to oil the top. Cover the dough with a damp cloth and let it rise in a warm place until has doubled in bulk (about 1 hour).

4. Punch down and shape into a loaf. Sprinkle the countertop with the sesame seeds and roll the loaf in the seeds. Place the loaf in a well-oiled loaf pan, 4 1/2 x 8 1/2 x 2 1/2 inches. Cover lightly with a damp cloth and let rise in a warm place until it has doubled in bulk (45 minutes to 1 hour).

5. Bake at 350°F for 45 minutes. Remove the bread from the pan and let it cool on a rack before storing. This bread is wonderful, warm from the oven, with Adzuki and Squash Soup (page 59).

Flaxseed Rye Bread

A large, dark loaf that is good for sandwiches.

1½ cups lukewarm water

2 tablespoons oil

2 tablespoons molasses

2 tablespoons carob powder

1 tablespoon dry active yeast

1 teaspoon sea salt

½ cup gluten flour or
2 tablespoons plus 1 teaspoon
Vital Wheat Gluten

¼ cup flaxseeds

1 cup whole rye flour

2¼ cups whole wheat bread
flour (approximately)

Yield: 1 loaf   Time: 3–4 hours

1. In a large bowl, combine the water, oil, molasses, carob powder, and yeast. Let the mixture sit for about 10 minutes to dissolve the yeast.

2. In a smaller bowl, mix together the sea salt, gluten flour or Vital Wheat Gluten, flaxseeds, rye flour, and about ½ cup of the wheat flour. Beat 100 strokes.

3. Add enough of the remaining wheat flour to make a kneadable dough. Turn the dough out onto a floured surface and knead for at least 10 minutes. Keep the kneading surface sprinkled with flour, kneading in just enough flour to keep the dough from sticking. A dough containing rye flour will always be stickier than a wheat dough, so don't add too much flour.

4. Oil the bowl in which you mixed the dough and return the dough to the bowl. Turn it over to oil the top. Cover the bowl with a clean, damp cloth and let the dough rise in a warm place until it has doubled in bulk (about 1 hour).

5. Punch down. Now either let the dough rise in the bowl another time or shape it into a loaf. Press the loaf down firmly in a well-oiled loaf pan, 4½ x 8½ x 2½ inches, to ensure that this large loaf does not rise too high. Oil the top of the loaf and let it rise until it has doubled in bulk.

6.. Bake at 350°F for 45 minutes. Remove the bread from the pan and let it cool on a rack before storing.

The first time I made this loaf, I let it rise too much in the pan and it fell over the sides. If that happens to you, just punch it down, reshape the loaf, and return it to the pan, pressing it down firmly. Let it rise again (this time only until doubled) and bake as usual.

Walnut Rye Bread

This bread is similar to one that I had in a fancy restaurant in France. It was served with goat cheese after the salad, which followed the main course.

Yield: 1 round loaf   Time: 3–4 hours

1. In a large mixing bowl, combine the water, oil, molasses, and yeast. Let sit for 5–10 minutes until the yeast is dissolved.

2. In a smaller bowl, mix together the salt, gluten flour or Vital Wheat Gluten, and 1 cup of the wheat flour. Beat 100 strokes with a wooden spoon. Stir in the remaining wheat flour, then add as much of the rye flour as necessary to make a kneadable dough. Turn the dough out onto a surface floured with some of the remaining rye flour, and knead for at least 10 minutes. Knead in as much flour as necessary to make a dough that is smooth, elastic, and not too sticky. Dough containing rye flour is always a little stickier than a 100 percent wheat flour dough, so don't add too much flour. When the dough is well kneaded, it should not stick to your hands or to the kneading surface.

3. Place the dough in an oiled bowl. Turn the dough over to oil the top. Cover the bowl with a clean, damp cloth and set it in a warm place to rise until the dough has doubled in bulk (about 1 hour). Punch down, knead in the walnuts, and either let the dough rise again or proceed to Step 4.

4. Shape the dough into a round loaf and place it on a cookie sheet that has been oiled and sprinkled with flour. Cover the loaf lightly with a damp cloth and let it rise until doubled in bulk.

5. Bake at 350°F for 45 minutes. Let cool on a rack.

1 cup warm water

1 tablespoon oil

¼ cup molasses

1 tablespoon dry active yeast

1 teaspoon sea salt

½ cup gluten flour or 2 tablespoons Vital Wheat Gluten

1½ cups whole wheat bread flour

1⅓ cups whole rye flour (approximately)

1 cup finely chopped walnuts

Sunflower Molasses Bread

1¹/₄ cups warm water

¹/₃ cup molasses

1 tablespoon oil

1 tablespoon dry active yeast

1 teaspoon sea salt

¹/₂ cup gluten flour or
2 tablespoons Vital Wheat
Gluten

3–3¹/₄ cups whole wheat bread
flour

¹/₂ cup sunflower seeds

This recipe makes a large, well-risen loaf of bread with a rich, dark color, a slightly sweet flavor, and the crunch of sunflower seeds.

Yield: 1 large loaf   Time: 3–4 hours

1. In a large bowl, combine the water, molasses, oil, and yeast. Let sit for 5–10 minutes until the yeast is dissolved.

2. In a smaller bowl, mix together the salt, gluten flour or Vital Wheat Gluten, and 1 cup of the bread flour. Add this mixture to the liquid mixture and beat with a wooden spoon for 100 strokes. Stir in enough of the remaining flour to make a kneadable dough. Turn the dough out onto a floured surface and knead in as much flour as necessary to make a dough that is not sticky. Continue kneading until the dough is smooth and elastic, at least 10 minutes.

3. Oil the bowl in which you mixed the dough. Place the dough in the bowl, then turn it over to oil the top. Cover the bowl with a clean, damp cloth. Let it rise in a warm place until it has doubled in bulk (about 1 hour).

4. Punch down. Knead in the sunflower seeds. Return the dough to its bowl, cover with the damp cloth, and either let it double again or just let it sit for 10–15 minutes.

5. Shape the dough into a loaf. Generously oil a loaf pan, 4¹/₂ x 8¹/₂ x 2¹/₂ inches, and sprinkle it with flour. Place the loaf in the pan. Sprinkle the top of the loaf with a few sunflower seeds and cover it lightly with the damp cloth. Let the loaf rise in a warm place until it has doubled in bulk (about 1 hour).

6. Uncover and bake at 350°F for 45 minutes. Remove the bread from the pan and let it cool on a rack before storing.

Focaccia

A herb-and-onion bread that is wonderful to serve with a large kettle of homemade soup and a salad for an easy but satisfying meal.

Yield: 1 flat loaf   Time: about 3 hours

1. Place the water in a large mixing bowl. Add the honey, 1 tablespoon of olive oil, 1 teaspoon of salt, and yeast. Let sit for 5–10 minutes until the yeast is dissolved.

2. In a smaller bowl, mix together the gluten flour or Vital Wheat Gluten and 1 cup of the bread flour. Add this flour mixture to the liquid mixture and beat 100 strokes with a wooden spoon. Then add as much of the remaining flour as necessary to make a kneadable dough. Turn the dough out onto a floured surface and knead for 10 minutes or more. Knead in as much flour as necessary to make a dough that is smooth, elastic, and not sticky.

3. Oil the bowl in which you mixed the dough. Place the dough in the bowl, then turn it over to oil the top. Cover the dough with a clean, damp cloth and let it sit in a warm place until it has doubled in bulk (about 1 hour). Punch it down.

4. Oil a 10-x-15-inch cookie sheet or a round pizza pan. Press the dough out until it covers the sheet or pan. Lightly cover with the damp cloth while you prepare the topping.

5. Heat 2 tablespoons of olive oil in a skillet. Add the onion, garlic, herbs, and 1/4 teaspoon of salt. Sauté for about 5 minutes, then cool for 3–4 minutes.

6. With your finger, poke 1/2-inch-deep holes at 1 1/2-inch intervals all over the top of the dough. Spread the warm (but not hot) onion mixture over the top of the dough and into the indentations. Cover it again with the damp cloth and let it continue to rise until it has doubled.

7. Bake at 350°F for about 20 minutes. To test if the bread is done, pinch a little of the top crust from the center. If it is done, it will not be gooey.

8. Serve the focaccia hot, either cut into squares or torn into chunks.

1 1/4 cups warm water

1 tablespoon honey (or malt syrup or fruit syrup)

1 tablespoon olive oil

1 teaspoon sea salt

1 tablespoon dry active yeast

1/2 cup gluten flour or 2 tablespoons Vital Wheat Gluten

2 3/4 cups whole wheat bread flour (approximately)

TOPPING:

2 tablespoons olive oil

1 1/2 teaspoons herbes de Provence (see page 102)

1 1/2 cups chopped onion (1 large onion)

5–6 cloves garlic, chopped

1/4 teaspoon sea salt

Burger Buns

Make your own buns to serve with teff and other healthful burgers.

1¼ cups lukewarm water

2 tablespoons concentrated
fruit sweetener

2 tablespoons oil

1 tablespoon dry active yeast

1 teaspoon sea salt

½ cup gluten flour or
2 tablspoons Vital Wheat
Gluten

2¾ cups whole wheat bread
flour (approximately)

Yield: 12 buns   Time: about 3 hours

1. In a large bowl, combine the water, sweetener, oil, and yeast. Let sit for 10 minutes to dissolve the yeast.

2. In a smaller bowl, mix together the salt, gluten flour or Vital Wheat Gluten, and 1 cup of the bread flour. Add this mixture to the liquid mixture and beat 100 strokes. Add as much of the remaining flour as necessary to make a kneadable dough. Turn the dough out onto a floured surface and knead for at least 10 minutes. Keep the surface sprinkled with flour to prevent the dough from sticking. Continue kneading until the dough is smooth, elastic, and only slightly sticky.

3. Oil the bowl in which you mixed the dough and return the dough to the bowl. Turn it over to oil the top. Cover the bowl with a clean, damp cloth and let the dough rise in a warm place until it has doubled in bulk (about 1 hour).

4. Punch down. Roll the entire piece of dough into a long cylinder (as if you were making a "rope" in clay for a coiled pot) and cut it into 12 equal pieces. Shape each piece into a ball and place them on a cookie sheet. Leave enough room between the pieces of dough for them to double in size. Slightly flatten each piece of dough with the palm of your hand. Let the dough rise until it has doubled in bulk (about 1 hour).

5. Bake at 350°F for 20 minutes. Cut the buns in half to serve with your favorite burger.

You can also shape this dough into hot dog buns. The baking time will be the same.

Whole Wheat English Muffins

Moist and slightly sweet.

Yield: 12–13   Time: about 3^1/$_2$ hours

1^1/$_2$ cups warm water
2 tablespoons oil
^{1}/$_4$ cup honey
1 tablespoon dry active yeast
1 teaspoon sea salt
^{1}/$_2$ cup gluten flour or 2 tablespoons Vital Wheat Gluten
3^1/$_2$ cups whole wheat pastry flour (approximately)
^{1}/$_4$ cup cornmeal

1. In a large bowl, combine the water, oil, honey, and yeast. Let sit for about 10 minutes to dissolve the yeast.

2. In a smaller bowl, mix together the salt, the gluten flour or Vital Wheat Gluten, and about 1 cup of the wheat flour. Beat 100 strokes with a wooden spoon.

3. Add enough of the remaining whole wheat flour to make a kneadable dough. Turn the dough out onto a floured surface and knead in as much flour as necessary to make a dough that will not stick to the kneading surface. Kneading will take about 10 minutes.

4. Place the dough in an oiled bowl. Turn the dough over to oil the top. Cover the bowl with a damp cloth and place it in a warm place until the dough has doubled in bulk (about 1 hour). Punch down.

5. Cut the dough into 12–13 equal pieces. The easiest way to do this is to roll the dough into a long cylinder, score it with a knife, and then cut it.

6. Sprinkle your work surface generously with cornmeal. Roll each of the pieces of dough into a ball. Place the balls of dough on the cornmeal-sprinkled surface and flatten each with the palm of your hand to a ^{1}/$_2$-inch-thick patty. Sprinkle the top with cornmeal. Cover the patties with a clean, damp cloth and let them rise until doubled in bulk (about 1 hour).

7. Carefully slide a spatula under a patty and place it in a heavy, unoiled skillet (cast-iron works well). Repeat until there are 3–4 muffins in the skillet (depending on the size of the skillet). Cook over medium-low heat for 5–7 minutes or until the bottoms are brown. Carefully turn them over and cook for 5–7 minutes more. Repeat until all the patties have been cooked.

8. Let the muffins cool. To serve, split with a fork and toast.

To speed up the cooking, use two skillets at a time.

VARIATION:

Add 1 tablespoon of cinnamon to the dough with the first cup of wheat flour. Then knead 1 cup of raisins into the dough after the first rising. Follow the rest of the recipe as written.

Whole Wheat Pizza Crust

This recipe also appears in my book Cooking with the Right Side of the Brain, *but it is so good that I wanted to include it here, too.*

¹/₂ cup warm water

2 tablespoons oil

1 teaspoon honey

2 teaspoons dry active yeast

1¹/₄ cups whole wheat flour
(bread or pastry flour)

Yield: 1 round 12¹/₂-inch crust or
1 rectangular 11-x-16-inch crust

Time: 1¹/₄ hour to prepare;
12–25 minutes to bake

1. Combine the water, oil, honey, and yeast in a medium bowl and let the mixture stand for about 10 minutes to dissolve the yeast.

2. Add 1 cup of the flour and mix well. Knead in the remaining flour. The dough will be soft and slightly sticky.

3. Place the dough in a lightly oiled bowl. Turn the dough over so that it is oiled on both sides. Then cover it with a damp cloth and let it rise in a warm place until doubled in bulk (45 minutes to 1 hour).

4. Transfer the dough to an oiled pizza sheet. Flatten and stretch the dough until it covers the pan evenly.

5. Cover the dough with the desired topping and bake according to the topping recipe.

TIPS FOR QUICK BREADS

Quick breads are baked goods, including breads, muffins, and biscuits, that are leavened with baking powder. The following tips will help you to make quick breads that are as delicious as they are healthful.

- Preheat the oven to the temperature specified in the recipe you have chosen.

- Prepare your loaf pan or muffin tin before you mix the batter.

- Prepare muffin tins and loaf pans by oiling them generously and then sprinkling them lightly with flour. Alternatively, you may spray them with a nonstick coating, or line your muffin tins with paper muffin cups.

- Beat the liquid mixture well, and stir or sift the dry ingredients until they are well mixed. Then add the dry ingredients to the liquid ingredients.

- Beat the batter just enough to combine all the ingredients; overbeating can make quick breads heavy or tough.

- Transfer the batter to the loaf pan or muffin tins as soon as the batter is mixed. Baking powder will lose its effectiveness upon standing too long. Immediately place the pan(s) in the oven.

Four-Grain Muffins

These muffins are surprisingly light and moist, but not very sweet.

Yield: 12 muffins

Time: 15 minutes to prepare; 15 minutes to bake

$1/3$ cup oat flour

$1/3$ cup barley flour

$1/3$ cup buckwheat flour

1 cup whole wheat pastry flour

$1/2$ cup sucanat

1 tablespoon baking powder

1 egg

2 tablespoons oil

$1 1/2$ cups soymilk

$1/2$ cup chopped nuts

1. Sift together the flours, sucanat, and baking powder.

2. In a large bowl, beat together the egg and the oil. Add about half of the soymilk and beat again. Add the flour mixture. Mix and add the remaining soymilk. Beat until the batter is mixed, but don't beat more than necessary. Fold in the nuts.

3. Spoon the batter into muffin tins that have been well oiled and lightly sprinkled with flour.

4. Bake at 350°F for 15 minutes or until a toothpick inserted into the center of a muffin comes out clean. Let muffins cool in the pan for about 10 minutes before removing them.

VARIATIONS:

- For a sweeter muffin, substitute raisins for the nuts and add 1–2 teaspoons of cinnamon.

- *Eggless variation:* Blend 1 package ($10 1/2$ ounces) of extra-firm silken tofu in a blender or food processor with the oil and 1 cup of soymilk. This will be your liquid mixture. Place it in a large mixing bowl. Add the flour mixture (Step 1), beat, fold in the nuts, and continue with Step 3 of the recipe.

- Bake on the center rack of the oven.

- Keep the oven closed until the cooking time given in the recipe has elapsed. The bread is done when it springs back after you press the center lightly with your finger. Another test of doneness is to stick a toothpick into the center. If it comes out clean (or, with some recipes, almost clean), the bread is done.

- Let quick bread sit in the pan for 5 minutes before removing it. This will help to keep it from breaking or crumbling. If the quick bread does not leave the pan easily, carefully run a blunt knife around the edges.

- Cool quick bread on a wire rack. Wait at least 15 minutes before slicing it with a serrated knife.

- Let quick bread cool before wrapping and storing.

- Quick bread can be left at room temperature for the first day. However, if there is any left, refrigerate the leftovers.

- Stale quick breads can be revived by toasting in a toaster oven. Cut muffins in half and toast them split side up.

- If you prefer sweeter quick breads, spread the ones given here with a little fruit-sweetened jam or honey.

- Nuts or any chopped dried fruit may be substituted for raisins, and raisins or other dried fruits may be substituted for nuts.

Potato Muffins

These slightly sweet muffins are good served with soup or with dinner.

Yield: 12 muffins	Time: 25 minutes

1 cup whole wheat pastry flour

1/2 cup barley flour

1 tablespoon baking powder

1/3 cup sucanat

2 tablespoons oil

1 egg

1 cup grated raw potato, lightly packed into the cup

1 cup soymilk

1. Sift together the pastry flour, barley flour, baking powder, and sucanat.

2. In a large bowl, beat together the oil and the egg. Add the grated potato and mix well. Add about 1/2 cup of the soymilk and beat again. Add the flour mixture to the egg/potato mixture. Mix and beat in the remaining soymilk just enough to blend.

3. Spoon the batter into muffin tins that have been well oiled and lightly sprinkled with flour.

4. Bake at 350°F for 15 minutes, or until a toothpick inserted into the center of a muffin comes out clean.

VARIATION:

Add 1 teaspoon of cinnamon to the flour mixture (Step 1) and fold 1/2 cup of raisins or nuts into the batter (Step 2).

Banana Muffins

These are really good!

Yield: 12 muffins	Time: 15 minutes to prepare; 20 minutes to bake

1 cup mashed, ripe bananas

1 egg

1/4 cup oil

1/3 cup concentrate fruit sweetener

1 teaspoon vanilla

1 1/4 cups soymilk

1 1/2 cups barley flour

1/2 cup oat flour

1 tablespoon baking powder

1 cup date pieces

1/2 cup chopped pecans or walnuts

1. In a large bowl, beat the mashed bananas and the egg with a wooden spoon until they are well mixed. Add the oil, sweetener, vanilla, and soymilk and beat until they are well mixed.

2. In a medium bowl, sift together the flours and the baking powder. Add the flour mixture to the liquid mixture. Mix well and fold in the dates and the nuts.

3. Spoon the mixture into muffin tins that have been well oiled and lightly sprinkled with flour. Oil the muffin tins around the top because the muffins will rise over the edges of the cups.

4. Bake at 350°F for 20 minutes or until a toothpick inserted into the center of a muffin comes out clean.

Patty's Bran Muffins

Patty developed this recipe for the bakery of a large natural foods store.

Yield: 2 dozen

Time: 20 minutes to prepare;
20 minutes to bake

1. In a large bowl, combine the sucanat, oil, molasses, and egg. Beat well. Add the soymilk and beat again.

2. In a medium bowl, mix together the bran, flour, baking soda, baking powder, and spices. Add the flour mixture to the liquid mixture and beat with a wooden spoon until the batter is just blended. Don't overbeat. Fold in the raisins, dates, and pecans.

3. Pour the batter into muffin tins that have been well oiled and lightly sprinkled with flour. Fill the tins three-quarters full.

4. Bake at 350°F for 20 minutes or until a toothpick inserted into the center of a muffin comes out clean.

$^1/_4$ cup sucanat

3 tablespoons oil

$^1/_4$ cup molasses

1 egg

1 cup soymilk

$1^1/_2$ cups bran

1 cups whole wheat pastry flour

$1^1/_2$ teapoons baking soda

$1^1/_2$ teaspoons baking powder

$^1/_4$ teaspoon nutmeg

$^1/_4$ teaspoon ground cloves

$^1/_2$ teaspoon cinnamon

$^1/_2$ cup raisins

$^1/_4$ cup chopped dates

$^1/_2$ cup chopped pecans

Oatmeal Apple Spice Muffins

Low-fat, dairyless, and eggless muffins made with whole grains.

1 cup oat flakes

1 1/2 cups whole wheat pastry flour

1 tablespoon baking powder

2 teaspoons cinnamon

1/2 teaspoon nutmeg

1/4 teaspoon cloves

1/3 cup sucanat

1 cup raisins

1 package (10 1/2 ounces) extra-firm silken tofu

2 tablespoons oil

1/2 cup apple juice

1 cup grated apple

Yield: 12 muffins

Time: 15 minutes to prepare; 20 minutes to bake

1. In a large bowl, combine the oat flakes, flour, baking powder, cinnamon, nutmeg, and cloves. Add the sucanat and mix. Then add the raisins and mix again.

2. In a blender or food processor, blend together the tofu, oil, and apple juice until the mixture is smooth and creamy. Add to the dry mixture. Add the grated apple and mix well. Make sure that all the flour is blended in. The batter will be thicker than most muffin batters.

3. Spoon the batter into muffin tins that have been well oiled and lightly sprinkled with flour.

4. Bake at 350°F for 20 minutes or until a toothpick inserted into the center of a muffin comes out clean.

Blueberry Muffins

These muffins are wheatless, dairyless, fruit-sweetened, and good!

2 cups barley flour

1/2 cup oat flour

1 tablespoon baking powder

1/2 teaspoon nutmeg

1 egg

1/3 cup oil

1/2 cup concentrated fruit sweetener

2 teaspoons vanilla

1 1/4 cups soymilk

1 1/4 cups blueberries (fresh or frozen)

Yield: 12 muffins

Time: 20 minutes to prepare; 15 minutes to bake

1. In a large bowl, sift together the flours, baking powder, and nutmeg.

2. In a mixing bowl, beat together the egg, oil, sweetener, vanilla, and soymilk. Add the liquid mixture to the dry mixture. Beat with a wooden spoon until the batter is smooth and well mixed. Fold in the blueberries.

3. Spoon the batter into muffin tins that have been well oiled and lightly sprinkled with flour. Oil around the top, too, because these muffins will rise a little bit over the sides on the cups.

4. Bake at 375°F for 15 minutes or until a toothpick inserted into the center of a muffin comes out clean. (If you hit a blueberry, it will stain the toothpick, of course, even if the muffins are done.)

Carrot Muffins

Eggless, fruit-sweetened muffins.

Yield: 12 muffins

Time: 15 minutes to prepare;
20 minutes to bake

1 cup whole wheat pastry flour

1 cup barley flour

1 tablespoon baking powder

1 teaspoon cinnamon

$^1/_2$ teaspoon nutmeg

$^1/_4$ teaspoon cloves

1 cup raisins

1 package (10$^1/_2$ ounces) soft silken tofu

$^1/_4$ cup oil

$^1/_2$ cup concentrated fruit sweetener

$^1/_4$ cup soymilk

1 teaspoon vanilla

1 cup grated carrots

$^1/_2$ cup sunflower seeds

1. Sift the pastry flour, barley flour, baking powder, cinnamon, nutmeg, and cloves together into a medium bowl. Add the raisins and mix well.

2. Place the tofu, oil, sweetener, soymilk, and vanilla in a blender or a food processor and blend until smooth and creamy. Transfer this mixture to a large bowl.

3. Add the flour mixture, and beat for just a few seconds with a wooden spoon. Fold in the carrots and the sunflower seeds.

4. Spoon the mixture into muffin tins that have been well oiled and lightly sprinkled with flour.

5. Bake at 350°F for 20 minutes or until a toothpick inserted into the center of a muffin comes out almost clean.

Amaranth Muffins

1 cup amaranth flour

1/2 cup whole wheat pastry flour

2 teaspoons baking powder

1 tablespoon vanilla

1 egg

1/2 cup soymilk

1/4 cup oil

1/4 cup concentrated fruit sweetener

1/2 cup raisins

1/2 cup chopped walnuts

Amaranth is so nutritious, it is really worth getting to know. These muffins are light textured and have the mild, nutty flavor of amaranth.

Yield: 12 muffins

Time: 15 minutes to prepare; 15–20 minutes to bake

1. In a medium bowl, sift together the amaranth flour, pastry flour, and the baking powder.

2. In a large bowl, beat together the egg, soymilk, oil, and sweetener.

3. While stirring with a wooden spoon, gradually pour the flour mixture into the liquid mixture. Beat for a few seconds, just until the mixtures are blended. Fold in the raisins and the walnuts.

4. Spoon the batter into muffin tins that have been well oiled and lightly sprinkled with flour.

5. Bake at 350°F for 15–20 minutes or until a toothpick inserted into the center of a muffin comes out clean.

Orange Corn Muffins

1 1/2 cups cornmeal

1 tablespoon baking powder

1/2 cup barley flour

1 teaspoon allspice

2 tablespoons grated orange peel from organically grown orange

1 package (10 1/2 ounces) firm silken tofu

1/3 cup concentrated fruit sweetener

1/4 cup oil

2/3 cup orange juice

1 cup raisins

Like most corn breads, these muffins are best hot from the oven.

Yield: 12 muffins

Time: 15 minutes to prepare; 15–20 minutes to bake

1. Place the cornmeal, baking powder, barley flour, and allspice in a mixing bowl and mix well. Add the orange peel and mix again.

2. Place the tofu, sweetener, oil, and orange juice in a food processor or blender and blend until smooth and creamy. Transfer this mixture to a large bowl.

3. Add the flour mixture and beat with a wooden spoon just until the mixtures are blended. Fold in the raisins.

4. Spoon the mixture into muffin tins that have been well oiled and lightly sprinkled with flour.

5. Bake at 350°F for 15–20 minutes or until a toothpick inserted into the center of a muffin comes out almost clean.

Peanut Butter Muffins

These wheatless muffins are not too sweet. Try them with fruit-sweetened jam or apple butter if you want a sweeter treat.

Yield: 12 large muffins

Time: 35 minutes to prepare; 20 minutes to bake

1. In a medium bowl, cream together the peanut butter, oil, and sweetener. Add the egg and beat well. Add the soymilk and the vanilla. Mix well.

2. In a large bowl, sift together the flours and the baking powder.

3. Add the peanut butter mixture to the flour mixture and beat with a wooden spoon until well blended. Fold in the peanuts.

4. Spoon the batter into muffin tins that have been well oiled and lightly sprinkled with flour.

5. Bake at 350°F for 20 minutes or until a toothpick inserted into the center of a muffin comes out almost clean.

$1/2$ cup peanut butter (smooth or crunchy)

$1/4$ cup oil

$1/2$ cup concentrated fruit sweetener

1 egg

$11/4$ cups soymilk

1 teaspoon vanilla

2 cups barley flour

$1/2$ cup oat flour

1 tablespoon baking powder

$1/2$ cup chopped unsalted dry-roasted peanuts

Banana Date Bread

This fruit-sweetened, moist bread contains neither eggs nor dairy products.

1 package (10¹/₂ ounces)
extra-firm silken tofu

1 cup mashed, ripe bananas

¹/₄ cup fruit juice (apple, white
grape, etc.)

2 teaspoons vanilla

¹/₂ teaspoon nutmeg, or to taste

2 tablespoons oil

1¹/₂ cups whole wheat pastry
flour

1 tablespoon baking powder

1 cup date sugar

1 cup date pieces

¹/₂ cup chopped walnuts

Yield: 1 loaf   Time: 20 minutes to prepare; 40 minutes to bake

1. In a blender or food processor, blend together the tofu, bananas, juice, vanilla, nutmeg, and oil until very smooth and creamy.

2. Sift the flour, baking powder, and date sugar together into a large bowl.

3. Add the creamed mixture and beat with a wooden spoon until it is just mixed. Fold in the date pieces and the nuts.

4. Turn the batter into an oiled and floured loaf pan, 4¹/₂ x 8¹/₂ x 2¹/₂ inches. The batter will be thick. Smooth the top with the back of your mixing spoon.

5. Bake at 350°F for 40 minutes or until a toothpick inserted into the center of the cake comes out clean. Let the cake cool in the pan for 10 minutes and then transfer it to a rack to finish cooling before you serve it or wrap it for storage.

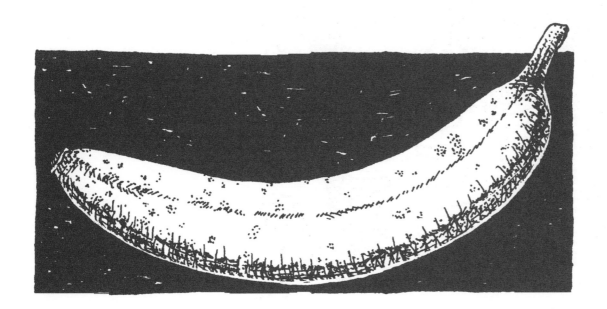

Pumpkin Bread

This quick bread is tender, moist, and spicy.

Yield: 1 loaf   Time: 15 minutes to prepare; 50 minutes to bake

1. In a large bowl, combine the pumpkin, egg, oil, and vanilla. Beat well.

2. Sift the flour, baking powder, cinnamon, allspice, nutmeg, and sucanat together into a medium bowl. If the sucanat is lumpy, you may need to rub it through the sifter.

3. Add the flour mixture to the pumpkin mixture, begin mixing with a wooden spoon, and add the soymilk while mixing. Beat just enough to make a smooth batter. Fold in the nuts.

4. Pour the batter into a well-oiled and floured loaf pan, $4^1/_2$ x $8^1/_2$ x $2^1/_2$ inches.

5. Bake at 350°F for 50 minutes or until a toothpick inserted into the center of the bread comes out clean. Let cool on a rack for at least 15 minutes before slicing with a serrated knife.

VARIATION:

A very good wheatless version uses $1^1/_2$ cups barley flour and $^1/_2$ cup oat flour in place of the whole wheat flour.

1 cup canned pumpkin

1 egg

2 tablespoons oil

1 teaspoon vanilla

2 cups whole wheat pastry flour

1 tablespoon baking powder

1 teaspoon cinnamon

1 teaspoon allspice

$^1/_2$ teaspoon nutmeg

$^1/_2$ cup sucanat

$1^1/_4$ cups soymilk

$^1/_2$ cup chopped pecans or walnuts

Cranberry Bread

This attractive quick bread is nice and tart.

Yield: 1 loaf   Time: 15 minutes to prepare; 40 minutes to bake

1. Sift together the flour, baking powder, and sucanat. If the sucanat is lumpy, rub it through the sifter.

2. In a large bowl, beat together the egg and the oil. Gradually add the orange juice and mix well. Add the vanilla and orange peel and mix well. Add the flour mixture to the liquid mixture and beat with a wooden spoon just enough to mix well. Fold in the cranberries.

3. Turn the batter into a well-oiled and floured loaf pan, $4^1/_2$ x $8^1/_2$ x $2^1/_2$ inches.

4. Bake at 350°F for 40 minutes or until a toothpick inserted into the center of the bread comes out clean (unless you hit a cranberry).

5. Let the bread cool in the pan for about 5 minutes, then remove it from the pan to cool on a rack. You may slice it with a serrated bread knife after about 15–20 minutes.

2 cups whole wheat pastry flour

1 tablespoon baking powder

$^1/_2$ cup sucanat

1 egg

2 tablespoons oil

1 cup orange juice

1 teaspoon vanilla

1 tablespoon orange peel

$1^1/_2$ cups cranberries

Barley and Oatmeal Bread

2 cups barley flour

1 cup oat flakes

1 tablespoon baking powder

1 egg

1/4 cup oil

1/3 cup concentrated fruit sweetener

1 cup soymilk

A wheatless quick bread that is slightly sweet, just right to serve with soup or a main course.

Yield: 1 loaf   Time: 20 minutes to prepare; 40 minutes to bake

1. In a medium bowl, combine the flour, oat flakes, and baking powder. Mix well.

2. In a large bowl, beat together the egg and the oil. Add the sweetener and beat again. Then slowly add the soymilk while continuing to beat.

3. Add the flour mixture to the liquid mixture and beat until the batter is well mixed.

4. Turn the batter into a well-oiled and floured loaf pan, 4$^{1}/_{2}$ x 8$^{1}/_{2}$ x 2$^{1}/_{2}$ inches.

5. Bake at 350°F for 40 minutes or until a toothpick inserted into the center of the loaf comes out clean.

Irish Brown Bread

4 cups whole wheat pastry flour

1 teaspoon sea salt

1 tablespoon baking powder

1/4 teaspoon baking soda

1/4 cup caraway seeds

1/2 cup raisins

2 cups soymilk

2 tablespoons lemon juice

This quick bread is unusual in that it is unsweetened. Try it when you make a simple meal of soup, salad, and bread. It is delicious hot from the oven. It is also good toasted for breakfast the next day.

Yield: 1 loaf   Time: 45 minutes

1. In a large bowl, mix together the flour, salt, baking powder, baking soda, and caraway seeds. Add the raisins and mix again.

2. In a medium bowl, mix together the soymilk and the lemon juice. Slowly stir the soymilk mixture into the flour mixture. The dough should be soft and sticky, but should hold its shape. If it is too soft, add a little more flour. Mix well, with a wooden spoon.

3. Turn the dough out onto a well-oiled and lightly floured cookie sheet. Shape it into a round loaf. With a sharp knife dipped in flour, cut an X about 1/2 inch deep into the top of the loaf.

4. Bake at 425°F for 30–40 minutes.

New Corn Bread

This wheatless, dairyless, eggless corn bread can be enjoyed even by people allergic to these foods. It is moist and delicious.

Serves: 4–8   Time: 20 minutes to prepare; 20–25 minutes to bake

1 package (10^1/$_2$ ounces) extra-firm tofu

^{1}/$_4$ cup oil

1 tablespoon cider vinegar

1 teaspoon sea salt

1^1/$_2$ cups cornmeal

^{1}/$_2$ cup oat flour

1 tablespoon baking powder

1 cup corn (fresh off the cob or unfrozen)

^{3}/$_4$ cup soymilk

1. In a blender or food processor, blend together the tofu, oil, vinegar, and salt until the mixture is smooth and creamy. Set aside.

2. In a large bowl, mix together the cornmeal, oat flour, and baking powder. Add the corn and mix well.

3. Add the tofu mixture to the cornmeal mixture and mix with a wooden spoon. Add the soymilk and mix well. Turn the batter into a well-oiled 9-inch cast-iron skillet. For a crispy crust, heat the skillet in the oven for a minute or two before filling it with the batter.

4. Bake at 400°F for 20 minutes or until the top of the corn bread is firm to the touch and a wooden toothpick inserted into the center comes out clean.

"Italian" Corn Bread

The Italian seasoning in this corn bread is a delicious change from the usual Southern or Southwestern variety.

Serves: 6   Time: 12 minutes to prepare; 18–20 minutes to bake

2 cups cornmeal

^{1}/$_2$ teaspoon sea salt

1 tablespoon baking powder

1 teaspoon basil

^{1}/$_2$ teaspoon oregano

^{1}/$_4$ cup Parmesan cheese or tofu-Parmesan

^{1}/$_4$ cup sun-dried tomato bits

1 cup corn (fresh off the cob or unfrozen)

^{1}/$_4$ cup oil

2 eggs

1^1/$_4$ cups soymilk or skim milk

1. Preheat the oven to 375°F.

2. Place the cornmeal, salt, baking powder, basil, oregano, cheese or tofu, and tomato bits in a large bowl and mix well.

3. Generously oil a 10-inch cast-iron skillet and place it in the oven for a few minutes while you finish mixing the batter.

4. Add the corn and the oil to the dry ingredients and mix again. Add the eggs and mix thoroughly, then add the milk and beat just until everything is well mixed.

5. Remove the hot skillet from the oven and pour in the batter.

6. Bake at 375°F for 18–20 minutes or until the top is firm and a knife inserted in the center comes out clean.

7. Serve with beans (kidney, pinto, Anasazi, etc.) and cooked kale or other greens.

Whole Wheat Biscuits

A Southern-style breakfast treat made healthier.

2 cups whole wheat pastry
flour

1 tablespoon baking powder

1/4 teaspoon sea salt

2 tablespoons oil

3/4 cup soymilk

1 tablespoon vinegar

Yield: about 12 biscuits   Time: 25 minutes

1. Sift the flour, baking powder, and salt together into a medium bowl. Mix with a spoon. Drizzle the oil onto the flour mixture and mix it with a fork until the oil is distributed throughout the flour mixture.

2. In a small bowl, mix together the soymilk and the vinegar.

3. Make a well in the center of the flour mixture and pour the milk mixture into the well, all at once. With a spoon, bring the flour mixture from around the sides of the bowl and stir it into the milk to make a soft dough. Lightly knead the dough on a floured surface for a few seconds to mix the ingredients.

4. On a lightly floured surface, pat the dough out to an even thickness of about 3/4 inch. With a floured 2-inch cookie cutter or a glass with a 2-inch opening (dip the rim of the glass in flour), cut the dough into rounds. Gather together the remaining scraps of dough and shape them into a ball. Flatten the dough once again and cut it into rounds.

5. Place the unbaked rounds so that they're touching in a well-oiled round cake pan.

6. Bake at 450°F for about 12 minutes or until brown.

7. Serve the biscuits hot from the oven. They are delicious with fruit-sweetened jam or apple butter. They are also good with Tahini Milk Gravy (page 98) and/or Sunday Brunch Tofu Scramble (page 41).

For a lighter biscuit, you may substitute 1 cup of unbleached white flour for 1 cup of the whole wheat flour.

Whole Wheat Crepes

These crepes are comparatively low in fat; they contain only two eggs, yet they are very thin and hold together well.

Yield: about 9–10 crepes   Time: 30 minutes

1 cup whole wheat pastry flour

2 eggs

1¼ cups soymilk

¼ teaspoon sea salt

1–2 tablespoons oil, as needed to cook crepes

1. In a medium bowl, combine the flour and eggs, and mix well with a fork. Slowly stir in the soymilk. Add the salt and beat with a wire whisk until the batter is smooth.

2. Drop a little less than ¼ cup of batter at a time onto a hot, oiled skillet or crepe pan. Tilt and rotate the skillet to distribute the batter evenly over the bottom of the pan. Cook the crepe until it is done on the bottom (lift the crepe by the edge and look: the bottom should be lightly flecked with brown). Turn the crepe over and cook briefly on the other side, a few seconds. Repeat this process with the remaining batter, oiling the skillet as necessary to prevent sticking.

3. If the batter thickens while you are making the crepes, thin it with a little extra soymilk. Stack the cooked crepes and cover them with a clean cloth until you are ready to fill them.

VERSATILE CREPES

Crepes are incredibly versatile. From breakfast to dinner to dessert, they can be the basis for many creative meals. For a breakfast that is both elegant and nutritious, stuff crepes with fresh fruit and top them with applesauce, yogurt, or fruit-sweetened jam. As a main dish or appetizer, try stuffing crepes with steamed vegetables (a good way to use up leftovers) and topping them with Golden Cashew Sauce (page 99) or Soy Cheese Sauce (page 100). A delicious way of using crepes creatively with vegetables is Eggplant-Stuffed Crepes (page 203). For dessert, tender crepes stuffed with raspberries or sliced bananas and topped with Carob "Cream" Sauce (page 268) are delectable. Or how about a crepe filled with finely chopped pineapple or mango and topped with Fresh Coconut Sherbet (page 269)?

Leftover crepes can be stored in the refrigerator for three to four days. Place them on a plate with a sheet of waxed paper between pairs of crepes and cover them. They can be quickly reheated in an unoiled skillet or filled and baked in a covered dish at 350°F for about 15 minutes or until warm.

Whole Wheat Dosas

1 cup whole wheat bread flour

1 teaspoon baking powder

1/4 teaspoon sea salt

1/2 teaspoon turmeric

1/4 cup finely minced onion
(1 small onion)

1 1/4–1 1/3 cups water

Oil to cook dosas

Thinner than pancakes and thicker than crepes, these savory Indian pancakes (pronounced DOH-shez) are delicious and easy to make.

Yield: 6–8 dosas   Time: 20 minutes

1. In a medium bowl, combine the flour, baking powder, salt, and turmeric. Add the onion and mix well. Add 1 1/4 cups water and beat for about one minute with a spoon. The batter should be like a pancake batter. If it is too thick or if it thickens while you are making the dosas, stir in some more water.

2. Drop a scant 1/4 cup of batter onto a small, heated, oiled skillet (a nonstick skillet works best). With a spatula, evenly spread the batter out to make the pancake thin and round. Cook the pancake over medium-high heat until it is set and golden on the bottom. Turn it over and cook the other side. Repeat until all the batter is used up.

3. To keep the dosas warm, stack them on a plate and cover them with a clean cloth. If necessary, they may be quickly reheated in an unoiled skillet.

4. Serve with curries or dal, accompanied by chutney.

Chick Pea Dosas

1 cup toasted garbanzo flour

1 cup water

1/2 teaspoon turmeric

1 clove garlic, pressed

1/8 teaspoon sea salt

Oil to cook dosas

Thin, savory pancakes made out of garbanzo flour nicely complement grain dishes.

Yield: 7–8 small pancakes   Time: 30 minutes

1. In a medium bowl, combine all the ingredients, except the oil. Beat with a wire whisk until there are no lumps.

2. Drop a scant 1/4 cup of batter onto a small heated, oiled skillet (a nonstick skillet works best). Rotate the skillet to spread the batter evenly. Cook over medium-high heat for about 3 minutes or until the pancake begins to brown. (Use a little lower heat than for regular pancakes or crepes.) Turn the dosa over and cook the other side. Repeat until all the batter is used up.

3. Stack on a plate and cover with a cloth to keep warm until serving time.

4. Serve as a bread to accompany grain dishes and curries, or fill with your choice of curried vegetables or grains and roll up like crepes.

Orient Express Pasta Salad (page 81) is enticingly exotic.

Assorted whole grain muffins (pages 121–127) are surprisingly light and moist.

Cranberry Bread (page 129) is tart and delicious.

Chapati

These North Indian flat breads are very simple to make. Use them with curries and Indian-style food, as flour tortillas with Mexican food, or as a good basic bread when you want a change from the ordinary.

Yield: 10–12 chapati   Time: 50 minutes

1 cup water

$1/2$ teaspoon sea salt

$2^1/_2$ cups whole wheat bread flour (approximately)

1. Place the water and salt in a large bowl. Gradually stir in enough of the flour to make a kneadable dough.

2. Turn the dough out onto a well-floured surface and knead in enough flour to make it smooth and not sticky. This should take 5–10 minutes.

3. Cover the dough with an inverted bowl and let it rest for about 30 minutes. (This is not absolutely necessary, but it makes the dough easier to roll out.)

4. Cut the dough into 10–12 pieces of equal size. Shape each piece into a ball, then press the ball between your hands to flatten it out. Place each flattened ball of dough on a floured surface and sprinkle with a little additional flour. With a rolling pin, roll out each piece of dough into a very thin round (about $1/_{16}$ inch thick).

5. Heat an unoiled skillet. One by one, cook the chapati over medium-high heat for about 1 minute on each side. As they are cooking, use a clean dish towel to press them down firmly against the bottom of the skillet. This will make them puff up. The chapati are done when they are lightly flecked with dark brown.

6. Stack the cooked chapati on a plate and cover them with a clean towel to keep them warm.

Chapati can be refrigerated and reheated.

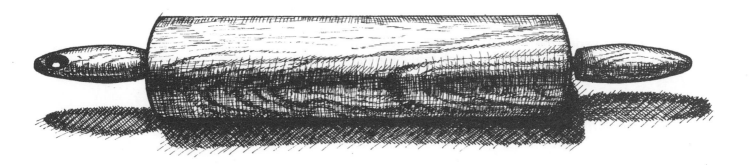

Parmesan Bread

1/4 cup olive oil

1/4 cup grated Parmesan cheese or tofu-Parmesan

8 thick slices whole grain French or Italian bread

This is a good alternative to garlic bread or any bread spread with butter or margarine. It is great with a hot bowl of homemade soup.

Serves: 8 — Time: 5 minutes

1. In a small bowl, mix together the olive oil and the cheese or tofu-Parmesan. Spread the mixture evenly over the bread.

2. Place the bread under the broiler or in a toaster oven and broil until hot and lightly browned around the edges.

VARIATIONS:

- *Parmesan Garlic Bread:* Add 6–8 cloves of pressed garlic to the cheese/oil mixture.
- *Garlic Herb Bread:* Add 1 teaspoon herbes de Provence (page 102) and 1/4 teaspoon sea salt to the garlic mixture; omit the cheese.

TIPS FOR PIE CRUSTS

By following these recipes, you can make wonderful 100 percent whole grain pie crusts that are crisp and tender with no saturated fats. Two recipes for wheatless pie crusts are provided for those with wheat allergies. Before you start, read the tips below, and get ready to make the perfect, healthful pie crust.

- Preheat the oven to the temperature specified in the recipe you are using.

- Mix the dough only as much as is necessary. Too much handling will make the dough tough.

- If the dough is too dry to hold together, sprinkle it lightly with water, or a mixture of water and oil. If it is too wet, sprinkle it with a little extra flour.

- Before rolling your crust out between two sheets of waxed paper, sprinkle the table or countertop lightly with water to keep the paper from slipping. Too much water will make the paper stick to your crust, however.

- Roll out your crust in all directions to make it nice and round.

- Bake both filled and unfilled pie crusts on the bottom rack of your oven.

- For a crisper crust, let the crust cool before filling.

- Let the filling cool a little before pouring it into the crust. If it is too hot, it will make the crust soggy.

Whole Wheat Pie Crust

This is a great recipe for a basic whole wheat crust. I have been making it for years, and it is still my favorite. This is the same recipe that appears in Cooking with the Right Side of the Brain, *but I am adding quantities of ingredients needed to make single-crust and small pies.*

Yield: 1 pie crust, as indicated   Time: 15 minutes to prepare; baking time depends on type of filling used

1. Place the flour in a medium bowl. Measure the oil and the hot water into a small bowl. Do not mix. Slowly pour the oil and water over the flour, mixing with a fork just enough to form a ball. If you are making a double crust, divide the dough into two portions, one piece slightly larger than the other.

2. Place the larger piece of dough between two sheets of lightly floured waxed paper and roll it out. Lightly sprinkle your work surface with water to keep the paper from slipping.

3. Carefully peel off the top sheet of waxed paper. Pick the dough up by the corners of the bottom paper and place it (paper side up) in the pie pan (a). Carefully peel off the paper (b). Fill the crust with the desired filling and roll out the remaining dough. Cover the pie with the top crust. Flute the edges (c), and cut some holes in the top crust to allow the steam to escape (d). Bake according to the directions given in the filling recipe you choose.

If you like, you can add a pinch of sea salt to any of the recipes at right.

FOR A DOUBLE 9-INCH CRUST:

1½ cups whole wheat pastry flour

⅓ cup oil

¼ cup hot water

FOR A SINGLE 9-INCH CRUST:

1 cup whole wheat pastry flour

¼ cup oil

3 tablespoons hot water

FOR A SINGLE 7½-INCH CRUST:

¾ cup whole wheat pastry flour

3 tablespoons oil

2 tablespoons hot water

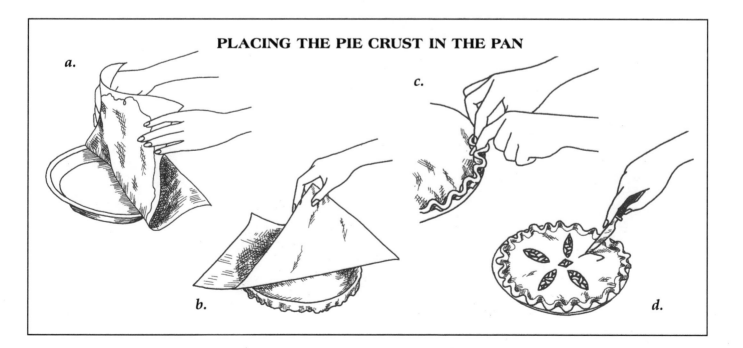

PLACING THE PIE CRUST IN THE PAN

a.

b.

c.

d.

Pecan Pie Crust

This crust is light, crisp, and tender.

3/4 cup whole wheat pastry flour

3/4 cup oat flour

1/2 cup pecans

1/4 cup oil minus 1 teaspoon

2 tablespoons water (approximately)

Yield: 1 single 9-inch crust

Time: 10 minutes to prepare;
20 minutes to bake

1. Place the flours and pecans in a food processor. Blend until the nuts are finely ground. Slowly add the oil while the blade is working and blend briefly, just to mix in the oil.*

2. Place the mixture in a medium bowl and stir in the water. Mix just enough to incorporate the water into the dough. Add enough water to make the dough hold together.

3. Roll out the dough between two pieces of waxed paper (see the drawing on page 137). Lightly sprinkle the counter with water to keep the paper from slipping. Peel off the top piece of paper. Pick up the dough, holding the bottom paper by the edges, and lay it in the pie pan with the dough facing the pan. Carefully peel off the paper. Flute the edges of the crust and pierce the sides and bottom of the crust with a fork to keep it from bubbling up as it bakes.

4. Bake at 350°F for 20 minutes or until golden brown.

*If you don't have a food processor, grind the nuts in a blender or finely chop them. Mix the nuts with the flour, stir in the oil, and mix well.

Potato Pie Crust

This crust is tender, but it is strong enough to hold its shape with the Onion Pie (page 199) and the Savory Butternut Squash Pie (page 197).

Yield: 1 single 9- or 10-inch crust   Time: 15 minutes

1 cup dry, unseasoned mashed potatoes

1/4 cup oil

1 cup whole wheat pastry flour

1 teaspoon baking powder

1/4 teaspoon sea salt

1 tablespoon water, or a little more if needed

1. Whip together the potatoes and the oil with a wire whisk or fork.

2. Mix together the flour, baking powder, and salt. Add the flour mixture to the potato mixture and blend with a fork or your hands. Do not overwork. If the dough is too dry to hold together, gradually add a little water. (If the mashed potatoes are fairly moist, you will not need to add any water.)

3. Roll the dough out between two pieces of waxed paper (see the drawing on page 137). Sprinkle the counter or tabletop with a few drops of water to keep the paper from slipping.

4. Carefully peel off the top sheet of paper. Lift the dough by the edges of the paper and place it (paper side up) in a pie plate. Carefully peel off the paper. Flute the edges of the pie crust, and fill and bake according to the recipe of your choice.

Peanut Butter Pie Crust

This is a good wheatless pie crust for peanut butter fans. Try it with dessert pies that would go well with peanut butter such as the Peanut Butter "Cream" Pie (page 252).

Yield: 1 single 9-inch crust   Time: 15 minutes to prepare; 10–12 minutes to bake

1 cup oat flour

3/4 cup peanut butter (smooth or crunchy)

2 tablespoons honey

1–2 tablespoons water, if necessary

1. Place the flour and the peanut butter in a large bowl. Using a fork and your hands, mix the two together. Add the honey, and mix as well as you can with a fork. Knead the dough in the bowl a few times with your hands until it is well mixed. If it doesn't hold together, add 1–2 tablespoons of water.

2. Roll the dough out between two pieces of waxed paper. Sprinkle a few drops of water on the counter to keep the paper from slipping. Peel off the top paper. Pick up the crust by the corners of the bottom paper and transfer it (dough side down) to a pie pan. Carefully peel off the paper. Flute the edges, and pierce the bottom and the sides of the crust all over with a fork.

3. Bake at 350°F for 10–12 minutes or until nicely browned.

Barley Walnut Pie Crust

This is a recipe for two slightly different wheatless pie crusts: a 7¹/₂-inch crust and a standard 9-inch crust. The smaller one is perfect for the Dried Fruit Pie (page 249).

Yield: 1 pie crust

Time: 15 minutes to prepare; 25 minutes to bake

FOR A 7¹/₂-INCH CRUST:

¹/₂ cup oat flour

¹/₄ cup barley flour

¹/₂ teaspoon cinnamon (optional)

1 cup walnuts

1 tablespoon oil

1 tablespoon maple syrup

FOR A 9-INCH CRUST:

1 cup oat flour

¹/₂ cup barley flour

1 teaspoon cinnamon (optional)

1 cup walnuts

3 tablespoons oil

2 tablespoons plus 1 teaspoon maple syrup

1. In a medium bowl, combine the oat flour, barley flour, and cinnamon (if desired).

2. Place the walnuts in a blender and finely grind them.

3. Mix the ground nuts with the flours. Stir in the oil and mix well. Stir in the maple syrup and mix again.

4. Press the dough evenly against the sides and the bottom of a lightly oiled pie pan.

5. Bake at 350°F for 25 minutes or until the crust is lightly browned.

VARIATION:

Substitute pecans for the walnuts.

8.
VEGETABLES

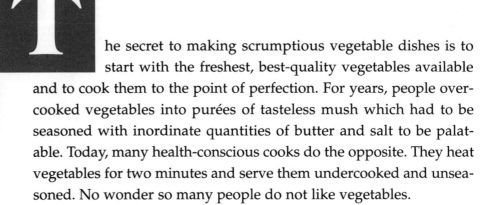

The secret to making scrumptious vegetable dishes is to start with the freshest, best-quality vegetables available and to cook them to the point of perfection. For years, people overcooked vegetables into purées of tasteless mush which had to be seasoned with inordinate quantities of butter and salt to be palatable. Today, many health-conscious cooks do the opposite. They heat vegetables for two minutes and serve them undercooked and unseasoned. No wonder so many people do not like vegetables.

There is, happily, a way to serve vegetables that are divinely good, still nutritious, and seasoned just right, but it is impossible to give you a chart of exact times for cooking them. The many factors affecting cooking time include the age of the vegetables, the size of the pieces, the type of cooking pan, and the amount of heat used.

The secret to perfectly cooked vegetables is to check them during cooking and remove them from the heat as soon as they are done. Once done, remove the lid, because they will continue to cook, even when taken off the heat.

Try to buy locally grown, organic produce. If the only vegetables you have had are from the supermarket, you will be surprised at how flavorful organic produce is. Also, buy vegetables that are in season. If you live in the North, use lots of root vegetables, cabbage, and winter squash in winter, and in summer buy the more succulent and tender vegetables such as tomatoes, sweet corn, and summer squash. Buying local, in-season produce is sound both ecologically and economically because it saves on shipping and packaging costs. It also assures you of the highest-quality, freshest, and best-tasting produce possible.

Dilled Carrots

Use big, sweet, organically grown carrots for the best flavor.

Serves: 5–6   Time: 20 minutes

1. Steam or pressure-cook the carrots until they are tender but still firm.

2. While the carrots are cooking, heat the oil in a skillet. Add the shallots and sauté until tender. Set aside.

3. When the carrots are tender, drain them of their cooking liquid, reserving 2 tablespoons. Place this in a cup, add the miso, and mix well to dilute the miso. Add the diluted miso to the carrots, along with the shallots and dill weed, and mix well.

This is a nice side dish to accompany grain dishes or meatless loaves.

$4^1/_2$ cups sliced carrots
(3 large, scrubbed carrots)

1 tablespoon olive oil

1 cup sliced shallots

2 tablespoons water (left over from steaming the carrots)

1 tablespoon yellow or white miso

$^1/_4$ cup finely chopped dill weed

Gingered Sweet Potatoes

Many people think that the usual candied sweet potatoes served for Thanksgiving are too sweet and rich. Here is a different, spicy version that is sweetened with date sugar.

Serves: 6–8   Time: 45 minutes

1. Either peel the sweet potatoes or scrub them and cut out any bad spots. Cut them into thick slices, and then into quarters. Steam the sweet potatoes until they are just tender, about 20 minutes. Or place them in a pressure cooker and heat until the regulator jiggles, then turn off the heat and let the cooker cool down on its own.

2. While the sweet potatoes are cooking, mix together the date sugar, ginger, cinnamon, and oil.

3. When the potatoes are done, place them in a mixing bowl. If there is any cooking liquid left, reserve it. Add $^3/_4$ of the date sugar mixture to the potatoes and mix well. Transfer the mixture to an oiled baking dish and sprinkle the remaining date sugar mixture over the top. Pour the water or leftover cooking liquid into the dish.

4. Cover and bake at 350°F for 20–25 minutes.

This dish may be made in advance through Step 3 and baked before serving. If it is cold when you bake it, add an extra 10–15 minutes to the baking time.

3 pounds sweet potatoes
(3 large potatoes)

1 cup date sugar

1 tablespoon finely grated fresh ginger

2 teaspoons cinnamon

2 tablespoons oil

$^1/_3$ cup water (or leftover cooking liquid)

Collard Greens with Sun-Dried Tomatoes

Serves: 4 Time: 10 minutes to prepare; 25 minutes to cook

1 pound fresh collard greens

1 cup water

20 sun-dried tomato halves, cut into small pieces

1 teaspoon basil

1/2 teaspoon sea salt

1 tablespoon plus 1 teaspoon lemon juice

3–4 chopped scallions

1. Wash the collards. Chop the stems into 1/4-inch pieces. Roll the leaves lengthwise and make a cut along the length of the roll. Now you can quickly chop them crosswise into bite-sized pieces.

2. Place the chopped collards in a large kettle (I use my cast-iron Dutch oven). Add the water, cover, and bring to a boil. Stir and reduce the heat. Add the tomato pieces, basil, salt, and lemon juice. Simmer, stirring occasionally, until the collards are tender (about 25 minutes more). Top with the scallions before serving.

Mustard Greens with Onions

1 tablespoon olive oil

1 cup chopped onion (1 medium onion)

1 pound fresh mustard greens

2 tablespoons lemon juice

1/2 teaspoon sea salt, or to taste

1 teaspoon herbes de Provence (see page 102)

Like kale and collards, mustard greens are an underappreciated but super-nutritious vegetable. They take longer to cook than spinach but much less time than either kale or collards.

Serves: 4 Time: about 20 minutes

1. Heat the oil in a large, heavy kettle. Add the onion, and sauté over low heat, about 5–10 minutes.

2. While the onion is cooking, wash the mustard greens. Chop the thickest part of the stem into 1/4-inch pieces, and chop the rest into bite-sized pieces. Add the greens to the kettle. They may fill it, but they will rapidly cook down.

3. Cover and turn the heat to high. When the pot is full of steam and the greens have begun to wilt (in 2–3 minutes), add the remaining ingredients. Stir and reduce the heat to medium-low. Cook for 5–10 minutes, stirring occasionally, until the greens are done.

Mustard greens, like kale and collards, are a traditional food of the Deep South, where they are served with corn bread and beans.

Kale with Sauerkraut

A nutritious and tasty side dish that goes well with beans.

Serves: 4   Time: 50 minutes

1. Wash the kale and chop it. Chop the thick stem ends finely so that they cook as fast as the leaves. Place the kale in a large, heavy pan with the remaining ingredients.

2. Cover and bring to a boil. Stir and reduce the heat. Cook over low heat, stirring occasionally, until the kale is tender.

Maybe it's because I was raised in the South, but I like to cook kale slowly, for about 45 minutes. I've seen many recipes with shorter cooking times, but I do not like the results. However, a pressure cooker can cut the cooking time. Just bring the pressure up, reduce the heat, and cook under pressure for 3–5 minutes. Then, let the pressure come down on its own.

8 ounces fresh kale

¹/₂ cup sauerkraut (fresh or canned)

¹/₂ cup water (use all or part of the water from the sauerkraut)

¹/₄ teaspoon caraway seeds

2 teaspoons balsamic vinegar

Herbed Brussels Sprouts

Serves: 4–6   Time: 25 minutes

1. To clean the Brussels sprouts, rinse them under running water, and remove any discolored leaves. Cut a thin slice off the bottom of each Brussels sprout and cut an X about ¹/₂ inch deep into each bottom.

2. In a heavy saucepan, heat the oil. Add the shallots and herbes de Provence, and sauté over low heat until the shallots are nearly tender, about 5 minutes. Add the water, lemon juice, vegetable broth powder, and tamari or salt. Add the Brussels sprouts, cover, and bring to a boil. Reduce the heat and simmer until the Brussels sprouts are tender, about 15 minutes or less if they are small and fresh.

1¹/₄ pounds Brussels sprouts

1 teaspoon olive oil

¹/₂ cup finely chopped shallots

1 teaspoon herbes de Provence (see page 102)

³/₄ cups water

1 tablespoon lemon juice

1 tablespoon vegetable broth powder

Tamari or sea salt to taste

Balsamic Beets

Add some color to your meal. This dish is good hot or cold.

4 medium beets

1 cup water

2 tablespoons balsamic vinegar

1 tablespoon honey

1 teaspoon tarragon

1/4 teaspoon sea salt

Serves: 4   Time: 45 minutes

1. Scrub the beets (unpeeled) and cut off the stem and root end. Cut the beets crosswise into 1/4-inch-thick slices and place them in a heavy pan.

2. Mix together the water, vinegar, honey, tarragon, and salt and pour this mixture over the beets in the pan. Cover and bring to a boil. Reduce the heat and simmer, stirring occasionally, until the beets are tender, 30–35 minutes.

Cauliflower Millet Purée

This dish is sometimes called "mock mashed potatoes" because it has a creamy color, mild flavor, and a texture similar to that of mashed potatoes.

1/2 cup millet

1 1/4 cups water

1/2 teaspoon sea salt

1 pound cauliflower, cut into flowerets

1 tablespoon yellow miso

2 tablespoons soymilk, if needed

Dash of cayenne pepper, or to taste

Serves: 4   Time: 35 minutes

1. Place the millet in a medium saucepan. Cover the millet with water and swish it around to wash it. Drain the millet through a fine wire strainer and return it to the pan.

2. Add the water and sea salt. Cover the pan and bring to a boil. Reduce the heat to low and cook for about 20 minutes, or until the water has been completely absorbed. Place the millet in a food processor.

3. While the millet is cooking, steam the cauliflower until it is very tender. Drain it well and place it in the food processor with the millet. Add the miso. Blend the mixture until it is smooth. If it is too dry, add the soymilk. Add the cayenne pepper and serve.

4. Serve as you would mashed potatoes. The purée is delicious plain or with a sauce or gravy of your choice.

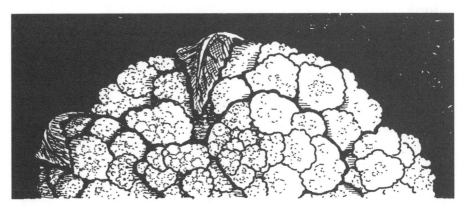

Sautéed Leeks

If you have never had leeks, imagine a green vegetable mildly seasoned with onions.

Serves: 2–4   Time: 30 minutes

1. To clean the leeks, cut off the root end and make an incision along the length of the leek. Spread the leaves apart and carefully rinse out any sand under running water.

2. Chop the leeks. You may use all of the white bulb and the lighter green part as well as much of the darker green part. Save the toughest dark green outer leaves and leaf tips for stock or a blended soup.)

3. Heat the oil in a skillet. Add the chopped leeks and the herbs. Sauté over high heat, stirring constantly, for about 3 minutes. Cover, reduce the heat to low, and continue to cook, stirring occasionally, for about 15 minutes more or until the leeks are tender. To test, taste some of the dark green part; if it is tender, the rest will be, too.

Sautéed leeks are a good accompaniment to grain and bean dishes.

3 medium leeks

1–2 tablespoons olive oil, as needed

1 teaspoon herbes de Provence (see page 102)

1/4 teaspoon sea salt

Green Beans with Garlic and Sunflower Seeds

Use garden-fresh green beans and cook them to the point of perfection and you will love this recipe.

Serves: 4   Time: about 30 minutes

1. Clean the green beans and break them into 1-inch pieces. Steam or pressure-cook them until they are just tender.

2. Heat the oil in a skillet and add the garlic and savory. Sauté for about 1 minute over low heat. Add the sunflower seeds and continue to sauté over medium heat until the sunflower seeds are browned. Add the salt and lemon juice. Mix well.

3. Add the cooked green beans to the skillet with the sunflower-garlic mixture and mix well. Top each serving with any sunflower seeds that are left in the pan.

1 pound fresh green beans

1 tablespoon sunflower oil

6 cloves garlic, minced

1 teaspoon summer savory

1/4 cup sunflower seeds

1/4 teaspoon sea salt

2 tablespoons lemon juice

Summer Squash with Peppers and Shallots

Serves: 4   Time: 15–20 minutes

1 tablespoon olive oil

3 medium yellow squash, sliced

1/3 cup chopped shallots

1 teaspoon basil

1/2 red or yellow bell pepper, diced

1/2 cup soymilk

1 tablespoon white or yellow miso

1 teaspoon arrowroot

2 tablespoons minced parsley

1. Heat the oil in a skillet. Add the squash, shallots, basil, and pepper. Sauté over medium heat for about 3 minutes.

2. Add 1/4 cup of the soymilk, cover, and reduce the heat. Let simmer over medium-low heat, stirring occasionally, for about 5 minutes or until the squash is tender.

3. In a small bowl, mix together the remaining soymilk, the miso, and arrowroot. Add this mixture to the squash, mix well, and bring to a boil. Sprinkle with the parsley and serve.

Amy's Summer Squash Casserole

Amy was one of my favorite cooking students. Here is a recipe that she invented.

Serves: 4–6   Time: 45 minutes

2 tablespoons toasted garbanzo flour

1 tablespoon oil

2 cups soymilk

1/4 cup nutritional yeast

1 teaspoon tamari

1 teaspoon dry mustard

1/2 teaspoon sea salt

Dash of cayenne pepper, or to taste

4 yellow squash, sliced

1/2 cup sliced sweet onion

Paprika garnish

1/2 cup whole grain cracker or bread crumbs

1. Place the garbanzo flour in a hot, unoiled skillet. Stir in the oil, then stir in the soymilk. Add the nutritional yeast, tamari, dry mustard, salt, and cayenne pepper. Continue to stir and cook over medium heat until the mixture thickens into a sauce.

2. Transfer the sauce to a large bowl and add the squash and onions. Mix well. Place in an oiled 7-x-11-inch baking dish. Sprinkle the top with paprika and then with the bread or cracker crumbs.

3. Bake at 350°F for 20 minutes or until the squash is just tender.

Zucchini Simmered in Mirin

Add an exotic touch to an ordinary vegetable.

Serves: 4   Time: 15–20 minutes

1. Heat oil in a large skillet. Add the onion and sauté over medium heat until it begins to become translucent.

2. Add the remaining ingredients, stir, and cover. Cook over medium-low heat, stirring often, until the vegetables are tender, about 8 minutes.

3. Mix well before serving to coat all the vegetables with the sauce.

1 teaspoon oil

1 cup chopped onion
(1 medium onion)

2 medium zucchinis, thinly sliced

1 red bell pepper, thinly sliced

2 cloves garlic, pressed

2 tablespoons lemon juice

3 tablespoons mirin

1 teaspoon basil

1/4 teaspoon sea salt

Baked Okra

I never liked okra until a woman from Louisiana taught me to fry it first and then bake it. Wanting to reduce the fat and save time, I decided to try just baking it. The results were just about the same: wonderful!

Serves: 4   Time: 35 minutes

1. Place the okra in a medium bowl and add the cornmeal, salt, and herbs. Mix until the cornmeal adheres to the okra.

2. Coat a shallow oven-proof pan (a pie pan or small cake pan works well) with the olive oil. Transfer the okra to the pan with a slotted spoon or your hands, letting any loose cornmeal fall back into the bowl. Bake at 375°F for about 25 minutes.

Serve as a side dish.

2 cups sliced okra

1/4 cup cornmeal

1/8 teaspoon sea salt

1/2 teaspoon basil

1/2 teaspoon oregano

1 tablespoon olive oil

Creamy Sweet Corn

This easy side dish is best with corn that is really fresh and sweet.

3–4 ears corn

1/4 cup soymilk

1 teaspoon honey

1 teaspoon basil

1 teaspoon sweet white miso, or to taste

Serves: 3–4   Time: 15 minutes

1. Cut the corn off the cobs and purée it in a blender or food processor.

2. Place the corn purée in a small, heavy saucepan. Add the soymilk, honey, and basil. Stirring constantly, cook the mixture over medium heat until it starts to simmer. Reduce the heat to low, cover, and cook for about 3 minutes longer. Add the miso, mix well, and serve.

Creamy Sweet Corn makes a good accompaniment to bean dishes. It is also good with the Tofu Sunflower Loaf (page 190).

Fried Green Tomatoes

This a traditional recipe from Kentucky that my mother made when I was a child. About once a year, I get an urge for fried green tomatoes and nothing else will do.

1/2–1 cup cornmeal

Sea salt to taste

4 medium green tomatoes, cut into thin slices

Oil as needed for frying

Serves: 4   Time: 30 minutes

1. In a small bowl, mix together the cornmeal and the salt. Dip the tomato slices, one at a time, into the seasoned cornmeal to coat them evenly on both sides.

2. Heat 1 tablespoon oil in a large skillet. Place as many tomatoes as will fit easily in the bottom of the skillet. Fry them over medium-high heat until they are browned on the bottom. Turn them over (adding more oil if necessary) and cook the other side until the cornmeal is golden brown and the tomatoes are tender.

9. MAIN DISHES

If you think that cutting back on fat and cholesterol means suffering through boring salads and plain steamed vegetables, it's time to take a new look at healthful cooking. By combining grains, bean, seeds, and fresh seasonal vegetables, the possibilities for satisfying, low-fat main dishes are limitless. Healthful cooking can be as hearty or as light as you like. There is no reason to give up good taste or to feel hungry in order to have a wholesome diet.

COOKING WHOLE GRAINS

Grains are easy to prepare and can be cooked in advance. Though cooked grains don't freeze well, they will keep for several days in the refrigerator.

All whole grains must be washed before cooking, with the exception of rolled or flaked grains (such as oat, wheat, rye, or barley flakes), couscous, and corn grits.

To wash, place the grain in the pot that you will cook it in. A heavy, medium-sized pan with a tight-fitting lid is best. Cover the grain with about 2 inches of water and swish it around. Drain it through a fine wire strainer. Repeat. If any hulls float to the top of the water, pour them off before draining through the strainer.

Return the grain to the pan and add the amount of water called for in the recipe. Some recipes call for boiling the water before adding the grain, but I don't see any difference in the result, so I don't do it.

Cover the pan, bring the water to a boil, then reduce the heat. Simmer until the water is absorbed. Fluff with a fork.

Don't stir the grain or needlessly open the lid while the grain is cooking; the result may be sticky grain. If you forget to check the cooking time when you start, you can quickly open the lid and peek in. If there is no water visible, poke a knife through the grain to see if there is still water in the bottom of pan.

When cooking large quantities of grains, I find the results are better when I cook them in batches of no more than 2 cups of dry grain.

On the facing page is a chart of approximate cooking times and yields for 1 cup of various grains. The less water you use, the shorter the cooking time and the chewier the texture of the grain.

Pressure-Cooked Rice

Rice is the primary staple of the macrobiotic diet, and pressure cooking is the way macrobiotic cooks prepare it. This recipe takes longer than cooking without pressure, and the resulting texture is much softer and stickier. (For cooking rice without a pressure cooker, see "Cooking with Whole Grains," beginning on page 152.)

2 cups brown rice*

3–4 cups water

1/2 teaspoon sea salt

Serves: 6   Time: about 1 hour

1. Place the rice in a pressure cooker. Cover with water and swish the rice around in the pan to wash it. Drain it through a wire strainer and return it to the pressure cooker

2. Add the water and the sea salt. Place the pressure cooker over high heat until the pressure regulator jiggles. Then reduce the heat to low and cook for 55 minutes. Remove the pressure cooker from the heat and let the pressure come down before opening the cooker.

*You may use long, medium, or short grain rice. The shorter the grain, the stickier the rice. If you use 4 cups of water to cook the rice, the rice will be softer and stickier than with 3 cups.

GRAIN (1 cup)	WATER	COOKING TIME	YIELD
Amaranth	2 1/2–3 cups	20–25 minutes	2 1/2 cups
Barley, pearled	2 1/2–3 cups	45–55 minutes	3–3 1/2 cups
Brown rice (long grain, Basmati, medium grain, and short grain)	2 cups	45 minutes	3 cups
Buckwheat groats (brown or white)	2 cups	20 minutes	2 1/2 cups
Bulgur wheat	2 cups	10–15 minutes	2 1/2 cups
Corn grits	4 cups	25–30 minutes	3 cups
Cornmeal	3 cups	30 minutes	2 1/2 cups
Couscous (whole grain; regular couscous is virtually instant)	3 cups	Bring water to boil, add couscous, cover, and let sit for 5 minutes.	3 cups
Millet (hulled)	2 1/2–3 cups	20–25 minutes	3 1/2 cups
Oats, whole (groats)	3–4 cups	45–60 minutes (see also Easy-Cooked Cereal, page 35)	3 cups
Oat flakes	2 cups	5 minutes	2 1/2 cups
Quinoa	2 cups	15–20 minutes	3 1/2 cups
Rye flakes	2 cups	5–10 minutes	2 1/2 cups
Rye, whole	3 1/2–4 cups	50–60 minutes	2 1/2–3 cups
Teff	3 cups	15 minutes	about 3 cups
Wheat flakes	2 cups	5–10 minutes	2 1/2 cups
Wheat, whole	3 1/2 cups	50–60 minutes (see also Easy-Cooked Cereal, page 35)	3 cups

Rice Curry

2 tablespoons oil

1 cup chopped onion
(1 medium onion)

1 cup chopped celery
(2 stalks)

1 tablespoon curry powder

1 teaspoon grated fresh ginger

1 cup brown Basmati rice

2 cups water

1/2 teaspoon sea salt

1/3 cup sliced almonds

Serves: 4   Time: 1 hour

1. Heat the oil in a skillet. Add the onion and celery. Sauté over medium heat for about 3 minutes. Add the curry powder and the ginger. Sauté for about 3 minutes more.

2. Wash and drain the rice and add it to the curry-vegetable mixture. Stir for about 2 minutes more. Add the water and the salt. Stir and cover. Bring to a boil, then reduce the heat and simmer, covered, over medium-low heat for 45 minutes or until the water is absorbed. Do not stir the mixture while it cooks.

3. While the rice is cooking, place the almonds in an oven-proof pan and bake at 350°F (a toaster oven works well for this) until they are lightly toasted (about 10 minutes). Fluff the rice and sprinkle the almonds over it just before serving.

This curry is good with Chick Pea Dosas (page 134), Vegetable Dal Curry (page 173), and Apple Chutney (page 93), or Fresh Mango Chutney (page 92).

Baked Rice Provençal

1 1/2 cups short grain brown rice

1 1/4 cups chopped onions
(1 1/2 medium onions)

1 teaspoon basil

1 teaspoon oregano

1/2 teaspoon sea salt

1 tablespoon vegetable broth powder

3 cups water

2 medium tomatoes, sliced

3 cloves garlic, pressed

1 tablespoon olive oil

Easy and tasty.

Serves: 4–6   Time: 10 minutes to prepare;
1 hour, 15 minutes to bake

1. Place the rice and the onions in a lightly oiled baking dish. In a medium bowl, combine the basil, oregano, salt, vegetable broth powder, and water. Mix well and pour over the rice. Stir and cover.

2. Bake the rice at 350°F for 1 hour.

3. Uncover the rice and top it with the tomatoes. In a small bowl, combine the olive oil and the garlic. Brush this mixture over the tomatoes. Cover. Return the mixture to the oven and bake for 15 minutes more.

4. Serve with bean and vegetable dishes.

Spicy Barley

If you have some leftover barley, this dish is quick to make.

Serves: 3   Time: 15 minutes

1. Heat the oil in a skillet. Add the shallots, garlic, basil, oregano, and cayenne pepper. Sauté over medium heat for 3–5 minutes.

2. Add the barley and salt, mix well, and cook until heated through. Then add the tomato and stir over medium-high heat until it is warm.

3. Sprinkle with the parsley and serve as a side dish to accompany beans, tofu, or tempeh.

VARIATIONS:

• Add 1/2 cup frozen peas to the skillet along with the barley.
• Substitute leftover rice or millet for the barley.

1 tablespoon olive oil

1/3 cup finely chopped shallots

4 cloves garlic, minced

1 teaspoon basil

1/2 teaspoon oregano

Dash of cayenne pepper, or to taste

2 cups cooked barley (see page 152)

1/4 teaspoon sea salt, or to taste

1 large tomato, chopped into small pieces

2 tablespoons minced parsley

Spinach and Millet Bake

Serves: 4   Time: 30 minutes to prepare; 30 minutes to bake

1. Wash the millet and drain it through a wire strainer. Place it in a heavy, medium-sized pan, add the water, and cover. Bring the water to a boil, reduce the heat, and simmer for 20 minutes or until all the water has been absorbed.

2. Meanwhile, blend together the tofu, salt, basil, oregano, and cayenne pepper in a blender or food processor until smooth and creamy. Scrape the sides of the container with a rubber spatula from time to time, if necessary. Set aside. Wash, drain, and chop the spinach.

3. When the millet is done, place it in a large bowl. Add the tofu mixture, the chopped spinach, the onion, and the garlic. Mix as well as you can with a wooden spoon and finish with your hands.

4. Press the mixture into a well-oiled 8-x-8-inch baking dish. Sprinkle the cheese on top and bake at 350°F for 30 minutes. Move the baking dish to the top rack and turn your oven to broil for a minute or two to brown the top. Cut into squares to serve.

This dish may be served plain or with a tomato sauce. It is good with steamed carrots or a carrot salad.

1 cup millet

2 cups water

1 package (10 1/2 ounces) extra-firm silken tofu

1 teaspoon sea salt

1 teaspoon basil

1/2 teaspoon oregano

Dash of cayenne pepper, or to taste

10 ounces spinach

1/3 cup finely chopped onion (1 small onion)

2 cloves pressed garlic

1/2 cup grated soy cheese or dairy cheese

Barley with Mushrooms and Walnuts

2 tablespoons light sesame oil

1 cup chopped onion
(1 medium onion)

1 teaspoon tarragon

1 cup barley

4½ cups water

2 tablespoons tamari

1½ cups oyster mushrooms
(about 7 mushrooms)

1½ cups white button
mushrooms
(about 7 mushrooms)

1 cup walnut pieces

Garnish: finely chopped fresh
parsley

The oyster mushrooms in this recipe give it a gourmet flair.

Serves: 4 as a main dish, 8 as a side dish   Time: about 50 minutes

1. Heat the oil in a large, heavy kettle. Add the onion and the tarragon. Slowly sauté the onion until it is tender. Add the barley and turn the heat to high. Stir the barley for a minute, then add the water and the tamari. Stir once and cover. When the water starts to boil, reduce the heat and simmer for 40 minutes.

2. While the barley simmers, clean and slice the mushrooms and prepare the rest of your meal. To clean the oyster mushrooms, rinse them in cool water, then break off and discard the tough bottom of the stem. It should break at the point where the flesh is tender.

3. After the barley has cooked for about 40 minutes, the water should be almost all absorbed. Add the sliced mushrooms to the pot, stir, and continue to simmer for about 10 more minutes.

4. While the mushrooms are cooking, place the walnuts in a shallow baking dish or on a cookie sheet and bake them at 350°F (a toaster oven works well) for about 5 minutes or until they are lightly roasted.

5. To serve, top the barley with the roasted walnuts and sprinkle with the parsley. As a main dish, serve with a steamed vegetable (asparagus is good) and a salad. As a side dish, serve with some baked tofu or tempeh and a salad.

Leftover cold barley (without the walnuts) is delicious for lunch on a bed of Boston lettuce topped with Umeboshi Cream (page 91).

Ratatouille Deluxe

Sun-dried tomatoes, white wine, and black olives make this ratatouille a real delight. It is an easy recipe to prepare for a dinner party.

Serves: 6   Time: about 1 hour

1. Heat the olive oil in a large, heavy kettle (a cast-iron Dutch oven works well). Add the onion, garlic, herbes de Provence, and basil. Sauté until the onions begin to become tender and translucent.

2. Add the bell pepper and eggplant. Stir over medium heat for 2–3 minutes, then add the tomato purée, sun-dried tomatoes, and tamari. Stir, cover, and bring the mixture to a boil. Reduce the heat and simmer for about 10 minutes.

3. Add the zucchinis, chick peas, black olives, and mushrooms. Continue to simmer slowly until the vegetables are tender.

4. Pour the wine into a measuring cup, add the arrowroot, and mix well to dissolve the arrowroot. Add the arrowroot-wine mixture to the stew. Bring to a boil, then reduce the heat and simmer a minute or two until the sauce has thickened. Add cayenne pepper.

5. Serve over whole grain pasta, brown rice, or millet, accompanied by a simple green salad.

2 tablespoons olive oil

1 cup chopped onion (1 medium onion)

2–5 cloves garlic, minced

2 teaspoons herbes de Provence (see page 102)

1 teaspoon basil

1 bell pepper, diced

1 medium–large eggplant (about 1¼ pounds), diced

1¾ cups tomato purée (1 large or 2 small tomatoes, blended in blender)

20–25 sun-dried tomato halves, cut into pieces

2–3 tablespoons tamari, to taste

2 medium zucchinis, sliced

2 cups cooked chick peas (see page 169)

1 cup sliced pitted black olives

1½ cups sliced mushrooms

⅓ cup white wine

1½ tablespoons arrowroot

Dash of cayenne pepper, or to taste

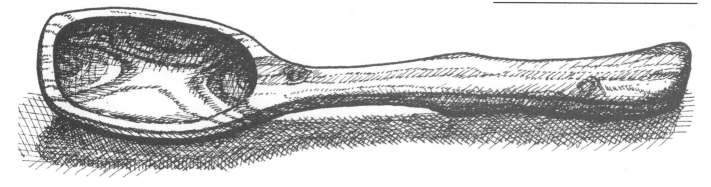

Quinoa Nori Rolls

These nori rolls are a delicious change from traditional nori maki; the quinoa and tahini work as well as sticky sushi rice and are more nutritious.

Serves: 8   Time: about 45 minutes to prepare; 2 hours to chill

SUSHI:

1 cup quinoa

2 cups water

1 tablespoon umeboshi vinegar

2 tablespoons tahini

2 tablespoons water

5 sheets toasted sushi nori*

FILLING:

1 small ripe avocado

1 tablespoon lemon juice

2 scallions, sliced lengthwise

DIPPING SAUCE:

1 tablespoon tamari

1 tablespoon lemon juice

1 teaspoon freshly grated ginger

1 clove garlic, pressed

1 tablespoon water

1. Place the quinoa in a saucepan and cover it with water. Swish it around to wash it and then drain it through a fine wire strainer. Return the quinoa to the pan and add 2 cups of water. Cover and bring the water to a boil. Reduce the heat and simmer without stirring for 15–20 minutes or until the water has been absorbed. Transfer the quinoa to a medium bowl.

2. Let the quinoa cool until it can be comfortably handled, but is still warm. Add the umeboshi vinegar, tahini, and 2 tablespoons of water. Mix well.

3. Cut the avocado in half, remove the pit, scoop out the flesh into a small bowl, and mash it. Add the lemon juice and mix well.

4. Place one sheet of toasted nori, one of the longer sides toward you, on a sushi mat, a woven placemat, or a clean dish towel.

5. Spread a fifth of the warm quinoa mixture over the nori, leaving a 2-inch strip uncovered on the two longer sides. Spread a fifth of the avocado mixture in a broad strip along the center of the quinoa mixture. Place a row of scallion slices along the center of the avocado (Drawing a).

a. The nori with quinoa-vegetable filling, before it is rolled.

6. Using the mat, roll the nori into a cigar shape (Drawing b). Press gently as you roll so that the nori roll is firm. Unroll the mat and roll the nori roll in a sheet of waxed paper.

7. Continue this procedure until the remaining sheets of nori have been used up. Place the wrapped nori rolls in the refrigerator to chill for about 2 hours. Chilling the rolls in the waxed paper tenderizes the nori and helps to hold everything together.

8. Prepare the dipping sauce: Combine all the ingredients in a small bowl.

9. To serve, slice the nori rolls into $1^1/_2$-inch-thick rounds using a very sharp knife (Drawing c). Serve with the dipping sauce.

Avocado-filled nori should be served the day they are made. However, if you wish to make nori rolls a day in advance, just substitute some matchstick-sliced carrots and cucumber for the avocado-lemon mixture.

*Toasted sushi nori (nori seaweed prepared for rolling sushi) is available in many natural foods stores. To toast your own, hold a piece of nori by the edge and quickly pass it over the heat of a stove burner until the nori turns a dark, translucent emerald green.

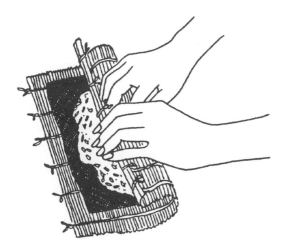

b. Using the sushi mat to roll the filling into the nori.

c. Slicing the quinoa nori roll.

Baked Lentil and Vegetable Stew

A hearty stick-to-the-ribs dish for a chilly fall evening.

1 cup dry green lentils

3 cups water

1 cup chopped onion
(1 medium onion)

2 cups chopped celery
(4 stalks)

1 cup sliced carrots
(2 medium carrots)

4 cups chopped rutabaga
(1 medium rutabaga)

1 pound Brussels sprouts
(cleaned and with an X cut in
the bottom of each)

4 bay leaves

1 tablespoon grated fresh
ginger

3 tablespoons tamari, or to
taste

Serves: 4–6

Time: 20 minutes to prepare;
1 hour, 15 minutes to bake

1. Combine all the ingredients, except for the tamari, in a large oven-proof pan (I use a cast-iron Dutch oven).

2. Mix well and bake at 350°F, stirring occasionally, until the lentils and vegetables are tender (about 1 hour, 15 minutes). If the stew begins to dry out, add some more water.

3. Before serving, add the tamari. Serve over brown rice or another grain.

Teff and Cabbage Stew

The teff thickens into a gravy in this richly flavored stew.

Serves: 4–5   Time: about 1 hour

1. Place the teff, water, and tamari in a large saucepan. Cover and bring to a boil. Reduce the heat and simmer for 15 minutes.

2. While the teff is cooking, heat the oil in a large skillet or a cast-iron Dutch oven. Add the onion, garlic, and ginger and sauté until the onion begins to become translucent. Add the cabbage and sauté for about 10 minutes more.

3. Combine the cabbage mixture with the teff. Cover and simmer over low heat for about 25 minutes.

$^1/_2$ cup teff

6 cups water

$^1/_4$ cup tamari

1 tablespoon oil

1 tablespoon toasted sesame oil

1 large onion, cut in half and then into thin slices

2 cloves garlic, minced

1 tablespoon grated fresh ginger

$^1/_2$ large or 1 small head cabbage, shredded (approximately 8 cups)

1 cup cooked chick peas (see page 169)

Potato Eggplant Curry

I once worked at a foundry that made bronze sculptures for a famous super-realist sculptor. One of my fellow workers, Mr. Singh, was an Eastern Indian. He taught me how to make this delicious curry.

2 tablespoons oil

1 rounded tablespoon curry powder

1 teaspoon ground cumin

1½ cups chopped onion (½ large Spanish onion)

2 baking potatoes, cut into ½-inch cubes

1 medium–large eggplant (about 1¼ pounds) cut into 1-inch cubes

¼ cup water, or more if needed

1 teaspoon sea salt, or to taste

Serves: 3–4   Time: about 1 hour

1. Heat the oil in a large, heavy kettle (a cast-iron Dutch oven works well). Add the curry powder, cumin, and onion. Sauté over medium heat for about 2 minutes. Add the potatoes and continue to stir for 2–3 minutes longer. Then add the eggplant and stir for 2–3 minutes longer.

2. Add the water and salt, stir, cover, and reduce the heat to low. Simmer, stirring occasionally, until the potatoes are done, about 40 minutes. The mixture should be dry, but if it begins to stick, add a little more water.

3. Serve the curry with Cashew "Sour Cream" (page 91) on the side and a green salad or Sambals (page 77). Chapati (page 135) and either the Apple Chutney (page 93) or the Fresh Mango Chutney (page 92) are authentic accompaniments.

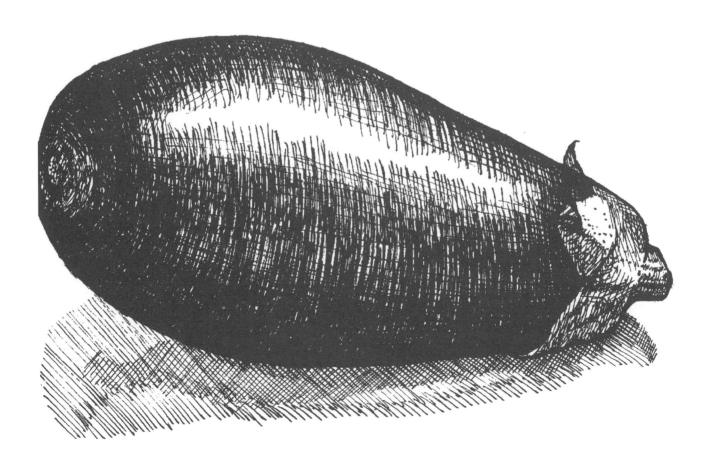

Hot Eggplant Mash with Rice

This recipe was inspired by a traditional Indian dish, which is usually served cold as a side dish (see Bunny's Eggplant Salad on page 79). This is wonderful served hot over rice.

Serves: 3–4   Time: 1 hour to bake eggplant; 15 minutes to prepare

1 medium eggplant (about 12 ounces)

1½ cups brown Basmati rice

3 cups water

⅓ cup Cashew "Sour Cream" (see page 91)

½ teaspoon sea salt

2 cloves garlic, pressed

1 ripe tomato, finely chopped

1 tablespoon finely chopped fresh mint

1. Rub the eggplant very lightly with oil. With a fork, pierce the skin of the eggplant all over at about 1-inch intervals. Place the eggplant on a cookie sheet and bake it at 350°F for about 1 hour or until the skin shrivels and the inside is very soft.

2. Meanwhile, wash the rice and drain it through a wire strainer. Place it in a heavy saucepan. Cover and bring to a boil. Reduce the heat and simmer over low heat for about 45 minutes or until the water has been absorbed.

3. While the eggplant and rice are cooking, prepare the Cashew "Sour Cream." Set aside.

4. When the eggplant is done, place it on a cutting board and cut it in half lengthwise. With a spoon, scrape the flesh out of each half, holding it with a towel so you don't burn yourself. Place the flesh in a bowl or saucepan, and mash it with a fork or potato masher.

5. Add the Cashew "Sour Cream," salt, and garlic and mix well. If the eggplant is still hot, you will not need to reheat it before serving. Otherwise, gently reheat the eggplant mixture by stirring it over medium heat until heated through. Do not boil.

6. To serve, spoon the eggplant mash over the rice. Garnish with the chopped tomato and the mint. Serve immediately.

Serve this dish with a bean dish and a salad.

Moroccan Couscous

STEW:

2 tablespoons olive oil

1½ cups chopped onion
(1 large onion)

3 cloves garlic, minced

3 bay leaves

1 teaspoon cumin

2 medium turnips, diced

1 cup chopped celery
(about 2 stalks)

1 cup sliced carrots
(2 medium carrots)

3 cups chopped cabbage

16-ounce can of tomatoes

2 medium zucchinis, cut into
thick slices

1 cups cooked chick peas
(see page 169)

3–4 tablespoons tamari, or to
taste

SAUCE:

¼ cup tomato paste

1 tablespoon olive oil

¼ cup water

1 teaspoon red pepper flakes

Dash of cayenne pepper, or to
taste

COUSCOUS:

2 cups whole wheat couscous

3 cups water

1. Heat the oil in a large kettle. Add the onion, garlic, bay leaves, and cumin. Sauté for about 5 minutes over low heat. Add the turnips, celery, carrots, and cabbage. Stir for a minute or two and add the tomatoes. Place the zucchinis on top of the other vegetables. Cover and simmer for about 15 minutes. Stir and continue to cook, stirring occasionally, until the vegetables are nearly tender, about 30 minutes.

2. Add the chick peas and the tamari. Continue to cook until the vegetables are tender. Don't hurry the cooking of this stew; slow cooking is what makes it good.

3. While the vegetables are cooking, prepare the sauce: Combine the tomato paste and olive oil in a small bowl. Add the water and mix well. Add the pepper flakes and mix again. This sauce is traditionally very hot; test before adding and mixing in cayenne pepper.

4. About 10 minutes before serving, prepare the couscous: Bring the 3 cups water to a boil in a medium saucepan. Add the couscous. Stir, cover, and remove the pan from the heat. Let sit for 5 minutes, or until the water is absorbed.

To serve, make a bed of couscous on a large platter or on individual serving plates. Make a well in the center of the couscous, pour the stew into the well, and serve the hot sauce on the side.

Basic Polenta

Serves: 3–4   Time: 30–35 minutes

1. Mix together the cornmeal, water, and salt in a heavy, medium-sized pan. Bring to a boil while stirring constantly. Reduce the heat and continue to cook and stir until the mixture thickens.

2. Reduce the heat to very low, cover, and continue to cook, stirring occasionally, for 30 minutes.

1 cup cornmeal

3 cups cool water

1/4 teaspoon sea salt

Corn Pudding

Serves: 4   Time: 20 minutes to prepare; 30 minutes to bake

1. In a heavy saucepan, mix together the cornmeal and the water. Bring to a boil while stirring constantly. Cover, reduce the heat, and simmer, stirring occasionally, for 15 minutes.

2. While the cornmeal is cooking, place the tofu in a blender or a food processor and blend until smooth and creamy. Scrape the sides of the container with a rubber spatula to make sure that the tofu is well blended.

3. Place the blended tofu in a mixing bowl. Add the corn, salt, vegetable broth powder, onion flakes, basil, cayenne pepper, and cooked cornmeal and mix well.

4. Generously oil an 8-x-8-inch baking dish. Turn the mixture into the dish, spreading it evenly, and top it with the soy cheese. Bake at 350°F for 30 minutes or until the top is browned and the pudding is set. Let stand for 10 minutes before serving.

1 cup cornmeal

3 cups water

1 package (10 1/2 ounces) firm silken tofu

2 cups corn (fresh off the cob or unfrozen)

1 teaspoon sea salt

2 tablespoons vegetable broth powder

1/4 cup dried onion flakes

1 teaspoon basil

Dash of cayenne pepper, or to taste

1/2 cup grated soy cheese (cheddar flavor)

Cornmeal Dumplings

1 cup cornmeal

1/2 teaspoon sea salt

1 teaspoon baking powder

1 package (10 1/2 ounces) extra-firm tofu

Dumplings are an old-fashioned food that is perfect today because they are easy, healthful, and satisfying. This recipe uses tofu instead of eggs.

Yield: 15–16 dumplings   Time: 25 minutes

1. In a mixing bowl, combine the cornmeal, salt, and baking powder.

2. Blend the tofu in a blender or a food processor until it is smooth and creamy. Use a rubber spatula, if necessary, to scrape the sides of the container so that the tofu is well blended.

3. Add the blended tofu to the cornmeal mixture and mix well.

4. Drop the dough by the tablespoonful into a kettle of gently boiling soup or stew. Cover and cook over medium heat for 10 minutes. To test whether dumplings are done, remove one from the stew and slice it. The inside should be breadlike and not gritty.

Cornmeal dumplings are great simmered in a pot of juicy beans. Add extra liquid to compensate for what the dumplings will absorb.

Kale and Cabbage Stew with Cornmeal Dumplings

1 tablespoon olive oil

1 1/2 cups sliced onion (1/2 large Spanish onion)

3 1/2 cups chopped cabbage

2 1/2 cups finely chopped kale

1 teaspoon caraway seeds

3 1/2 cups water

3–4 tablespoons tamari

1 tablespoon balsamic vinegar

1 recipe Cornmeal Dumplings (above)

This recipe goes perfectly with the Cherry Tomato Salad (page 73).

Serves: 3–4   Time: about 1 hour, 20 minutes

1. Heat the oil in a large, heavy kettle (I use a cast-iron Dutch oven). Add the onion and sauté over medium heat until the onion begins to become translucent (3–4 minutes). Add the cabbage, kale, and caraway seeds and stir for about 2 minutes. Add the water, tamari, and vinegar. Bring to a boil, cover, and reduce the heat.

2. Simmer over low heat, stirring occasionally, for about 45 minutes or until the vegetables are tender.

3. When the vegetables are almost tender, prepare the dumpling batter. Raise the heat to medium so that the stew is at an easy boil. (If the stew is not hot enough, the dumplings will fall apart.) Drop the batter into the stew by the tablespoonful. There should be about 15 dumplings resting on the surface of the stew. Cover and cook for 10 minutes.

4. If the stew is not to be served immediately, remove the dumplings with a slotted spoon to a separate bowl. When time to serve (best within an hour of being made), reheat them with the stew.

Anasazi Bean Stew
with Cornmeal Dumplings

Serves: 4   Time: overnight to soak beans; about 2 hours to cook

1. Wash and pick over the beans. Place them in a bowl with water to cover them and let soak for overnight or 8–10 hours.

2. Drain the beans. Place them in a large, heavy kettle. Add fresh water. Cover and bring to a boil. Reduce the heat and simmer $1^{1}/_{2}$ hours or longer until the beans are almost tender.

3. Add the onions, celery, carrots, kombu, bay leaves, savory, and tomato purée. Mix and continue to simmer until the beans and vegetables are tender, about 45 minutes. Remove the kombu, slice it into bite-sized pieces, and return to pot. Add the vinegar and tamari.

4. While the vegetables are cooking, prepare the dumpling batter. Have the stew at an easy boil over medium heat and drop spoonfuls of the batter onto the surface of the stew. Cover and cook for 10 minutes.

5. Transfer the dumplings to a bowl with a slotted spoon. Stir the stew to mix it well. Serve it surrounded by the dumplings. Delicious with cooked greens and a tomato salad.

$1^{1}/_{2}$ cups Anasazi beans

3 cups water

2 cups chopped onions (2 medium onions)

1 cup chopped celery (2 stalks)

$1^{1}/_{2}$ cups sliced carrots (2–3 medium carrots)

1 strip kombu, 6–7 inches, rinsed

3 bay leaves

2 teaspoons summer savory

2 cups tomato purée (3–4 medium tomatoes, blended)

1 tablespoon balsamic vinegar

2 tablespoons tamari

1 recipe Cornmeal Dumplings (see facing page)

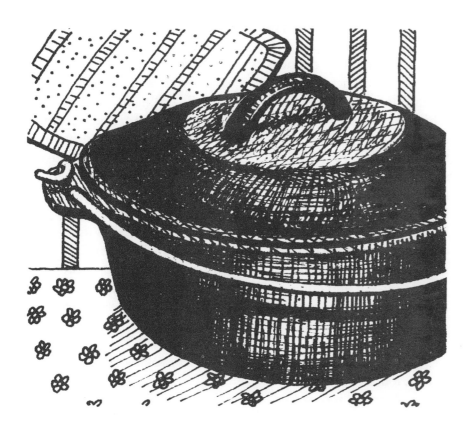

DRIED LEGUMES

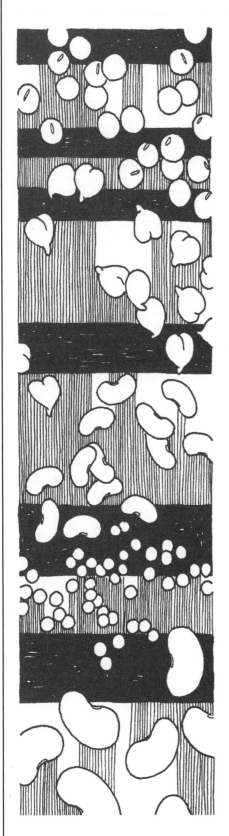

The virtues of dried legumes (beans and peas) are many. They are one of the most nourishing, yet least expensive foods. Their protein content is especially high, and they are a good source of iron and many other nutrients. In contrast to the protein derived from animal sources, legumes contain neither cholesterol nor saturated fat. There is also great diversity among legumes. I once bought a sample of each kind of bean that was available in Montreal and ended up with 23 varieties! Each variety has its own distinctive flavor, shape, and color. And they all taste good!

Despite their many virtues, legumes have one drawback, which has limited their popularity: namely, a tendency to cause flatulence. Legumes contain two unusual starches which are not easily broken down by the enzymes normally found in the intestines. These starches break down slowly, ferment, and form gastro-intesinal gas. However, with a little care in eating habits, food combinations, and cooking methods, I've found that most people can eat and enjoy legumes without experiencing the unpleasantness associated with them.

In fact, a little attention to menu planning and eating habits can help ensure you of good digestion of all your meals. The following list contains some general suggestions I follow when using beans as well as some tips on cooking beans that I have found render them more digestible.

- Soaking dried legumes before cooking them improves their digestibility and decreases their cooking time.

- After soaking, cook dried beans in fresh water. Discard the soaking water or use it to water your plants.

- The best way I know of to make beans easy to digest is to sprout them a little before cooking them. This changes some of the indigestible starches to digestible sugars. The sprouts do not have to be very long; a 1/4-inch sprout is enough to make a difference. Sprouting beans, even just slightly, also makes them cook faster. See page 74 for how to sprout beans.

- Beans are most easily digested when they are well cooked. Long, slow cooking, as in an electric slow-cooking pot, is ideal.

- Most cookbooks recommend adding salt or tamari at the end of cooking because it is thought that salt added earlier will keep the beans from becoming tender. However, some cooks prefer to add salt to the cooking water with the beans. They say that it does not significantly influence the cooking time or the tenderness of the beans, and that it makes the beans more flavorful. I add salt near the end of cooking.

- I have found that a tablespoon or so of vinegar added to a pot of beans as they are cooking makes them easier to digest. It also enhances their flavor.

- Miso, sauerkraut, and yogurt are good choices to serve in the same meal with beans because they are foods that aid digestion.

- Seasoning a bean dish with winter or summer savory is a traditional cooking method that seems to make beans more digestible.

- Space your meals far enough apart. Nibbling in between meals slows down the digestion of previously eaten foods, giving them time to ferment in the digestive system, causing gas and discomfort.

- Drinking with meals also inhibits digestion. When you drink with your meals, the time that the food spends in your mouth is much shorter.

Less saliva is produced and the food is less thoroughly chewed. Digestive enzymes in the mouth, stomach, and intestines are diluted by beverages; thus, digestion is slowed. Also, the stomach must make more acid to retain the proper environment for digestion. All of these factors increase the likelihood of fermentation and gas in the digestive system.

- Keep your meals simple. When I have legumes, I don't eat potatoes, fruit, sweeteners (such as molasses with baked beans), or desserts in the same meal. An ideal meal centered on beans would consist of the beans, a grain or bread, a green salad, and a cooked vegetable.

- Eat dried beans in small amounts, especially to begin with. Many people who cannot tolerate a large quantity of legumes have no difficulty when eating small portions ($1/2$ cup or less). When beans become a regular part of the diet, I have found a person's system adapts and digestion becomes easier.

- Fennel tea (unsweetened) relieves gas and aids digestion, which makes it a nice beverage to serve after a meal containing beans. It has a fresh, aniselike flavor. Fennel seed may be chewed after meals for the same purpose.

HOW TO COOK DRIED LEGUMES

The cooking method for all types of dried legumes, including sprouted legumes, is the same. Only the cooking time varies.

Although soaking is not essential for every type of legume, all types profit from it. The list below outlines how to soak and cook dried legumes. For instructions on cooking beans in an electric slow-cooking pot, see page 170.

1. Wash and pick over the beans or peas. Be careful to remove any dirt and small stones that may be mixed in with them.

2. Place the washed beans in a bowl big enough to hold at least double their volume, and add twice as much water as dried beans. Soak the beans 8 hours or overnight. After soaking, you may either cook them or sprout them, as desired.

3. To cook them, drain the beans, place them in a large kettle, and cover them with about $1^1/2$ inches of fresh water (or at least 2–$2^1/2$ cups of water for each cup of beans).

4. Cover the kettle, and bring the water to a boil, watching that they don't boil over. Reduce the heat and slowly simmer the beans until they are tender.

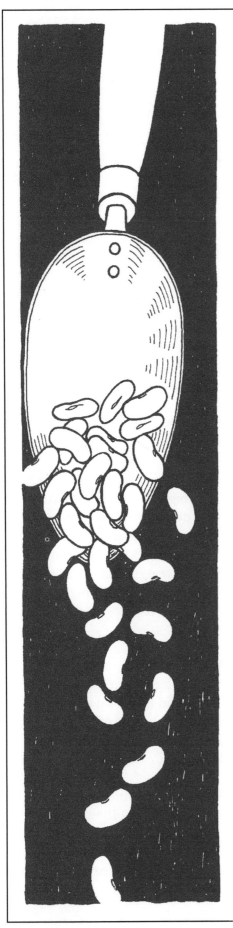

5. As the beans cook, stir them occasionally and add more water, if needed.

6. When the beans are done, they will be very tender and the cooking liquid will have thickened into a flavorful sauce.

Tips and Suggestion

- One cup of dried beans yields 2$\frac{1}{2}$–3 cups cooked. While it is a good idea to cook more than you will need for one meal, don't go overboard and cook more than you will be able to use.

- If you do cook more beans than you need, they can be frozen.

- A strip of kombu added to a pot of beans adds minerals and a pleasant flavor.

- Vegetables and seasonings may be added to a kettle of beans during the last 30 minutes of cooking.

- Good seasonings for beans include tamari, miso, vinegar, lemon, bay leaves, garlic, savory, cayenne pepper, basil, chili powder, cumin, parsley, and scallions.

COOKING BEANS IN A SLOW-COOKER

Wash and pick over the desired amount of beans. For the average household, 1–2 cups of beans is plenty. One cup of dry beans will yield about 2$\frac{1}{2}$–3 cups cooked.

Place the beans in a bowl that gives them room to more than double in size. Add enough water to cover the beans by about 1$\frac{1}{2}$ inches and let them soak overnight (8–10 hours).

Drain and rinse the soaked beans and place them in an electric slow-cooker. Add enough water to cover them by 1 inch. Cover the pot and turn it on high. Let the beans cook for 1–2 hours. Turn the pot to low and let the beans continue to cook until they are very tender (8–12 hours, depending on the type of bean).

During the last hour of cooking, you may add seasonings such as tamari, vinegar, bay leaves, winter or summer savory or other herbs, and garlic. A 6-inch strip of kombu may also be added during the last hour or two of cooking. If the beans become too dry near the end of cooking, add a little more water. When the beans are tender, you may add a tablespoon of olive oil, some fresh parsley, or minced scallions.

COOKING TIMES FOR LEGUMES

Here is a list of approximate cooking times for some of the most commonly used beans. Times will vary depending on the freshness of the beans (fresh beans cook more quickly) and the water that you use. Beans cooked in hard water take longer to become tender.

Legume	Unsoaked	Soaked overnight	Sprouted, 2–3 days
Adzuki beans	1 hour or more	40 minutes	30 minutes or less
Anasazi beans	1 hour or more	45 minutes	about 20 minutes
Black (turtle) beans	2–3 hours	1–1½ hours	45 minutes or more
Black-eyed peas	1½ hours	1 hour or less	30 minutes
Chick peas (garbanzos)	Not recommended	2–3 hours	1 hour or more
Great Northern beans	3 hours	1½–2 hours	45 minutes or more
Green peas, split	1 hour or less		They will not sprout.
Kidney beans	1½–2 hours	1 hour	30 minutes or more
Lentils, green	45 minutes	30 minutes or less	10 minutes
Lentils, red	20 minutes	10 minutes	5 minutes
Mung beans	45 minutes–1 hour	35–45 minutes	20 minutes
Pinto beans	3 hours	2 hours	30 minutes or more
Soybeans	Not recommended	3–4 hours	1½ hours or more

Bean and Eggplant Stew

2 tablespoons olive oil

3 bay leaves

1 teaspoon basil

1/2 teaspoon oregano

1/2 large Spanish onion, sliced

3 cloves garlic, minced

1 medium–large eggplant
(about 1 pound), diced

3 cups cooked Anasazi or Great
Northern beans, unseasoned
(see page 169)

1 1/2 cups cooking liquid from
beans

20 sun-dried tomato halves,
cut into pieces

1 teaspoon sea salt

1 tablespoon wine vinegar

This stew is really delicious. It tastes as though it should be a traditional specialty from some little village in Italy, but it's not, as far as I know.

Serves: 4   Time: 1 hour

1. Heat the oil in a large, heavy kettle. Add the bay leaves, basil, oregano, and sliced onion. Sauté over medium-low heat until the onion begins to be translucent. Add the garlic and the eggplant and continue to sauté for 5 minutes longer.

2. Add the cooked beans, the cooking liquid from the beans, sun-dried tomato pieces, salt, and vinegar. Cover and simmer, stirring occasionally, until the eggplant is tender.

3. Serve over Basic Polenta (page 165), accompanied by a green salad.

Split Pea Purée

1 cup green split peas

1 tablespoon balsamic vinegar

2 bay leaves

3 1/2 cups water

2 tablespoons olive oil

1 cup chopped onion
(1 medium onion)

1 teaspoon summer savory

2 tablespoons white or yellow
miso

Simple, economical, and good.

Serves: 4   Time: about 1 hour, 20 minutes

1. Wash and pick over the peas. Place them in a kettle and add the vinegar, bay leaves, and water. Cover and bring to a boil. Reduce the heat and simmer, stirring occasionally, until the peas have formed a purée and all the water has been absorbed.

2. After the peas have cooked for about 1 hour, heat the oil in a skillet and add the onion and savory. Sauté the onion over low heat until tender. Add the cooked onion to the peas. Simmer for a few minutes longer and then add the miso. Mix well.

3. Serve on a bed of rice or other grain, accompanied by steamed vegetables and a salad.

Vegetable Dal Curry

Easy and delicious, especially when served with Whole Wheat Dosas (page 134) and Fresh Mango Chutney (page 92) for an Indian feast. Dal may also be served simply over brown Basmati rice.

Serves: 4–6   Time: 1 hour

1. Heat the oil in a large, heavy kettle. Add the onion, curry powder, coriander, and cumin. Sauté over medium heat until the onion begins to become translucent.

2. Add the carrots and the cauliflower, and stir for a few seconds. Then add the lentils and the water. Mix well. Raise the heat and bring the mixture to a boil. Lower the heat, stir, and cover. Simmer for about 40 minutes, stirring occasionally, until the lentils have formed a thick purée. Add the salt and mix well.

2 tablespoons oil

1 cup chopped onion
(1 medium onion)

1 tablespoon curry powder

1 teaspoon coriander

1/2 teaspoon cumin

1 1/2 cups sliced carrots
(2 medium–large carrots)

1/2 medium head cauliflower,
cut into flowerets

1 cup red lentils, rinsed and
drained

2 1/2 cups water

1 teaspoon sea salt, or to taste

Baked Beans

Everyone likes baked beans for a picnic, but I find the sweetener in traditional recipes makes the beans hard to digest. In this recipe, the sweetness comes from slowly cooked onions, spices, and natto miso.

Serves: 4   Time: overnight to soak beans;
                    1–1 1/2 hours to cook beans; 20–25 minutes to bake

1. Wash and pick over the beans. Place them in a bowl with water to cover and let them soak overnight. Drain and rinse the beans and place them in a large pot with the water. Bring to a boil, cover, reduce the heat, and simmer, stirring occasionally, until they are very tender (1 hour or longer).

2. While the beans are cooking, heat the olive oil in a skillet. Add the onion and the garlic, and sauté over low heat for at least 30 minutes or until the onion is very tender. The long, slow cooking of the onion is what brings out its sweetness.

3. Add the sautéed onion and the remaining ingredients to the beans. Mix well. Place in a well-oiled baking dish. Cover and bake at 350°F for 20–25 minutes.

1 cup Anasazi beans

2 1/2 cups water

2 tablespoons olive oil

1 large onion, chopped
(preferably Spanish)

5–6 cloves garlic, minced

1 teaspoon cinnamon

1/2 teaspoon allspice

3 tablespoons natto miso

1/4 cup tomato paste

Tofu Vegetable Stew

1 pound firm tofu

1/4 cup tamari

1/4 cup mirin

1 cup water

2 cloves garlic, pressed

1 cup sliced carrots
(2 medium carrots)

1 bell pepper, sliced

2 medium zucchinis, sliced

2 cups sliced mushrooms
(about 9 mushrooms)

1/3 cup water

1 1/2 tablespoons arrowroot

2–3 scallions, chopped

This stew has lots of flavor because the vegetables simmer in the liquid in which the tofu has marinated.

Serves: 3–4   Time: 45 minutes to marinate; 30 minutes to bake; 15 minutes to prepare

1. Cut the tofu into small pieces, 1 x 1/2 x 1/4 inches.

2. In a shallow dish, mix together the tamari, mirin, 1 cup water, and garlic. Add the tofu, covering it with the liquid, and marinate for at least 45 minutes.

3. Meanwhile, wash and slice the vegetables.

4. Remove the tofu with a slotted spoon and place it on a well-oiled cookie sheet. Bake at 400°F for about 15 minutes or until the bottom of the tofu pieces are brown. Turn them over and bake about 15 minutes longer.

5. While the tofu is in the oven, pour the marinating liquid into a large saucepan. Add the carrots, pepper, zucchini, and mushrooms. Cover and bring the liquid to a boil. Reduce the heat and simmer until the vegetables are just tender (about 10 minutes). Remove from the heat.

6. In a small bowl, mix together the 1/3 cup water and the arrowroot. Add the mixture to the vegetables with the scallions. Bring to a boil, stirring constantly. Simmer for a few seconds until the sauce thickens. Add the baked tofu and mix.

7. Serve over brown rice, millet, buckwheat, quinoa, or pasta.

USING TOFU

Tofu is soybean curd. (For a discussion of how tofu is made, see page 19.) In Japan and China, it is used in innumerable ways. Tofu has no cholesterol, and it's rich in B vitamins and high in protein.

There are several kinds of tofu. I use firm (Chinese-style) tofu most often, and when a recipe calls for crumbled tofu, this is the style to use. Firm tofu is good for frying, grilling, stir-frying, and in sandwiches.

Silken and soft (Japanese-style) tofu are also available. Soft tofu has an almost creamy texture, and silken tofu is extra-soft and smooth.

Soft tofu is too soft for many of the recipes in this book. It can be used in recipes that call for blended tofu, but omit any water that is called for in blending the tofu.

Silken tofu is very mild and delicious in desserts and sauces. It contains more water and less protein than the other types and is not suitable for frying or grilling. If you substitute silken tofu for recipes in this book that call for firm tofu, the texture of the finished product will be different from what I intended.

Greg's Kapusta

One year, I was the assistant prop master for the Sarasota Opera. The prop master was Greg Ecenia, a former ballet dancer who now does props for theaters and films. He is of Russian descent, and this recipe is an old family favorite that I made meatless.

Serves: 4   Time: about 1¹/₂ hours

1. Heat the olive oil in a large, heavy kettle. Add the onions and sauté over medium heat for about 5 minutes. Add the crumbled tofu and continue to cook over medium heat for about 10 minutes, stirring often to keep it from sticking.

2. Add the remaining ingredients and stir constantly until the mixture gets juicy enough to keep it from sticking, about 5–10 minutes.

3. Cover, reduce the heat to low, and simmer, stirring occasionally, for about 1 hour or until the cabbage is tender.

Kapusta is delicious served over rice, millet, or buckwheat.

VARIATION:

For tofu with a meatier consistency, follow the instructions for Pressed Tofu (below) and substitute it for the regular tofu called for.

1 tablespoon olive oil

2 cups chopped onions (2 medium onions)

1 pound firm tofu, crumbled

3 bay leaves

3 cloves garlic, minced

1 teaspoon tarragon

4 cups chopped cabbage (1 small cabbage)

1 cup drained and rinsed sauerkraut

1 medium tomato, coarsely chopped (or 1 cup canned tomatoes)

¹/₄ cup tamari

Pressed Tofu

Use pressed tofu when you want a firmer, meatier texture than regular tofu.

Serves: 4–6   Time: 20–25 minutes

1 pound tofu

1. Crumble the tofu into a large kettle of boiling water. Bring the water back to a boil and cook for 1 minute.

2. Drain the tofu through a colander lined with a clean dish towel (Drawing a).

3. Run some cold water over the tofu to cool it for easier handling. Twist the towel and press the tofu to squeeze out the water until it has a crumbly texture like that of ground beef (Drawing b).

a.

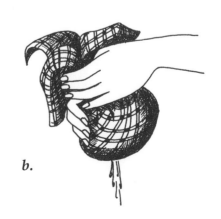

b.

Tropical Breeze Sweet-and-Sour Tofu

I made this recipe for a dinner party and my friends really liked it. If you wish, you may cut it in half to serve four.

3 pounds firm tofu

1½ cups tropical fruit juice (mango, passion fruit, papaya, or a mixture of)

3 cloves garlic, pressed

1 teaspoon coriander

¼ cup vinegar (wine, cider, or rice)

2 tablespoons tamari

1½ cups water

½ cup yellow or white miso

2 tablespoons oil

1½ cups chopped onions (1½ medium onions)

1 red bell pepper, sliced

¼ cup arrowroot

Serves: 8–10

Time: 2–3 hours to marinate tofu; 15 minutes to prepare; 35 minutes to bake

1. Cut the tofu into small rectangles that are ¼–½ inch thick. Place them in a shallow dish.

2. Mix together the fruit juice, garlic, coriander, vinegar, and tamari. In a small bowl, add about ¼ cup of the water to the miso to dilute it. Mix it well and add it to the juice mixture. Pour the liquid over the tofu and marinate the tofu for 2–10 hours; the longer it marinates, the stronger the flavor. If you marinate it longer than 2 hours, place it, covered, in the refrigerator.

3. After the tofu has marinated, remove it from the liquid (reserving the liquid to make the sauce) and place it on two well-oiled cookie sheets. Bake at 375°F for 30–40 minutes or until the tofu is nicely browned. Turn it over once during the baking so that it will brown on both sides.

4. While the tofu is baking, heat the oil in a large, heavy kettle and add the onion. Sauté the onion over medium-low heat for about 5 minutes. Add the pepper and continue to sauté, stirring occasionally, until the vegetables are tender.

5. Add the arrowroot to the marinating liquid and stir until it is dissolved. Pour the liquid into the kettle with the sautéed vegetables and bring it to a boil while stirring. When the mixture thickens, add the baked tofu and simmer for a few minutes.

6. Serve over a bed of cooked grain or over whole grain pasta.

Vegetable Casserole

Healthy and delicious.

Serves: 4–6   Time: about 1 hour

1. Peel or scrub the potatoes and dice them. Cook them until they are tender, either in a pressure cooker, or in a pan in a small amount of water. Mash the potatoes and set aside.

2. Place the tofu in a food processor and add the miso and cayenne pepper. Blend until smooth and creamy. Scrape the sides of the food processor with a rubber spatula so that all the tofu is well blended.

3. Add the tofu blend to the potatoes and mix together with a wooden spoon.

4. Steam the green beans and the carrots until just barely tender (still crisp). Place them in a lightly oiled 8-x-8-inch baking dish. Add the salt, olive oil, and garlic and mix well.

5. Spread the potato mixture over the vegetables. Sprinkle with soy cheese. Bake at 350°F for 20 minutes. Move the baking dish to the top rack and turn the oven to broil for 2–3 minutes to brown the top. Let cool for 10 minutes before serving so that the casserole is easier to dish up.

VARIATION:

Substitute 4 cups of your choice of lightly steamed mixed vegetables for the carrots and green beans.

---

2 pounds potatoes

1 package (10$\frac{1}{2}$ ounces) firm silken tofu

$\frac{1}{4}$ cup yellow or white miso

Dash of cayenne pepper, or to taste

2 cups sliced carrots (3 medium carrots)

2 cups green beans, broken into 1-inch pieces

$\frac{1}{2}$ teaspoon sea salt, or to taste

1 tablespoon olive oil

3 cloves garlic, pressed

$\frac{2}{3}$ cup grated soy cheese

Dominique's Creamy Millet Casserole

Mild and creamy millet covered with a cloud of mushrooms and topped with a garnish of piquant red peppers and onions.

Serves: 4–5   Time: 35 minutes to prepare; 40 minutes to bake

3 cups cooked millet
(see page 152)

$^1/_2$ cup soymilk

$^1/_2$ teaspoon sea salt

1 teaspoon basil

1 pound tofu

1 tablespoon oil

4 tablespoons tamari

1 clove garlic

$^1/_4$ cup water

1 cup sliced mushrooms (about 4–5 medium mushrooms)

GARNISH:

1–2 tablespoons oil

1 cup onion, chopped
(1 medium onion)

1 large red bell pepper, diced

1 teaspoon basil

$^1/_4$ teaspoon cayenne pepper, or to taste

1. Place the cooked millet, soymilk, salt, and basil in a food processor and blend until creamy. (The mixture is probably too stiff to blend in a blender.) Transfer the mixture to an oiled baking dish such as a 7-x-11-inch Pyrex dish or a 10$^1/_2$-inch cast-iron skillet.

2. Crumble the tofu and place it in the food processor with the oil, tamari, garlic, and water. Blend until smooth and creamy, then transfer the mixture to a medium bowl. Add the mushrooms and mix well. Spread this mixture over the millet.

3. In a skillet, prepare the garnish: Heat the oil and sauté the onion over medium heat for 3–5 minutes. Add the bell pepper, basil, and cayenne pepper. Sauté 2–3 minutes more. Distribute this mixture evenly over the tofu mixture in the baking dish. Bake at 350°F for 40 minutes.

4. Let cool 10–15 minutes before serving so that it will hold together when it is dished out. Serve with a green vegetable.

Quinoa Casserole

Serves: 3-4   Time: 25 minutes to prepare; 35–40 minutes to bake

1. Wash the quinoa and drain it through a wire strainer. Place it in a pan with the water. Cover and bring to a boil, reduce the heat, and simmer for about 20 minutes or until the water is absorbed.

2. Meanwhile, heat the oil in a skillet. Add the celery, onion, and basil, and sauté until the vegetables are almost tender.

3. When the quinoa is done, place it in a mixing bowl. Add the sautéed vegetables and the remaining ingredients. Mix well, using your hands if necessary. Pack the mixture into an oiled loaf pan (4$^1/_2$ x 8$^1/_2$ x 2$^1/_2$ inches) or casserole dish. Bake for 35–40 minutes at 350°F.

4. Serve plain or top with the Quick and Light Fresh Tomato Sauce (page 96). Add a green salad or some steamed broccoli, and you have a great meal.

Cover any leftover casserole and store it in the refrigerator in the pan. When it is cold, you can slice it. Heat some oil in a skillet and brown the slices on both sides. They're delicious.

1 cup quinoa

2 cups water

1 tablespoon oil

1 cup chopped celery (2 stalks)

1 cup chopped onion (1 medium onion)

1 teaspoon basil

1 pound tofu, mashed

$^1/_4$ cup white miso

$^1/_4$ cup tahini

$^3/_4$ cup sliced pitted black olives

Dominique's Meal in a Casserole

The millet cooks along with the other ingredients in one dish.

Serves: 4   Time: 15 minutes to prepare; 45 minutes to bake

1. Place all the ingredients (except the boiling water) in a casserole dish. Mix well. Pour the boiling water over the mixture and cover.

2. Bake at 350°F for 30 minutes, stir, and bake about 15 minutes longer, or until the liquid has been absorbed. Fluff with a fork, discard the bay leaves, and let cool for at least 10 minutes before serving.

3. Serve with Tahini Brown Sauce (page 97) or Tahini Milk Gravy (page 98) and a green salad.

1 cup chopped onion (1 medium onion)

1 cup tempeh, cut into small cubes (4 ounces or $^1/_2$ slab)

3 cloves garlic, pressed

1 cup uncooked millet

1 cup sliced carrots (2 medium carrots)

$^1/_4$ teaspoon sea salt

3 bay leaves

1 teaspoon grated fresh ginger

1 tablespoon toasted sesame oil

3 cups boiling water

Buckwheat and Sweet Potato Casserole

An unusual flavor combination that works really well together.

1 cup toasted buckwheat groats (kasha)

2 cups water

2 medium sweet potatoes, scrubbed and cubed

1 tablespoon oil

1¼ cups chopped onion (1 large onion)

1 teaspoon tarragon

4 cloves garlic, pressed

2 tablespoons tamari

1 tablespoon yellow miso

¼ cup liquid from cooking potatoes (or all or part soymilk)

½ cup grated soy cheese (cheddar flavor)

Serves: 4   Time: 30 minutes to prepare; 20 minutes to bake

1. Rinse the buckwheat and drain it through a wire strainer. Bring the water to a boil. Add the buckwheat, cover, and reduce the heat. Simmer without stirring for 15–20 minutes, or until the water has been absorbed.

2. While the buckwheat is cooking, pressure-cook or steam the sweet potatoes until they are tender enough to mash. Set aside with the cooking liquid.

3. Heat the oil in a skillet. Add the onion and the tarragon, and sauté until the onion is tender. Add the sautéed onion to the cooked buckwheat. Add the garlic and the tamari and mix well. Place this mixture in an oiled 8-x-8-inch baking dish. Set aside.

4. Mash the sweet potatoes with a potato masher or fork and add the miso and cooking liquid or soymilk. Mix well. Spread the sweet potato mixture over the buckwheat. Sprinkle with the grated soy cheese and bake at 350°F for 15–20 minutes. Move dish to top rack and turn the oven to broil for 2–3 minutes to brown the top.

5. Serve with a green salad.

Mediterranean Rice Casserole

Serves: 3–4   Time: 20 minutes to prepare; 20 minutes to bake

1. Heat the oil in a large skillet. Add the onion, garlic, and herbes de Provence. Sauté over medium heat for 3–4 minutes or until the onion is nearly tender. Add the zucchinis and the tomato bits, and sauté for about 3 minutes more. Add the tofu, the vegetable broth powder, about 1/2 cup of the olives, and 1/4 cup of the brine from the olives. Mix well and stir over medium heat for a minute or two or until the mixture is thoroughly heated.

2. Lightly oil a 2-quart casserole dish. Spread half the rice in the dish. Top with the vegetable mixture, then cover the vegetable mixture with the remaining rice. Decorate the top with the remaining olives. Sprinkle the remaining tablespoon or so of liquid from the olives evenly over the top of the casserole.

3. Cover and bake at 350°F for 20 minutes.

4. Serve with a green salad.

2 tablespoons olive oil

1 cup onion, chopped

3 cloves garlic, minced

1 teaspoon herbes de Provence (see page 102)

2 medium zucchinis, sliced

15 sun-dried tomato halves, cut into pieces

1 cup firm tofu, crumbled

1 tablespoon vegetable broth powder

5-ounce jar pimento-stuffed green olives in brine, sliced

1/3 cup liquid from the olives

3 1/2 cups cooked brown rice (see page 152)

Nondairy Potatoes au Gratin

3 baking potatoes

1 package (10½ ounces) soft silken tofu

1 cup soymilk

3 tablespoons white or yellow miso

1 tablespoon umeboshi paste

½ large sweet onion, sliced very thin

1 teaspoon herbes de Provence (see page 102)

1½ slices whole grain bread

¼ cup sesame seeds

This recipe is as flavorful as the old favorite, but I have lightened it to make it more healthful.

Serves: 4

Time: 20 minutes to prepare; 1 hour, 20 minutes to bake

1. Wash the potatoes well, scrubbing them with a vegetable brush. Don't peel them. Slice them as thin as possible. Set aside.

2. In a blender or food processor, blend together the tofu, soymilk, miso, umeboshi paste, and herbs. Set aside.

3. Generously oil a 9-inch cast-iron skillet or casserole. Line the bottom of the skillet with half of the potatoes. Separate the onion slices into rings and arrange them over the potato slices. Pour in half the tofu mixture. Repeat the layers, using the remaining potatoes, onion, and tofu mixture.

4. In a blender or food processor, grind the bread to make crumbs. Mix together the bread crumbs and the sesame seeds and sprinkle the mixture over the top of the casserole. Cover and bake at 350°F for 1 hour. Remove the cover and bake for 20 minutes more.

This dish is delicious served with lightly steamed broccoli and the Cherry Tomato Salad (page 73).

VARIATION:

Substitute thinly sliced turnips or rutabaga for one of the potatoes.

New Potatoes and Green Beans with Sun-Dried Tomato Spread

This easy dish is a meal in itself.

Serves: 2–3   Time: 1 hour, 10 minutes*

1. Prepare the Sun-Dried Tomato Spread. Let it stand while you prepare the vegetables.

2. Wash the potatoes and cut them in 1¹/₂-inch chunks if they are too big. Wash the beans and break them into 1-inch pieces.

3. Place the potatoes and green beans in a pressure cooker with about 1 cup of water. Bring the pressure up and then remove the pressure cooker from the heat. Let the pressure come down on its own.

   If you don't have a pressure cooker, place the potatoes in a pan with about 1¹/₂ inches of water in the bottom, cover, and bring to a boil. Reduce the heat and simmer, stirring occasionally, until they are tender. Add more water if they begin to stick.

4. Steam the green beans separately until tender.

5. To serve, place the cooked potatoes and green beans on a plate. Top with a mound of the Sun-Dried Tomato Spread and surround with slices of avocado. Serve immediately.

*This recipe can be put together in 15 minutes flat if the tomato spread is already made and you cook the vegetables in a pressure cooker.

1 recipe Sun-Dried Tomato Spread (see page 46)

1¹/₂ pounds new potatoes (Red Bliss variety is nice)

1 pound green beans

Slices of ripe avocado

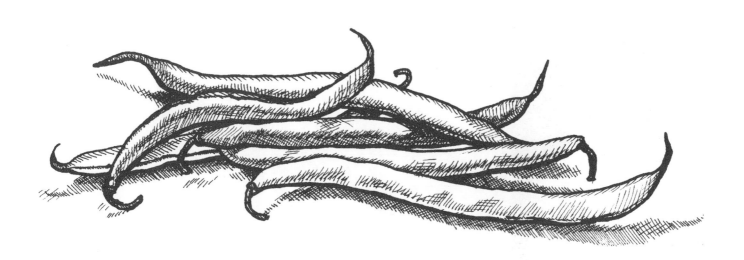

Ground Seitan

12-ounce package Arrowhead Mills Seitan Quick Mix

1½ cups water

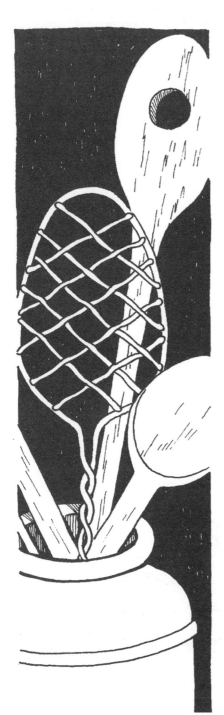

Here is an easy and versatile way to prepare Arrowhead Mills Seitan Quick Mix. Instead of simmering in a broth as the package directs, this recipe makes a large quantity of ground seitan by baking. It can be seasoned (see recipe on facing page) and frozen for later use.

Yield: 6 cups   Time: 20 minutes to prepare; 30 minutes to bake

1. In a large bowl, mix together the Seitan Quick Mix and the water, beating with a wooden spoon. Turn the dough out onto a counter- or tabletop and knead until thoroughly mixed and elastic, about 5 minutes. You do not need to flour the work surface.

2. Oil a cookie sheet and place the seitan on it. Let it rest for about 5 minutes. Stretch and flatten the seitan into a slab that is about ½ inch thick. The raw seitan is very elastic. It will spring back as you try to flatten it, so just get it as close to ½ inch thick as you can without being fussy.

3. Bake the seitan at 350°F for 30 minutes. After 15 minutes of baking, pierce any bubbles that have formed in the seitan with a fork. Continue baking for another 15 minutes.

4. Remove the baked seitan from the oven and invert a large bowl over it. You may need to fold the seitan or push it together to make the bowl fit over it. Let the seitan stand covered by the bowl until it is cool enough to handle (about 20 minutes).

5. Tear the seitan into chunks and place about a third of them in a food processor. Grind the seitan until it has the consistency of ground beef. Transfer the ground seitan to a bowl, and grind the remaining seitan in two more batches.

6. Let cool before storing. Use the ground seitan to make Seasoned Ground Seitan (facing page) or freeze it in 2-cup portions to season and use as you like.

Seasoned Ground Seitan

When you make ground seitan from the mix, it is convenient to season it so it will be ready to use. Seasoned ground seitan can be added to chili, spaghetti sauces, lasagne, meatless loaves, or just about anything that usually calls for ground beef. It adds protein, flavor, and texture without a lot of fat

Yield: about 8 cups   Time: 20 minutes

1. Heat the oil in a very large skillet or a heavy kettle. Add the onion, garlic, and bay leaves. Sauté over medium-low heat until the onion is nearly tender. Add the thyme, sage, and celery seeds and continue to sauté until the onion is tender.

2. Add the ground seitan, the tamari, yeast, and water or tomato juice. Mix well. Let cool before storing.

3. Use as much seasoned ground seitan as you need and freeze the rest in 2-cup containers.

2 tablespoons olive oil

1 large Spanish onion, chopped (about 3¹/₄ cups)

12 cloves garlic

5 bay leaves

1 teaspoon thyme

1 teaspoon sage

¹/₂ teaspoon celery seeds

1 recipe Ground Seitan (see page 184)

¹/₄ cup tamari

¹/₄ cup nutritional yeast

¹/₂ cup water or tomato juice

SEITAN QUICK MIX

Seitan is a low-fat, high-protein, meaty-textured food made of wheat gluten. It can be made at home, but it is very time-consuming. Arrowhead Mills Seitan Quick Mix takes most of the work out of making seitan, or you can buy prepared seitan at natural foods stores. Seitan made from a mix will keep as long as a week in the refrigerator, or it can be frozen for later use. The traditional method for cooking seitan (whether made from a mix or not) takes about 2 hours, but it needs no attention as it cooks. A quick, microwave method is described on the box of mix. I prefer the traditional method.

Tips for Using Prepared Seitan

- Thin slices of seitan can be added to any vegetable stir-fry.

- Thinly sliced seitan is also delicious in sandwiches.

- Add chunks of seitan to any vegetable or bean stew.

- Seitan may be brushed with a tamari-and-garlic mixture and pan-fried or broiled to serve like steaks. Serve with one of your favorite sauces.

- Ground seitan can be used wherever the texture of ground beef is desirable: in chili, pasta dishes, sloppy Joe mixes, etc.

Shepherd's Pie

2 cups Seasoned Ground
Seitan (page 185)

3½ cups corn, cut fresh off the
cob or frozen (no need to thaw)

2 tablespoons finely chopped
parsley

2 cups mashed potatoes,
seasoned to taste

½ cup grated soy cheese
(optional)

Paprika

1–2 teaspoons olive oil

*If you have some Seasoned Ground Seitan on hand, this recipe is very easy
to make.*

Serves: 4   Time: 25 minutes to prepare;
                             about 30 minutes to bake

1. Lightly oil an 8-x-8-inch baking dish. Spread the seasoned ground seitan in the dish. Make a layer of corn over the seitan. Sprinkle with parsley. Spread the mashed potatoes over the corn. Top the potatoes with soy cheese, if desired, or sprinkle with paprika, and/or drizzle with a little olive oil.

2. Bake at 350°F for 30 minutes. Move baking dish to the top rack and turn the oven to broil to brown the top. Let stand for 10 minutes before serving. Serve with a salad.

Marinated Baked Tempeh

8-ounce package of tempeh

½ cup water

2 tablespoons tamari

2 cloves garlic, pressed

1 tablespoon mirin

1 tablespoon grated fresh
ginger

1 tablespoon vinegar (rice,
wine or cider)

½ cup water

1 rounded tablespoon
arrowroot

Serves: 2   Time: 15 minutes to prepare; 30 minutes
                             to marinate; 30 minutes to bake

1. If the tempeh is frozen, let it thaw. Cut the tempeh into small rectangles (about 2 x ½ x ½ inches). Place the tempeh in a shallow dish such as a cake pan.

2. In a small bowl, mix together ½ cup water, the tamari, garlic, mirin, ginger, and vinegar. Pour this marinade over the tempeh and let it stand for at least 30 minutes.

3. Remove the tempeh from the liquid, reserving the marinade to make a sauce, and place the tempeh on an oiled cookie sheet. Bake at 375°F for 30 minutes or until nicely browned. Halfway through the baking, turn the tempeh over so that it browns on both sides.

4. Add the remaining water to the marinade. Add the arrowroot and mix well to dissolve it. Pour the mixture into a small saucepan. Bring the liquid to a boil while stirring constantly. Remove the sauce from the heat and add the baked tempeh.

5. Serve over rice, millet, wild rice, or pasta. Accompany with some steamed or stir-fried vegetables. The first time that I made this, I served it with wild rice, steamed broccoli, and Moroccan Carrot Salad (page 79). It was a colorful and delicious meal.

Bulgur Pecan Balls

Meatless balls to serve in your favorite sauce with pasta or rice.

Serves: 5–6   Time: 25 minutes to prepare; 30 minutes to bake

1. Place the bulgur in a medium saucepan. Add the water, cover, and bring to a boil. Reduce the heat and simmer for 10–15 minutes or until all the water has been absorbed.

2. Meanwhile, coarsely grind the pecans in a blender and place them in a medium bowl. Place the tofu and the tamari in a blender or a food processor and blend until smooth and creamy. Use a rubber spatula to push the tofu down into the blades so that it is well blended. Add the blended tofu to the pecans. Add the garlic, thyme, and gluten flour or seitan mix.

3. Add the cooked bulgur to the other ingredients in the bowl. Mix well.

4. Drop the mixture, 1 heaping teaspoonful at a time, onto a well-oiled cookie sheet. Shape into mounds with your hands or another spoon (they will not be perfectly round). Bake at 350°F for 30 minutes or until the balls are firm and brown.

5. Place the Mushroom Wine Sauce or tomato sauce into a large saucepan and add the balls. Simmer the balls in the sauce for about 5 minutes before serving.

6. Serve over rice or pasta, accompanied by a green salad.

*Use any tomato or spaghetti sauce that you like; you need at least 3–4 cups.

1/2 cup bulgur

1 cup water

1/2 cup pecans

1 package (10 1/2 ounces) extra-firm silken tofu

1–2 tablespoons tamari, or to taste

1 clove garlic, pressed

1 teaspoon lemon thyme or thyme

1/4 cup gluten flour or Arrowhead Mills Seitan Quick Mix

1 recipe Mushroom Wine Sauce (page 98) or a tomato sauce*

Simple Rice Patties

Serves: 3–4

Time: 45 minutes to cook rice;
20 minutes to cool; 20 minutes to prepare

1 cup uncooked short grain
brown rice

2 cups water

1/4 cup tahini

1 teaspoon basil

1/4 teaspoon oregano

1/2 cup finely chopped onion
(1 small onion)

1–2 cloves garlic, pressed

1 tablespoon vegetable broth
powder

1/4 teaspoon sea salt, or to taste

1/3 cup finely chopped parsley

2 tablespoons oil, or as needed
to brown patties

1. Wash the rice and drain it through a wire strainer. Place the rice in a heavy, medium-sized pan. Add the water, cover, and bring to a boil. Reduce the heat and simmer for about 45 minutes, or until all the water has been absorbed.

2. Add the tahini, basil, oregano, onion, garlic, vegetable broth powder, salt, and parsley. Mix well. Let the rice mixture cool until it can be comfortably handled. Shape into six to eight patties.

3. Heat enough oil to brown the patties in a skillet. Place the patties in the skillet and cook over medium heat until nicely browned on the bottom. Turn them over and cook the other side.

4. Serve with a sauce (a tomato sauce is good), a steamed vegetable, and a salad.

Simple Millet Croquettes

These mild-flavored croquettes are delicious with walnut gravy.

Serves: 3–4

Time: 20 minutes to cook millet;
20 minutes to cool; 10 minutes to prepare

1 cup millet

2 1/2 cups water

1/2 teaspoon sea salt

1/2 teaspoon cumin

1 cup finely chopped onion
(1 medium onion)

2 tablespoons oil, or as needed
to brown patties

1. Rinse the millet and drain it through a wire strainer. Place the millet in a heavy, medium-sized pan. Add the water, cover, and bring to a boil. Reduce the heat and simmer for 20 minutes or until the water has been absorbed.

2. Remove the millet from the heat and let it stand, covered, until it is cool enough to handle.

3. Add the salt, cumin, and onion to the millet and mix well.

4. Shape the millet mixture into eight patties. Heat the oil in a skillet. Add about four of the patties and cook them over medium heat until they are golden brown on the bottom. Turn them over and cook the other side. Cook the remaining patties.

5. Serve with Spicy Peanut Sauce or Walnut Onion Gravy (page 101). Accompany with a steamed vegetable and a salad.

Linda's Sun Burger

This wonderful recipe is from my neighbor Linda Wagner.

Serves: 3–4   Time: 40 minutes

1. Place the sunflower seeds in a blender or food processor and grind them. Place the ground seeds in a medium bowl. Add the remaining ingredients. Mix well, using your hands if necessary. Let sit for 15 minutes.

2. Shape the mixture into patties. Heat some oil in a skillet and cook over medium heat as many patties as will fit easily in the skillet. When they are brown on the bottom, turn them over and brown the other side. Repeat with the remaining patties.

3. Serve either on whole grain hamburger buns with all the trimmings or with a sauce. They are delicious with Almost-Instant Tomato Sauce (page 96).

1 cup sunflower seeds

1 cup grated carrot
(1 large carrot)

$^{1}/_{2}$ cup finely chopped celery
(1 stalk)

$^{1}/_{3}$ cup finely chopped onion
(1 small onion)

1 cup whole grain bread crumbs

$^{1}/_{4}$ cup T.V.P. (textured vegetable protein)

2 tablespoons nutritional yeast

1 egg

2 tablespoons tamari

1 teaspoon sage

1–2 tablespoons oil, as needed to cook patties

Tofu Sunflower Loaf

Serves: 4–5   Time: 15 minutes to prepare; 30 minutes to bake

1 pound firm tofu

1 cup sunflower seeds

1 cup whole grain bread crumbs

1/2 cup finely chopped onion (1 small onion)

2 cloves garlic, pressed

2 eggs

1 teaspoon herbes de Provence (see page 102)

2 tablespoons tamari

1/4 cup grated Parmesan cheese or tofu-Parmesan

1. Crumble the tofu into a large bowl. Coarsely grind the seeds in a food processor or blender. Add the ground sunflower seeds and all the remaining ingredients to the tofu. Mix well, using your hands if necessary.

2. Pack the mixture into a well-oiled loaf pan, 4$1/2$ x 8$1/2$ x 2$1/2$ inches, pressing firmly so that it holds together. Bake at 350°F for 30–40 minutes or until the loaf is firm and brown.

For a good, easy meal, top with a tomato sauce and serve with corn on the cob and a big green salad.

Red Lentil Loaf

Economical, low in fat, and nutritious. Tastes good, too!

Serves: 4   Time: 20 minutes to prepare; 40 minutes to bake

1 cup red lentils

2 cups water

1 cup cooked brown rice (see page 152)

1 cup oat flakes

1 egg or egg replacer

1 cup grated carrot

3 tablespoons tamari

2 scallions, chopped

2 cloves garlic, pressed

1 teaspoon sage

1. Wash and pick over the lentils. Place them in a pan with the water. Cover and bring to a boil. Reduce the heat and simmer, stirring occasionally, until the water is absorbed (about 15 minutes).

2. While the lentils are cooking, mix together the rice, oat flakes, egg or egg replacer, carrot, tamari, scallions, garlic, and sage in a large bowl. When the lentils are cooked, add them to the other ingredients and mix well.

3. Oil a loaf pan, 4$1/2$ x 8$1/2$ x 2$1/2$ inches, and sprinkle the sides and bottom with a few oat flakes to keep the loaf from sticking. Pack the loaf mixture into the pan and bake at 350°F for 40 minutes. Let the loaf stand for 5–10 minutes before slicing.

4. Serve with a sauce, a steamed vegetable, and a green salad. Red Pepper Sauce (page 99) is a delicious complement.

Almond Rice Loaf

Serves: 6   Time: 20 minutes to prepare; 45 minutes to bake

1. Place the almonds in a blender and coarsely grind them. Transfer them to a mixing bowl.

2. Crumble the tofu and add it to the almonds. Mash the tofu with a fork.

3. Add the remaining ingredients and mix well, using your hands if necessary.

4. Generously oil and flour a loaf pan, 5$^1/_2$ x 9$^1/_2$ x 3 inches. Firmly pack the loaf mixture into the pan. Bake at 350°F for 45 minutes, or until the loaf is firm. Let the loaf stand for 10–15 minutes. Run a knife around the sides of the pan to loosen the loaf, then turn it out of the pan.

5. Slice the loaf and top with the sauce of your choice. This loaf is especially good with Carrot Sauce (page 92). Accompany with a steamed vegetable and a salad.

2 cups raw unsalted almonds

1 pound tofu

2 cups cooked brown rice (see page 152)

1 cup finely chopped onion (1 medium onion)

3 tablespoons tamari

2 tablespoons tahini

3 cloves garlic, pressed

1 teaspoon sage

1 teaspoon thyme

$^1/_2$ teaspoon celery seeds

Dash of cayenne pepper, or to taste

Quinoa Loaf

Serves: 6   Time: 20 minutes to cook quinoa; 15 minutes to prepare loaf; 45 minutes to bake

1. Place the quinoa in a medium saucepan and cover it with water. Swish the quinoa around in the water to wash it and then drain it through a fine wire strainer. Return the quinoa to the saucepan and add 2 cups of water. Cover and bring to a boil. Reduce the heat to low and cook for 15–20 minutes or until the water has been absorbed. Transfer the quinoa to a medium bowl.

2. Crumble the tofu and add it to the bowl. Mash it with a fork. Place the cashews in a blender and coarsely grind them. Add them to the bowl. Add the remaining ingredients and mix everything well, using your hands if necessary.

3. Generously oil and flour a loaf pan, 5$^1/_2$ x 9$^1/_2$ x 3 inches. Firmly pack the loaf mixture into the pan. Bake at 350°F for 45 minutes. Let the loaf stand for 10–15 minutes. Run a knife around the sides of the pan to loosen the loaf, then turn it out of the pan.

4. Slice the loaf and top with the sauce of your choice. This loaf is especially good with Carrot Sauce (page 92) or Green Sauce (page 97). Accompany with a steamed vegetable and a salad.

1 cup uncooked quinoa

2 cups water

1 pound tofu

1 cup raw unsalted cashews

1 cup grated carrot

$^1/_2$ cup finely chopped onion (1 small onion)

4 tablespoons tamari

$^1/_4$ cup tahini

1 teaspoon thyme

1 teaspoon sage

Moussaka

A healthful version of a traditional Greek favorite.

1 large eggplant
(1³/₄–2 pounds)

1 teaspoon sea salt

1 tablespoon olive oil

2 cups chopped onions

6 cloves minced garlic

1 teaspoon basil

1 teaspoon oregano

¹/₂ teaspoon cinnamon

1¹/₂ cups canned unsalted
tomato purée

2 tablespoons tamari

1 cup lentils, cooked and
drained (see page 169)

TOPPING:

1 package (10¹/₂ ounces) firm
silken tofu

2 tablespoons yellow miso

Dash of cayenne pepper, or to
taste

¹/₄ teaspoon nutmeg

¹/₄ teaspoon turmeric

Serves: 6

Time: 1 hour, 20 minutes to prepare;
about 45 minutes to bake

1. To eliminate excess liquid, slice the eggplant into rounds no thicker than ¹/₄ inch. Sprinkle each slice lightly with salt and stack them in a large bowl. Let stand for about 1 hour. Drain off the liquid, then briefly rinse the slices under running water and pat them dry with a clean dish towel.

2. While the eggplant stands, heat the oil in a large skillet. Add the onions, garlic, basil, oregano, and cinnamon. Sauté until the onions begin to become tender. Add the tomato purée, tamari, and lentils. Mix well and simmer for about 5 minutes.

3. To make the topping, place the tofu, miso, cayenne pepper, nutmeg, and turmeric in a blender. Blend until smooth and creamy. If necessary, scrape the sides of the blender with a rubber spatula so that the tofu is well blended.

4. To assemble, lightly oil a 7-x-11-inch baking dish. Place a third of the eggplant in the dish, overlapping the slices. Spoon half of the tomato mixture over the eggplant slices. Make another layer of eggplant, and then top it with the remaining sauce. Finish with the remaining eggplant. Spread the topping over the casserole and bake at 350°F for 45 minutes or until the eggplant is tender. Let sit for 10 minutes before slicing.

5. Serve with homemade bread and a big green salad. Some fresh mint in the salad dressing is nice with this dish.

This dish may be prepared the day before serving. Assemble the casserole, except for the topping, and refrigerate until ready to bake. Bake the casserole at 350°F for 15 minutes, and then top with the tofu mixture. Continue to bake until the eggplant is tender, about 45 minutes longer.

Vegetable Lasagne

In this easy dish, the noodles cook while the lasagne bakes.

Serves: 4–6   Time: 30 minutes to prepare; 45 minutes to bake

1. Heat olive oil in a large, heavy kettle.

2. Add the onion, garlic, basil, oregano, and cloves. Sauté over medium heat for 1–2 minutes and then add the celery. Sauté for 2 more minutes and then add the carrots. Sauté for 1–2 minutes more and then add the zucchini and the yellow squash. Stir, cover, and cook over medium-low heat, stirring occasionally, until the vegetables begin to become tender. Add the mushrooms. Sauté until all the vegetables are barely tender.

3. Add the tomatoes and the tomato paste. Mix well. Add the tamari and the honey or fruit sweetener and mix again. Set aside.

4. Prepare the filling in a food processor or powerful blender: Blend together the tofu, garlic, and salt. Scrape the sides of the container with a rubber spatula so that the mixture is thoroughly blended. Set this filling aside.

5. Lightly oil a 7-x-11-inch baking dish. Spread a thin layer of the sauce (about 1 cup) over the bottom of the dish. Place a layer of uncooked lasagne noodles over the sauce.* Spread the filling over the layer of noodles. Top with half of the remaining sauce. Sprinkle with a quarter of the Parmesan cheese or tofu-Parmesan.

   Make another layer of noodles, going perpendicular to the first layer so that the lasagne holds together well. Top that layer with the remaining sauce. Sprinkle with the remaining Parmesan and then top with the mozzarella.

6. Cover with foil and bake at 350°F for 35 minutes. Uncover and bake for 10 minutes longer. Remove the lasagne from the oven and let it sit for 10–15 minutes before slicing.

*To break the uncooked lasagne noodles neatly to the proper size, place them flat on the kitchen counter with the excess hanging over the edge. Hold the noodle firmly down against the counter with one hand and snap off the excess with the other.

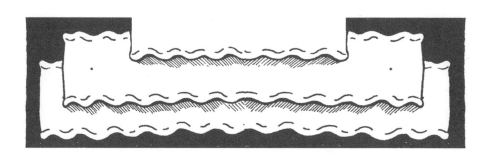

SAUCE:

2 tablespoons olive oil

1½ cups chopped onion

4 cloves garlic, minced

1 teaspoon basil

1 teaspoon oregano

¼ teaspoon ground cloves

2 stalks celery, finely chopped

1½ cups sliced carrots

1 medium zucchini, sliced

1 yellow squash, sliced

2 cups sliced mushrooms

1-pound can tomatoes

6-ounce can tomato paste

1 tablespoon tamari, or to taste

1 tablespoon honey or concentrated fruit sweetener

FILLING:

1 package (10½ ounces) extra-firm silken tofu

1 clove garlic

¼ teaspoon sea salt

8 ounces whole wheat lasagne noodles

TOPPING:

½ cup grated Parmesan cheese or tofu-Parmesan

1 cup grated low-fat mozzarella or tofu-mozzarella

Spinach Quiche

This quiche contains no eggs.

1 single unbaked 7½-inch Whole Wheat Pie Crust (see page 137)

10 ounces fresh spinach

1 package (10½ ounces) extra-firm silken tofu

2 tablespoons yellow miso

¼ cup dried onion flakes

1 teaspoon basil

½ teaspoon oregano

¼ teaspoon nutmeg

Dash of cayenne pepper, or to taste

½ cup grated soy cheese (cheddar flavor)

Serves: 4 Time: 20 minutes to prepare; 40 minutes to bake

1. Prepare the pie crust.

2. Wash, drain, and chop the spinach. Place it in a large pot, cover, and cook for 3–4 minutes or until it is wilted. Drain the spinach well and press it with the back of a spoon to expel any excess liquid. Place the drained spinach in a large bowl. Set aside.

3. Place the tofu and miso in a blender or a food processor and blend until smooth and creamy. Scrape the sides of the blender or food processor occasionally with a rubber spatula so that all the tofu is well blended.

4. Add the tofu mixture to the cooked spinach. Add the onion flakes, basil, oregano, nutmeg, and cayenne pepper. Mix well.

4. Fill the pie crust with the spinach-tofu mixture. Top with the soy cheese. Bake at 350°F for 40 minutes or until the crust is brown and the filling is firm. Let cool for 5–10 minutes before slicing.

VARIATIONS:

- A friend made this quiche omitting the nutmeg and replacing it with 1 teaspoon of curry powder. It was delicious.
- To fill a 9-inch crust, increase the spinach to 1 pound and add a little salt to taste.

Italian Eggplant Quiche

The only things really Italian about this recipe are the ingredients and the inventor: My friend Dominique is half Italian.

Serves: 6

Time: 35 minutes to bake eggplant; 30 minutes to prepare; 45 minutes to bake

1. Prepare the pie crust.

2. Slice the eggplant into ½-inch-thick rounds. Place the slices on a lightly oiled cookie sheet. Bake at 350°F for 35 minutes.

3. Place the cooked eggplant slices in a food processor and blend until smooth.

4. Transfer the eggplant purée to a mixing bowl and add the garlic, flour, sun-dried tomatoes, basil, oregano, and salt. Mix well.

5. Spread the eggplant mixture in the pie crust. Top with the fresh tomato slices and sprinkle with basil.

6. Bake at 350°F for 40 minutes. Top with the soy cheese and bake for 5–10 minutes more.

7. Let the pie stand for 10–15 minutes before slicing.

1 single unbaked 9-inch Whole Wheat Pie Crust (see page 137)

1 medium–large eggplant (about 1¼ pounds)

2 cloves pressed garlic

3 tablespoons whole wheat pastry flour

20 sun-dried tomato halves, cut into small pieces

1 teaspoon basil

1 teaspoon oregano

1 teaspoon sea salt

TOPPING:

1 large tomato, cut into ½-inch-thick slices

½ teaspoon basil

4 slices soy cheese or ½ cup grated soy cheese

Koo Koo

10 ounces fresh spinach

1 teaspoon sea salt

2 eggs, beaten

1/2 cup walnuts, ground in a blender

1/4 cup dried onion flakes

1 clove garlic, pressed

1 teaspoon basil

1/2 teaspoon oregano

1 tablespoon tamari

2 tablespoons whole wheat pastry flour

I enjoy trying to adapt recipes from my favorite restaurants. This crustless spinach pie is lower in fat than the one served at Fandangos, a restaurant in Sarasota which specializes in Middle Eastern cuisine and jazz.

Yield: 7 1/2-inch pie; serves: 4

Time: 1 hour to prepare; 35 minutes to bake

1. Wash and drain the spinach. Leave it in the sink and sprinkle with salt. Take large handfuls of spinach and rub them between your hands so that the salt is evenly distributed. (This will take only a minute.) Let sit for at least 45 minutes.

2. One handful at a time, squeeze the spinach firmly to extract the excess liquid, as in wringing out a sponge. Chop the pressed spinach, then place it in a large bowl.

3. Add the remaining ingredients and mix as well as you can with a spoon. Finish mixing with your hands, squeezing the mixture as you mix.

4. Press the mixture into a 7 1/2-inch pie pan that has been lightly floured and sprinkled with flour. Press the mixture into the pan as well as you can with your hands, then use the flat bottom of a glass to press it some more until the top is even and the mixture fits nicely into the pan.

5. Bake uncovered at 350°F for 20 minutes, then cover with foil and bake for 15 minutes more.

6. Serve warm; Koo Koo is wonderful plain or with Creamy Dill Sauce (page 102). For a delicious meal, serve it with Barley with Mushrooms and Walnuts (page 156) and Moroccan Carrot Salad (page 79).

Savory Butternut Squash Pie

This pie has a wonderful flavor and a beautiful rich color.

Serves: 6

Time: 45 minutes to bake squash;
20 minutes to prepare; 45 minutes to bake pie

1. Prepare the pie crust.

2. Cut the squash in half lengthwise. With a spoon, scrape out the seeds and the strings. Place the squash, cut side down, on a lightly oiled cookie sheet and bake at 350°F for 45 minutes or until it is easily pierced with a fork. Let the squash cool for easier handling.

3. Heat the oil in a large skillet and add the onion, garlic, and herbs. Sauté until the onion is tender.

4. When the squash is cool enough to handle, scrape out the flesh and mash it with a fork or potato masher. Measure out 3½ cups of the mashed squash and add it to the onion mixture. Add the salt, flour, and the egg. Mix well.

5. Fill the pie crust with the squash mixture. Sprinkle the pie with the soy cheese. Bake at 350°F for 45 minutes.

For a delicious meal, serve with Cherry Tomato Salad (page 73) and steamed green beans.

Any leftover squash may be mixed with a little sautéed onion and garlic and seasoned with white miso or salt and served as a side dish the next day.

1 Potato Pie Crust (see page 139)

1 medium–large butternut squash

1 tablespoon oil

1¼ cups chopped onion (1 medium–large onion)

6 cloves garlic, minced

1½ teaspoons herbes de Provence (see page 102)

1 teaspoon sea salt

2 tablespoons whole wheat pastry flour

1 egg, beaten

½ cup soy cheese

Parsnip Pie

1 single 9-inch Whole Wheat
Pie Crust (see page 137)

2 pounds parsnips

2 leeks

1 tablespoon olive oil

8 cloves garlic, minced

2 tablespoons yellow or white
miso

1/4 teaspoon nutmeg

1 egg

Dash of cayenne pepper, or to
taste

1/2 cup grated soy cheese
(cheddar flavor) or dairy
cheddar cheese

A winter vegetable pie.

Serves: 6–8   Time: 45 minutes to prepare; 1 hour to bake

1. Prepare the pie crust.

2. Scrub the parsnips and slice them, discarding the stems and ends. Steam or pressure-cook them until they are tender enough to mash easily (15–20 minutes for steaming; in the pressure cooker, raise the heat until the regulator jiggles, then cool off the cooker). Drain the cooked parsnips and place them in a large bowl. Mash them with a potato masher.

3. Cut the root end off the leeks and slit them lengthwise. Wash the leeks under running water, rinsing out any sand or dirt. Chop the leeks, using only the tender green part and the white part. (Save the dark green part for soup stock.)

4. Heat the oil in a skillet. Add the leeks and the garlic and sauté for about 10 minutes or until the leeks are tender.

5. Add the sautéed leek mixture to the mashed parsnips. Add the miso, nutmeg, egg, and cayenne pepper. Mix well.

7. Fill the pie crust with the parsnip mixture. Top it with the soy cheese.

8. Bake at 350°F for 1 hour, or until the filling is firm and the crust is brown.

Bulgur Pecan Balls (page 187) with Quick and Light Fresh Tomato Sauce (page 96) over whole wheat pasta, served with a side dish of Zucchini Simmered in Mirin (149).

Served on a bed of brown rice, Tempeh Chick Pea Curry (page 232) is nutritious and spicy.

New Potatoes and Green Beans with Sun-Dried Tomato Spread (page 183), a complete meal in one dish.

Onion Pie

Simple and delicious.

Serves: 6   Time: 1 hour to prepare; 45 minutes to bake

1. Prepare the pie crust.

2. Heat the oil in a large skillet. Add the onions and the herbs. Sauté over medium heat, stirring frequently, for about 20 minutes or until brown.

3. Add the flour and mix well. Slowly pour in the milk while stirring. Turn the heat to high and stir until the mixture has thickened. Add the salt and the cayenne pepper. Let the mixture cool slightly, then add the egg and mix well.

4. Transfer the onion mixture to the pie crust. Top with the cheese and bake at 350°F for 45 minutes. Let set for about 10 minutes before cutting and serving.

1 Potato Pie Crust (see page 139)

2 tablespoons olive oil

6 cups sliced onions (2 large Spanish onions)

1 1/2 teaspoons herbes de Provence (see page 102)

1/4 cup whole wheat pastry flour

1 cup soymilk

1 teaspoon sea salt

Dash of cayenne pepper, or to taste

1 egg, beaten

1/2 cup grated soy cheese (cheddar flavor) or dairy cheddar cheese

Louise's Pizza Marseilles

This recipe is perfect for a party, well worth the time it takes to prepare it.

2¹/₂ pounds onions (about
3 large Spanish onions)*

1 medium head garlic

2 tablespoons olive oil

1¹/₂ teaspoons herbes de
Provence (see page 102)

¹/₂ teaspoon sea salt

1 Whole Wheat Pizza Crust
(see page 120)

15 sun-dried tomato halves

Water to soak tomatoes

6-ounce can pitted black olives

Serves: 3–6   Time: 2¹/₂ hours

1. Peel and slice the onions and the garlic. The garlic cloves are easier to peel if you smash them with the side of your knife first.

2. Heat the oil in a large, heavy kettle. Add the onions and the garlic and sauté over medium-low to low heat, uncovered, stirring occasionally, for about 2 hours or until the vegetables have reduced to about a quarter of the quantity that you started with. Don't hurry; the secret to this recipe is long, slow cooking.

3. After about 1 hour of cooking, begin making the crust. About 15 minutes before the dough has finished rising (it will double in bulk), place the tomato halves in a small bowl and cover them with water. Let them soak while the crust finishes rising. Add the herbs and the salt to the onions, mix well, and continue to cook them.

4. When the dough has risen and the onions are very tender, stretch and pat the dough onto a well-oiled 11-x-16-inch cookie sheet (see crust recipe). Cool the onion mixture, then spread it over the crust. Slice the soaked tomatoes and the olives. Arrange the tomatoes and olives over the onions.

5. Bake on the lower rack of the oven at 375°F for about 12 minutes or until the bottom of the pizza is brown (lift the edge of the pizza to check). Cut pizza into squares and serve with a green salad.

*The quantity of onions does not have to be exact, but don't use less than 2¹/₂ pounds; it is better to have too much than too little to cover the crust.

Crispy Crust Veggie Pizza with Tofu-Cream Topping

Serves: 3–6   Time: 1¼ hours

1. Make the Whole Wheat Pizza Crust. While the dough is rising, prepare the other ingredients.

2. Heat the oil in a skillet. Add the onion, garlic, and basil. Sauté over medium heat until the onion is almost tender. Add the tomato purée and the salt. Simmer for about 10 minutes. Set aside.

3. Place the tofu, miso, and cayenne pepper in a blender or food processor. Blend until smooth and creamy. Scrape the sides of the blender or food processor with a rubber spatula if necessary so that the tofu is well blended. Set aside.

4. When the dough has risen, generously oil an 11-x-16-inch cookie sheet. Stretch and pat the dough onto the cookie sheet. The dough will be thin, but it will cover the sheet. Spread the tomato sauce evenly over the dough and then distribute the chopped broccoli and zucchini over the sauce. Now pour the tofu cream evenly over the pizza, covering as much of the surface as possible.

5. Bake on the bottom rack of the oven at 375°F for about 12 minutes or until the bottom of the crust is nicely browned (lift the edge of the pizza to check). When the crust is brown, place the pizza on the top rack of the oven and turn it to broil for about 3 minutes to lightly brown the top. Watch carefully so that it doesn't burn. Cut into squares and serve.

---

1 Whole Wheat Pizza Crust (see page 120)

1 tablespoon oil

1 cup chopped onion (1 medium onion)

4 cloves garlic, minced

1 teaspoon basil

1 cup tomato purée (canned, unsalted)

¼ teaspoon sea salt

1 package (10½ ounces) soft silken tofu

2 tablespoons yellow or white miso

Dash of cayenne pepper, or to taste

1 cup finely chopped broccoli flowerets

1 cup finely chopped zucchini (1 small zucchini)

½ teaspoon oregano

Artichoke and Fresh Tomato Pizza

This pizza is easy because it does not need a sauce.

1 Whole Wheat Pizza Crust
(see page 120)

6 cloves garlic, pressed
(or less, to taste)

1/2 teaspoon sea salt

1 teaspoon oregano

1 teaspoon basil

1 tablespoon olive oil

16-ounce can artichoke hearts,
drained and finely chopped

3–4 tomatoes

1/2 cup grated soy cheese or
low-fat mozzarella cheese

Yield: 12 small slices;
serves: 4

Time: 1 hour, 15 minutes for crust;
15 minutes to prepare; 15 minutes to bake

1. Make the pizza crust. While the dough rises, prepare the topping. Press the garlic into a medium bowl. Add the salt, herbs, and oil. Add the artichoke hearts and mix well.

2. Cut the tomatoes into slices 1/4–1/2 inch thick. Select 12 nice, big slices and set aside. Reserve the small slices from the ends to use in a soup, sauce, or stew.

3. After the dough for the crust has risen, place it in the middle of a well-oiled 11-x-16-inch cookie sheet. Stretch and pat the dough until it covers the bottom and sides of the sheet. If the sheet has no sides, build up the edges a little thicker. Distribute the artichoke mixture evenly over the crust Arrange the tomato slices in one layer over the artichoke mixture. Top with the grated cheese.

4. Bake at 375°F for 15 minutes or until the crust is a crispy golden brown (lift the edge of the pizza to check).

5. To serve, cut the pizza into squares, one tomato slice per piece. Serve hot.

Curry-Stuffed Dosas with Mango Chutney

1 recipe Vegetable Dal Curry
(see page 173)

1 recipe Fresh Mango Chutney
(see page 92)

1 recipe Whole Wheat Dosas*
(see page 134)

Serves: 4   Time: 1 1/2 hours

1. Make the curry. While it is cooking, make the chutney and let it chill until the meal is ready to eat. When the curry is almost finished, start making the dosas.

2. To assemble, place a heaping tablespoonful or two of the curry on a dosa and fold it over to cover the filling. Repeat with the remaining dosas. Serve the curry on the side.

For a real feast, accompany with brown Basmati rice, and Sambals (page 77). For dessert, serve with a tray of Almond Candy (page 243) and Halvah (page 244).

*There is enough curry to fill almost two recipes of dosas. Therefore, you may want to double the recipe for the dosas. Any leftovers can be refrigerated and reheated later in an unoiled skillet.

Eggplant-Stuffed Crepes

Yield: 7–8 crepes   Time: 20 minutes to make crepes;
                    1 hour to bake eggplant; 30 minutes to prepare

1. Make the crepes and set them aside while you make the filling.

2. Wash the eggplant and pierce the skin with a fork. Lightly oil the skin and place the eggplant in a baking dish. Bake at 350°F for about 1 hour or until shriveled and very tender. Let it cool for easy handling.

3. In a large skillet, heat the oil. Add the onion and the herbs. Sauté until the onion is almost tender and then add the mushrooms and the sun-dried tomatoes. Sauté until the mushrooms are tender. Cut the baked eggplant in half lengthwise and scrape out the flesh. If the flesh is firm, chop it. Add the eggplant flesh to the skillet with the other ingredients. Add the tamari, then cover and let stand while you make the sauce.

4. Blend together in a blender the tofu, miso, and cayenne pepper, until the mixture is smooth and creamy. Add 1/4 cup of the sauce to the eggplant mixture. Check the seasoning and add more tamari or salt, if you prefer. Reheat the eggplant mixture and keep it warm.

5. Place the sauce in a small saucepan and heat it, but do not boil.

6. If the crepes are cold, place them in an oven-proof dish, cover them with foil, and place them in a 400°F oven for 3–5 minutes or until warm.

7. Place a warm crepe on the countertop, spoon some filling down the center, and roll it up. Place the crepe in a warm serving dish. Top with warm sauce and sprinkle with a little parsley. Repeat until you have used up the filling.

These crepes are good with steamed green beans and Cherry Tomato Salad (page 73).

1 recipe Whole Wheat Crepes
(see page 133)

FILLING:

1 medium eggplant

1 tablespoon olive oil

1 1/4 cups chopped onion
(1 medium onion)

1 teaspoon herbes de Provence
(see page 102)

2 1/2 cups sliced mushrooms
(about 15 medium mushrooms)

15 sun-dried tomato halves,
cut into small pieces

1 tablespoon tamari, or to taste

SAUCE:

1 package (10 1/2 ounces) firm
silken tofu

2 tablespoons white or yellow
miso

Dash of cayenne pepper, or to
taste

2 tablespoons minced fresh
parsley

Buckwheat-Stuffed Cabbage Rolls

1 medium head white cabbage

1 cup water

FILLING:

1 tablespoon oil

1 cup chopped onion
(1 medium onion)

3 cloves garlic, minced

1 teaspoon thyme

1 cup toasted buckwheat

2 cups water

2 tablespoons tamari

SAUCE:

3 cups tomato purée
(3 medium tomatoes, coarsely
chopped, then blended)

1 cup sauerkraut

2 tablespoons tomato paste

Buckwheat and cabbage go perfectly together, a traditional combination in Eastern Europe. Making cabbage rolls is easy and really delicious—worth every minute it takes to prepare them.

Yield: 8 cabbage rolls; serves: 4–8   Time: 45 minutes to prepare;
45 minutes to bake

1. Wash the cabbage, removing any tough or damaged outer leaves. Cut out the core and discard it. Place the cabbage, core side down, in a large kettle and add the water. Cover and bring to a boil. Reduce the heat and simmer for about 10 minutes.

2. Remove the cabbage and let it cool for easier handling. Save the remaining water for use in soups or stews.

3. While the cabbage cools, prepare the filling: Heat the oil in a large skillet. Add the onion, garlic, and thyme. Sauté over medium heat for 3–5 minutes, stirring occasionally. Add the buckwheat and stir. Add the water, cover, and reduce the heat. Cook for 15–20 minutes or until the water has been absorbed. Add the tamari and mix well. Set aside uncovered to cool.

4. Carefully pull 16 leaves off the steamed cabbage. Cut away the thick, tough part from the base of each leaf (Drawing a). Choose the eight largest leaves and place the remaining leaves inside them to make a double layer.

5. When the filling is cool enough to handle, take a heaping table-spoonful and pack it onto the center of a small leaf (Drawing b). Fold the top and bottom of the large leaf over the filling, then fold the two sides over the seam (Drawing c). Place the cabbage roll, seam side down, on the countertop. Repeat until you have used up all the leaves that you removed. Save the remaining cabbage to use in soups or stews.

6. Mix together the tomato purée and the sauerkraut and place this mixture in a 7-x-11-inch baking dish. Place the cabbage rolls, seam side down, on the tomato-sauerkraut mixture (Drawing d). Cover the pan with foil. Bake at 350°F for 45 minutes to 1 hour or until the cabbage is tender.

7. Transfer the cabbage rolls to a serving plate. Add the tomato paste to the tomato-sauerkraut mixture that is left in the bottom of the pan. Mix well. Spoon the sauce over the cabbage rolls and serve.

These cabbage rolls go well with Dilled Carrots (page 143) or Summer Squash with Peppers and Shallots (page 148).

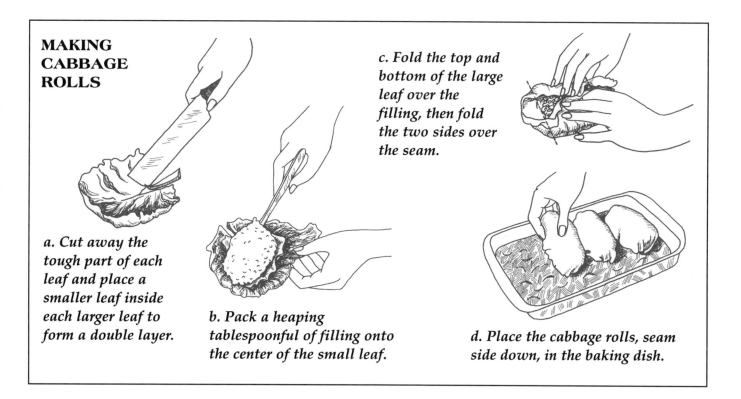

MAKING CABBAGE ROLLS

a. Cut away the tough part of each leaf and place a smaller leaf inside each larger leaf to form a double layer.

b. Pack a heaping tablespoonful of filling onto the center of the small leaf.

c. Fold the top and bottom of the large leaf over the filling, then fold the two sides over the seam.

d. Place the cabbage rolls, seam side down, in the baking dish.

Tex-Mex Corn Cakes

These pretty little vegetable pancakes taste and look a lot like omelets.

Serves: 4   Time: 35 minutes

1. In a blender or food processor, combine the tofu, water, garlic, salt, and baking powder. Blend until smooth and creamy. Transfer the mixture to a medium bowl and add the remaining ingredients. Mix well.

2. Heat some oil in a skillet (I use a nonstick skillet with only a few drops of oil). Drop the batter by the heaping tablespoonful onto the skillet. The pancakes should be small; if you try to make them too big, they will fall apart. Cook over medium-high heat until brown on the bottom. Turn them over and cook the other side. Repeat until the batter is used up.

3. Serve warm with Fresh Salsa (page 94) and sliced avocado on the side.

$1^1/_2$ cups mashed tofu, packed into the cup

$1/_2$ cup water

1 clove garlic

$1/_2$ teaspoon sea salt

2 teaspoons baking powder

1 cup grated zucchini, packed into the cup ($1/_2$ medium zucchini)

$1/_4$ cup red bell pepper, finely chopped

1 teaspoon basil

1 cup cornmeal

1–2 tablespoons oil, as needed to cook pancakes

Black-Bean-Stuffed Yellow Peppers

4 bell peppers (yellow, red, or green)

Water for steaming the peppers

1 tablespoon olive oil

1 cup chopped onion (1 medium onion)

1 tablespoon chili powder

1 teaspoon cumin

1 teaspoon basil

1/2 teaspoon oregano

2 cups cooked and drained black beans (see page 169)

1 tablespoon wine vinegar

2 1/2 cups cooked brown rice (see page 152)

1 teaspoon sea salt

1 medium ripe tomato, chopped (about 1 cup)

8 slices cheddar-flavor soy cheese (optional)

The yellow peppers are especially pretty with the black beans, but if you like, you can use green or red peppers, or a mixture of all three.

Serves: 4–8   Time: about 45 minutes

1. Cut the peppers in half lengthwise and remove the seeds. Place the peppers, cut side down, on a steaming rack in a large pan. Add about 1/2 inch of water to the pan, cover, and bring to a boil. Reduce the heat and steam the peppers for 5–10 minutes or until they are nearly tender but still hold their shape well.

2. Heat the olive oil in a skillet. Add the onion and sauté over medium heat until it is nearly tender. Add the chili powder, cumin, basil, and oregano. Continue to sauté until the onion is tender. Add the beans and the vinegar and mix well. Add the rice, salt, and chopped tomato, and mix again.

3. Fill the steamed peppers with the bean mixture. Top each pepper half with a slice of soy cheese, if you like, and place the peppers in a shallow baking dish. Bake, covered, at 350°F for about 15–20 minutes or until peppers are tender.

4. Serve these peppers with the Fresh Salsa (page 94), Tex-Mex Corn Cakes (page 205), and a big green salad.

Stuffed Peppers à la Provençale

The ingredients that flavor this recipe are used abundantly in the cuisine of the South of France.

Serves: 3   Time: 45 minutes

1. Cut the peppers in half lengthwise and remove the seeds. Place the peppers, cut side down, on a steaming rack in a large pan. Add about 1/2 inch of water to the pan, cover, and bring to a boil. Reduce the heat and steam the peppers for 5–10 minutes or until they are nearly tender but still hold their shape well.

2. Heat the olive oil in a skillet. Add the celery, the onion, and the herbs. Sauté over medium heat for 3–4 minutes. Add the tomatoes and the 2 tablespoons water. Cover and continue to cook, stirring occasionally, until the vegetables are tender but still firm.

3. In a large bowl, mix together the sautéed vegetables, rice, olives, and goat cheese. Taste the mixture and add salt, if necessary, depending on the saltiness of the olives and the cheese.

4. Fill the steamed peppers with the rice mixture. Sprinkle the tops with the Parmesan cheese or tofu-Parmesan. Place the stuffed peppers in a shallow baking dish. Add the 1/4 cup of water, cover with foil, and bake for 15 minutes or until the peppers are heated through. Don't overcook them, or they will fall apart. Remove the foil when the peppers are done, move the baking dish to the top rack, and turn the oven to broil for a minute or two to brown the tops.

5. Serve these peppers plain, with sliced tomatoes and a steamed vegetable, or with a tomato sauce and a green salad.

This recipe can easily be doubled. It is a nice dish to serve guests.

---

3 large green bell peppers

Water for steaming the peppers

1 tablespoon olive oil

1/2 cup chopped celery
(1 stalk)

1 cup chopped onion
(1 medium onion)

1 teaspoon herbes de Provence
(see page 102)

12 sun-dried tomato halves,
cut into small pieces

2 tablespoons water

3 cups cooked brown rice
(see page 152)

3/4 cup sliced pitted black olives

3 ounces fresh goat cheese

Sea salt to taste (if necessary)

1/4 cup grated Parmesan cheese
or tofu-Parmesan

1/4 cup water

Broccoli-Stuffed Potatoes

Serves: 4–8   Time: 1 hour 45 minutes

4 baking potatoes

2 cups finely chopped broccoli

1 tablespoon oil

1 cup finely chopped onion

1 cup Golden Cashew Sauce
(see page 99)

1 tablespoon yellow or white
miso

1/2 teaspoon tarragon

Dash of cayenne pepper, or to
taste

Dash of sea salt, or to taste

Paprika garnish

1/2 cup soy cheese (cheddar
flavor) or cheddar cheese

1. Scrub the potatoes and cut out any bad spots or eyes. Pierce the skins with a fork in a few places to keep them from exploding. Bake the potatoes at 375°F for 1 hour or until a fork easily penetrates the centers.

2. While the potatoes are baking, lightly steam the broccoli until it is just tender. Set aside.

3. Heat the oil in a skillet and sauté the onion over medium heat until it is tender. Set aside.

4. Prepare the sauce.

5. When the potatoes are done, let them stand until they are cool enough to handle, then cut them in half lengthwise. With a spoon, scoop out the center of each potato half, leaving enough around the edges (about 1/4 inch) to make a shell that does not fall apart. Place the potato flesh in a medium bowl. Mash the flesh with a fork or a potato masher. Add 1 cup of the sauce and the miso. Mix well. Add the steamed broccoli, the sautéed onion, and the tarragon, and mix again. Season with salt and cayenne pepper.

6. Stuff the potato shells with the broccoli mixture. Sprinkle with paprika and top with the soy cheese or cheddar cheese. Place potato shells in an oven-proof dish. Bake, uncovered, at 375°F for about 15 minutes or until the potatoes are heated through and the cheese is melted.

Leftover stuffed potatoes are great reheated for lunch.

Zucchini Foster

It took a lot of work to make a stuffed zucchini recipe that I was happy with. Everyone who tried the early attempts gave me suggestions on how to improve them. The Foster family from Nokomis, Florida, gave me lots of suggestions, which I did not follow, but I named the successful recipe after them anyway.

Serves: 4–8   Time: 30 minutes to prepare; 30–40 minutes to bake

1. Place the sunflower seeds in a shallow oven-proof pan. Bake them at 350°F for about 15 minutes or until they are lightly toasted, stirring occasionally so that they brown evenly. Remove them from the oven and let them cool

2. Meanwhile, heat the oil in a skillet. Add the onion and sauté for about 3 minutes. Add the green pepper and the herbs, and sauté over medium heat until the vegetables are tender.

3. Place the toasted sunflower seeds and the sun-dried tomatoes in a blender and coarsely grind them. Add this mixture to the sautéed vegetables. Add the rice and tamari and mix well.

4. Clean the zucchinis with a brush under running water, then cut them in half. With a teaspoon, carefully scoop out the flesh, leaving a shell that is strong enough to hold its shape ($^1/_4$–$^1/_2$ inch thick).

5. Fill the zucchini shells with the rice mixture. Place the shells in an oiled rectangular baking dish and cover with foil. Bake at 350°F for 30–40 minutes or until the zucchini shells are tender but still hold their shape.

6. Serve with New Corn Bread (page 131) and a nice big salad.

$^1/_2$ cup sunflower seeds

1 tablespoon oil

$^1/_2$ cup finely chopped onion (1 small onion)

$^1/_2$ cup finely chopped green pepper ($^1/_2$ medium pepper)

1 teaspoon herbes de Provence (see page 102)

15 sun-dried tomato halves

1$^1/_2$ cups cooked short or medium grain brown rice (see page 152)

2 tablespoons tamari

4 medium zucchinis (about 2 pounds)

Stuffed Eggplant

This is a nice recipe to serve for a special occasion.

Serves: 2–4   Time: 20 minutes to prepare; 35 minutes to bake

1 eggplant, smaller than medium (about 12 ounces)

2 tablespoons olive oil

1 cup chopped onion (1 medium onion)

2 cloves garlic, minced

1 cup chopped mushrooms (about 4–5 medium mushrooms)

1 teaspoon basil

1/2 teaspoon oregano

1/4 cup sun-dried tomato bits

2 tablespoons tamari

3/4 cup whole wheat bread crumbs

1/4 cup tahini

2–3 tablespoons water

1. Cut the eggplant in half. Then, with a sharp paring knife, cut out the flesh, leaving a shell about 1/2 inch thick. Dice the flesh and set it aside to use in the stuffing.

2. Heat the olive oil in a skillet, add the onion and the garlic, and sauté over medium heat until the onion begins to become tender. Add the diced eggplant, mushrooms, basil, and oregano. Stir, cover, and continue to cook for about 5 minutes, stirring occasionally, until the vegetables are tender. Add the sun-dried tomato bits and the tamari. Mix well, cover, and remove from the heat. Let stand for a minute to allow the dried tomatoes to soften. Add 1/2 cup of the bread crumbs and the tahini and mix well.

3. Fill the eggplant shells with the stuffing mixture. Top with the remaining 1/4 cup of bread crumbs, and place the stuffed eggplant halves in a shallow baking dish. Add 2–3 tablespoons of water to the bottom of the pan and cover it with foil. Bake at 350°F for about 35 minutes or until the shell is tender but still holds its shape. Uncover, move pan to the top rack, and broil the top for 1–2 minutes to brown the bread crumbs. Let cool for a few minutes before serving.

This dish is good with plain brown rice (or plain wild rice) and slices of fresh, ripe tomato. Add a green salad if you like.

Stuffed Mushrooms

Serves: 4   Time: 20 minutes to prepare; 30 minutes to bake

1. Wash and dry the mushrooms and carefully remove their stems. Chop the stems and set aside.

2. Heat the oil in a skillet. Add the garlic and the herbs and sauté until the garlic begins to brown. Add the chopped mushroom stems, and sauté until tender. Add the bread crumbs and the T.V.P. Stir. Add the tamari and mix well. Remove the pan from the heat.

3. Place the mushroom caps in a lightly oiled baking dish or cake pan. Stuff the mushroom caps with the crumb mixture. Lightly press the stuffing into the caps and mound it as high as you can. Cover and bake at 350°F for 30 minutes. Sprinkle with the parsley.

4. Serve as a side dish, appetizer, or part of a main dish. To serve as part of a main dish; start with a bed of brown rice or wild rice, or a mixture. Top the rice with the sauce of your choice (Tahini Milk Gravy, page 98, is good). Arrange the mushrooms on the sauce-covered rice and sprinkle with parsley. Serve with a steamed vegetable and a salad.

1 pound large mushrooms (8–10 large mushrooms)

2 tablespoons olive oil

2 tablespoons minced garlic

1 teaspoon herbes de Provence (see page 102)

1 cup whole grain bread crumbs, lightly packed

1/4 cup T.V.P. (textured vegetable protein)

1 tablespoon tamari

1 tablespoon minced fresh parsley

Buckwheat-Stuffed Acorn Squash

A good dish for a late autumn supper.

Serves: 4   Time: about 45 minutes to bake squash; 20 minutes to prepare; 10 minutes to bake.

1. Cut the acorn squashes in half lengthwise and scoop out the seeds and the stringy parts.

2. Place the squash halves, cut side down, on a lightly oiled cookie sheet and bake for 20 minutes at 350°F. Turn the halves over and bake for about 25 minutes more or until they are tender but still firm enough to hold their shape.

3. While the squash halves are baking, heat the oil in a skillet. Add the onion and the celery, and sauté over medium heat until they are almost tender. Add the yellow squash and continue to cook until the vegetables are tender Add the garlic and stir for a minute more. Transfer to a medium bowl.

4. Add the remaining ingredients and mix well. Pack this mixture into each squash cavity. Bake for about 10 minutes more.

5. Serve with Herbed Brussel Sprouts (page 145) and Balsamic Beets (page 146).

2 large acorn squashes

1 tablespoon olive oil

1 cup finely chopped onion

1 cup finely chopped celery

1 cup finely diced yellow squash (1 medium squash)

4 cloves garlic, pressed

1 cup cooked buckwheat (see page 152)

1/2 cup tomato purée

1 teaspoon basil

1 teaspoon oregano

1/2 teaspoon cinnamon

1 1/2 tablespoons tamari

Stuffed Butternut Squash

1 medium–large butternut squash (about 4¹/₂ pounds)

1 cup brown rice

2 cups water

1 cup chopped pecans

1 tablespoon oil

2 medium leeks

1 teaspoon tarragon

1 teaspoon sea salt

2 tablespoons vegetable broth powder

1 slice whole grain bread

2 teaspoons oil

Serves: 4–6   Time: 45 minutes to bake squash and cook rice

1. Cut the squash in half lengthwise and scoop out the seeds and the stringy part. Place squash, cut side down, on a lightly oiled cookie sheet. Bake at 350°F for about 45 minutes or until squash can be easily pierced with a fork but is firm enough to hold its shape.

2. While the squash is in the oven, wash the rice and drain it through a wire strainer. Place it in a pan with the water, cover, and bring to a boil. Reduce the heat to a simmer and cook the rice for about 45 minutes or until the water has been absorbed.

3. Place the pecans in an oven-proof pan and bake at 350°F for about 10 minutes or until lightly toasted.

4. While the rice is cooking, cut off the root ends of the leeks, then slit the leeks lengthwise and rinse them well under running water. Discard the toughest green part of the leeks (or save it for soups) and chop the white part and the tender green part.

5. Heat 1 tablespoon of oil in a skillet. Add the chopped leeks and the tarragon. Sauté them over medium heat until they are tender (about 10 minutes).

6. When the squash is done, scrape out the flesh, leaving a shell about ¹/₂ inch thick. Place the squash shells on a cookie sheet and the flesh in a large bowl. Mash the flesh with a fork. Add the cooked rice, toasted pecans, leeks, salt, and vegetable broth powder. Mix well and stuff the shells with this mixture.

7. Tear up the bread and place it in a blender. Blend to make crumbs. Add the 2 teaspoons of oil and blend again. Sprinkle the crumbs over the stuffed squash.

8. Bake at 350°F for about 20 minutes or until the bread crumbs are toasted. Transfer the squash to a serving platter.

9. Serve with Balsamic Beets (page 146), Louise's Red and White Cabbage Salad (page 76), homemade bread or rolls, and an apple pie for a fall or winter feast.

Crusty Garden Bake

This dish is a vegetable cobbler.

Serves: 4   Time: 30 minutes to prepare; 15 minutes to bake

1. Steam the vegetables until they are nearly tender. Set aside while you prepare the sauce.

2. Place the tofu, miso, savory, soymilk, and cayenne pepper in a food processor or blender. Blend until smooth and creamy. Mix the sauce with the vegetables (drained of their cooking liquid). Set aside while you make the crust.

3. Place the biscuit mix in a medium bowl. Stir in the oil with a fork until it is evenly distributed. Add the water and mix to form a dough. Set aside.

4. Place the vegetable-sauce mixture in an 8-x-8-inch baking dish. Drop teaspoonfuls of the dough evenly over the surface of the vegetables. With the back of the spoon, spread the dough to cover the surface. It's all right if some spots don't get covered because the dough will even out as it rises. Sprinkle with the sesame seeds.

5. Bake at 425°F for about 15 minutes or until the crust is lightly browned and the sauce is bubbly.

2 cups chopped cabbage

1½ cups sliced carrots
(2 medium carrots)

1 cup chopped celery
(2 stalks)

1 cup chopped onion
(1 medium onion)

1 cup diced potato,
(1 medium potato)

SAUCE:

1 package (10½ ounces) firm silken tofu

¼ cup white or yellow miso

1 teaspoon summer savory

½ cup soymilk

Dash of cayenne pepper, or to taste

CRUST:

1 cup Arrowhead Mills Multi-Grain Biscuit Mix

2 tablespoons oil

⅓ cup water

2 tablespoons sesame seeds

Holiday Dinner Loaf

2 pounds firm tofu

1/4 cup tamari

2 teaspoons herbes de Provence
(see page 102)

4–6 cloves garlic, pressed

1/2 cup gluten flour or
Arrowhead Mills Seitan Quick
Mix

STUFFING:

2 cups pecans

1 tablespoon oil

1 cup chopped onion
(1 medium onion)

1 cup chopped celery
(2 stalks)

3 slices whole grain bread,
cut into 1/2-inch cubes (3 cups)

1 cup water

2 teaspoons Vecon natural
vegetable stock (if unavailable
at your natural foods store,
substitute 2 tablespoons
tamari)

1 egg or egg replacer

1 1/2 teaspoons sage

This stuffed loaf is a wonderful alternative to the traditional turkey dinner. There are a lot of steps to this recipe, but it is easy to make.

Serves: 10   Time: 1 hour to prepare; 1 hour to bake

1. Place 1 pound of tofu in a food processor with the tamari and blend until smooth and creamy. Transfer to a large bowl. Place the remaining pound of tofu in the food processor and blend until smooth and creamy. Transfer to the mixing bowl with the other tofu. Add the herbes de Provence, the garlic, and the gluten flour or seitan mix. Mix well.

2. Generously oil and flour a loaf pan, 12 x 4 1/2 x 3 inches.* Spread three-quarters of the tofu mixture evenly over the bottom and sides of the pan; reserve the remainder to use later to cover the top. Use your hands or the back of a spoon dipped in cool water to smooth out the tofu mixture and make sure that it is firmly pressed against the sides of the pan. Bake at 350°F for 10 minutes. Set aside while you make the stuffing.

3. Place the pecans in a shallow baking dish and bake them at 350°F for 10–15 minutes until they are lightly toasted. Stir them occasionally while they are baking so that they brown evenly. Coarsely grind the toasted nuts in a blender or food processor. Set aside.

4. Heat oil in a skillet. Add the onion and celery. Sauté over medium heat for about 5 minutes or until the vegetables begin to become tender. Place the sautéed vegetables in a large bowl. Add the bread cubes and mix well.

5. In a saucepan, bring the water to a boil. Add the Vecon vegetable stock and stir until the paste is dissolved. Pour over the bread cubes and vegetables. Add the ground pecans and mix. Add the egg or egg replacer and the sage and mix thoroughly.

6. Pack the stuffing into the center of the tofu-lined loaf pan. Spread the top with the remaining tofu. Press around the edges with the back of a spoon to seal the edges. Bake at 350°F for 50 minutes. When the loaf is done, it should be firm and brown.

7. Let the loaf cool in the pan for at least 15 minutes before unmolding onto a serving platter. Slice and serve.

8. This loaf may be prepared a day in advance and baked beginning an hour and 20 minutes before serving. Bake for an extra 10–15 minutes if the loaf is cold.

9. Serve with all (or some) of the trappings of a traditional holiday dinner (see Holiday Dinner, below).

* This size loaf pan, longer than most, works so well with this recipe that it is worth looking for one if you don't already have one. However, you may also use a casserole dish or two small loaf pans.

Holiday Dinner

One year, I invited the whole production crew of a movie that my husband was working on to my house for Christmas dinner. At first, I was concerned that the menu might be too unusual for a group of people who were not especially interested in natural foods, but I decided not to compromise and made the healthiest feast I could.

It turned out to be one of the most appreciated large dinners I have ever made. Everyone loved it, and there were almost no leftovers. Here is the menu, perfect for Thanksgiving, Christmas, or any other fall or winter feast.

HORS D'OEUVRES:

- Tamari Roasted Almonds (purchased at a natural foods store or made according to the recipe in *Cooking with the Right Side of the Brain*)

- Tahini Dressing (page 91) made as a dip with less water, served with baked rice crackers (not puffed rice cakes)

- Creamy Dill Sauce (page 102) made as a dip using firm silken tofu, served with a raw vegetable platter

DINNER:

- Cranberry Quick Bread (page 129)

- Pumpkin Bread (page 129)

- Holiday Dinner Loaf (page 214)

- Mushroom Wine Sauce (page 98)

- Cranberry Sauce (page 93)

- Onion Pie (page 199)

- Herbed Brussels Sprouts (page 145)

- Balsamic Beets (page 146)

- Gingered Sweet Potatoes (page 143)

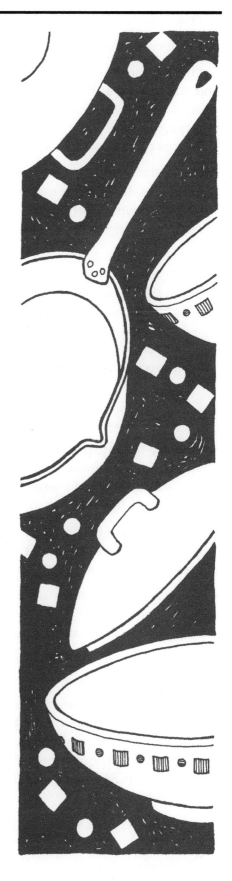

DESSERT:

- Holiday Fruitcake (page 258)

- Fruit and Nut Squares (page 245)

- Raspberry "Cream" Pie Supreme (page 253)

It took me two whole days to make this meal: one to plan, shop, and start cooking; the second to finish. It was an evening meal, so I cooked all day. If you are not experienced cooking on such a scale, you may prefer to take three days or have a helper. Listed below are some tips on how to proceed:

- Check the recipes for the quantities they serve, and double them if necessary. Remember that when you serve many dishes, people will eat smaller portions of everything. For example, to serve 15, I recommend these quantities:

    1 dinner loaf
    1 of each of the dips
    1 of each of the breads
    1 of each of the desserts
    1 recipe cranberry sauce
    1 recipe sweet potatoes
    2 recipes beets
    2 recipes Brussels sprouts
    2 onion pies
    2 recipes mushroom sauce (mine went really fast)

- Go over the ingredients in every recipe and make a list of what you will need. Running out to the store in the middle of cooking is a waste of time and energy. Buy everything you need one or two days before the meal.

- The dinner loaf (except for baking), the fruitcake, the beets, the filling for the onion pie, the two dips, the sweet potatoes, and the mushroom wine sauce all can be made in advance.

- The day of the dinner, prepare the vegetables for the vegetable platter, prepare the Brussels sprouts (but don't cook them), make the two pies, and bake the quick breads.

- Before your guests arrive, make the vegetable platter and the tahini-and-rice-cracker platter. Put the almonds in a serving dish.

- One hour and 20 minutes before dinner, begin baking the previously prepared dinner loaf. About 15–20 minutes before it's done, put the onion pie and sweet potatoes in the oven to reheat. Cook the Brussels sprouts about 20 minutes before serving time and reheat the mushroom sauce. The beets and the cranberry sauce are good served cold.

- Other recipes that would be good with a holiday dinner are Curried Pumpkin Soup in the Shell (page 69) and Donna's Pumpkin Pie (page 248).

10. QUICK MEALS

Don't let a busy schedule keep you from enjoying healthy food. A good diet will enhance your life, giving you the stamina and energy you need to function at your highest level.

Learning a new way to cook or learning to cook for the first time does take time and effort, but what new skill doesn't? When you become adept at cooking with natural foods, you will see how fast and easy it can be. I can make a great meal from scratch without a microwave in less than 30 minutes, and I'm sure that with a little practice you can, too.

The recipes in this section can all be prepared in 30 minutes or less, but don't limit yourself to these recipes. There are recipes in other parts of this book that may seem time-consuming at first glance but that require very little effort or tending. Casseroles, for instance, are quick to prepare; most of the time is in the baking. Bean dishes similarly call for a long period of unattended cooking. And there are many possibilities for making an entire meal out of a soup or salad and some whole grain bread.

TIPS FOR QUICK COOKING

These tips will help you to cook rapidly and efficiently:

- The most important step in preparing quick and healthful meals is to have some precooked beans and grains on hand. At least once a week, cook a large pot of beans and another of grain. Lightly salted, they will keep in your refrigerator through the week to be used in different ways. Each week, try a different bean and grain.

- Cooking grains and beans requires very little attention, which allows you to do other things while they cook. For example, brown rice takes about 45 minutes, during which time you can take a quick shower, prepare other dishes, or do some chores.

- An electric slow-cooker is wonderful for cooking beans without tending them. Turn it on when you go out for the day, and when you come home, the beans are ready.

- Plan several meals in advance and buy everything you need in a single shopping trip.

- I like to plan how I am going to cook my meal as I drive home. That way when I start, I know which utensils to use and how to proceed.

- In preparing your meal, begin with the foods that take the longest to cook. While they are cooking, you can prepare the faster foods or make a sauce or salad.

- A pressure cooker is a great time-saver for soups, vegetables, and beans.

- You will be amazed at how quickly you can chop vegetables with a Japanese vegetable knife. Be careful because it is very sharp.

- Keep the utensils that you use frequently out on top of the counter or hanging nearby.

Asparagus Orientale

Although this dish is quick to make, it is quite elegant and very delicious.

Serves: 2–3   Time: 25 minutes

1. Prepare the Umeboshi Cream and set aside.

2. Bring a large kettle of water to a boil and cook the pasta al dente.

3. As soon as you begin heating the water, wash the asparagus and snap off the tough ends. (You may use these ends for a soup stock or in a blended soup.) Cut the stalks into 1/2-inch pieces, leaving the tips a little longer. Place the stalks in a skillet and place the chopped red pepper over them. Place the tips around the edges of the pan on top of the other vegetables. (This will keep the tips from overcooking.) Pour 1/4 cup water into the skillet. Cover and bring to a boil. Reduce the heat and simmer for about 3 minutes or until the asparagus stalks are just tender.

4. When the pasta is done, drain it and add it to the vegetables, along with the sesame oil and tamari or shoyu. Add the scallions and toss well.

5. Place the pasta-vegetable mixture on individual serving plates. Garnish each plate with a large dollop of Umeboshi Cream. Serve immediately.

---

1 recipe Umeboshi Cream (see page 91)

Water for cooking pasta

6 ounces rice spaghetti or udon noodles

1 pound fresh asparagus

1 red bell pepper, finely chopped

1/4 cup water

1 teaspoon toasted sesame oil

2 tablespoons tamari or shoyu, or to taste

1 or 2 scallions, chopped

Sunny-Day Pasta

Water for cooking pasta

8 ounces corn pasta: shells or spirals

1 tablespoon oil

1 cup chopped onion (1 medium onion)

1/3 cup sunflower seeds

3 medium carrots, cut into matchsticks (about 1 1/2 cups)

1 teaspoon basil

2 tablespoons tamari

2 tablespoons nutritional yeast

1 tablespoon balsamic vinegar

1 clove garlic, pressed

1 ripe tomato, chopped

1/2 cup finely chopped parsley

Yellow corn pasta, colorful vegetables, and sunflower seeds are delightful in this easy dish.

Serves: 3–4   Time: 25 minutes

1. Bring a large kettle of water to boil for cooking the pasta.

2. Meanwhile, heat the oil in a skillet. Add the onion and sunflower seeds. Sauté until the onion begins to become tender. Add the carrots and the basil and sauté until the carrots are tender (about 5 minutes longer).

3. When the water boils, cook the pasta al dente.

4. While the pasta cooks, mix together the tamari, yeast, vinegar, and garlic in a small bowl. Pour this mixture over the sautéed vegetables in the skillet. Add the tomato and the parsley. Mix well and heat, but do not simmer.

5. When the pasta is done, drain it and add it to the vegetable mixture in the skillet. Toss well and serve. Accompany with a big green salad.

Pasta and Chick Peas with Miso Pesto

Hearty, tasty, and quick.

Serves: 3–4   Time: 15–20 minutes

1. Bring a large pot of water to boil for the pasta.

2. Meanwhile, place the chick peas in a colander and set aside.

3. Place the walnuts, garlic, basil, water, and miso in a blender. Blend until smooth. Set aside.

4. Cook the pasta al dente. Drain it through the colander over the chick peas, and return the cooked pasta and chick peas to the pot in which you cooked the pasta. Add the pesto sauce and toss well, using two forks. Sprinkle with parsley and Parmesan cheese, if you like.

5. Serve immediately with a big salad of lettuce and tomatoes.

Water for cooking pasta

10 ounces whole grain spaghetti or fettucini

2 cups cooked chick peas (see page 169)

1/2 cup walnuts

3–4 cloves garlic, peeled

2 ounces fresh basil (1–1 1/2 cups leaves packed into cup)

1/2 cup water

2 tablespoons yellow or white miso

2 tablespoons chopped fresh parsley

Grated Parmesan cheese or tofu-Parmesan (optional)

Alan's Spaghetti

This recipe is super-quick!

Serves: 3–4   Time: 20 minutes or less

1. Bring a large pot of water to boil for the spaghetti.

2. Meanwhile, place the frozen peas in a colander and set aside.

3. Finely chop the tomatoes, saving the juice and transferring it to a medium bowl along with the tomatoes.

4. When the water boils, cook the spaghetti al dente, then drain it through the colander over the peas. Immediately return the pasta and peas to the pot in which you cooked the pasta and add the finely chopped tomatoes with their juice and the chopped herbs. Press the garlic into the mixture and add the tamari. Toss well and serve immediately. Top with Parmesan cheese or tofu-Parmesan, if desired.

Water for cooking spaghetti

10 ounces whole grain spaghetti

1 cup frozen peas

3 medium ripe tomatoes

2 tablespoons chopped fresh basil

2 tablespoons chopped fresh parsley

3–4 cloves garlic

2 tablespoons tamari

Grated Parmesan cheese or tofu-Parmesan (optional)

Pasta with Peanuts and Vegetables in Honey Mustard Sauce

Serves: 3   Time: 25 minutes

1½ cups sliced carrots

1 stalk broccoli (peel and slice the stem and cut the top into flowerets)

1 medium yellow squash, sliced

1 medium zucchini, sliced

1 cup water from steaming vegetables

Water for cooking pasta

8 ounces whole grain pasta (angel-hair pasta would be good)

¼ cup cool water

1½ tablespoons arrowroot

½ teaspoon toasted sesame oil

1 rounded tablespoon Dijon-style mustard

2 tablespoons tamari, or to taste

1 tablespoon honey

2 cloves garlic, pressed

½ cup dry-roasted unsalted peanuts

1. Steam the carrots and broccoli for 5 minutes, then add the squash and zucchini and continue to steam until all the vegetables are tender but still crisp. Reserve any water left over from the steaming and pour it into a measuring cup. Add or subtract water to make 1 cup.

2. In a large pot, bring water to boil and cook the pasta al dente.

3. Meanwhile, mix together ¼ cup of water, the arrowroot, sesame oil, mustard, tamari, honey, and garlic in a small bowl. Transfer this mixture to the pan in which you cooked the vegetables. Add the cup of water left over from steaming the vegetables, stir gently, and bring to a boil. When the sauce has thickened, add the peanuts and the vegetables. Mix gently.

4. When the pasta is done, drain it and top it with the vegetable-peanut mixture. Serve immediately.

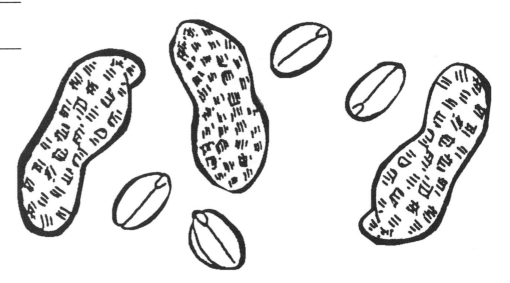

Jean's Macaroni

My husband, Jean, didn't invent this recipe, but he likes it, which is fine with me because it is quick, easy, and nutritious.

Serves: 3   Time: 20–25 minutes

1. Heat the oil in a large skillet. Add the onion and sauté until it begins to become tender, then add the garlic and basil. Sauté for a minute or two longer and then add the mushrooms. Sauté until the onions and mushrooms are both tender and then add the olives, if you like.

2. In a large pot, bring water to a boil and cook the macaroni al dente.

3. While the macaroni is cooking, blend together the tofu, miso, and tomato sauce in a food processor or a blender until the mixture is smooth and creamy.

4. When the macaroni is done, drain it well and add it to the vegetables in the skillet. Add the sauce and mix well. Add the tamari and the cayenne pepper. Mix well.

5. Serve with a big green salad.

2 tablespoons olive oil

1 cup chopped onion, (1 medium)

3 cloves garlic, minced

1 teaspoon basil

2¹/₂ cups sliced mushrooms (about 10–12 medium mushrooms)

1 cup sliced pitted black olives (optional)

Water for cooking macaroni

3 cups whole grain macaroni (rice macaroni is good)

1 package (10¹/₂ ounces) silken tofu (soft or firm)

2 tablespoons yellow miso

1 cup tomato sauce (fresh or canned)

1 tablespoon tamari, or to taste

Dash of cayenne pepper, or to taste

Chili Mac

This is an easy and hearty dish that the whole family will like.

Serves: 4–6	Time: 25 minutes

Water for cooking macaroni

10 ounces whole grain macaroni

2 tablespoons olive oil

1½ cups chopped onion (1 large onion)

1 cup chopped celery (2 stalks)

½ bell pepper, chopped

1 jalapeño pepper, seeded and minced (or use cayenne pepper or salsa to taste)

1 teaspoon chili powder

1 teaspoon cumin

1 teaspoon basil

1-pound can tomatoes

2 cups cooked red kidney beans or pintos with cooking liquid (see page 169)

¼ cup tamari

1. Bring a large pot of water to boil for cooking the macaroni.

2. Meanwhile, heat the oil in a large skillet or a cast-iron Dutch oven. Add the onion, celery, bell pepper, jalapeño pepper, chili powder, cumin, and basil. Sauté until the vegetables are tender. If you are substituting salsa or cayenne pepper for the jalapeño pepper, add it with the tamari (Step 3).

3. Cook the macaroni al dente; drain. Add the canned tomatoes, cooked beans with their liquid, and tamari to the sautéed vegetables. Add the macaroni and mix well. Reheat if necessary.

4. Serve with a big green salad.

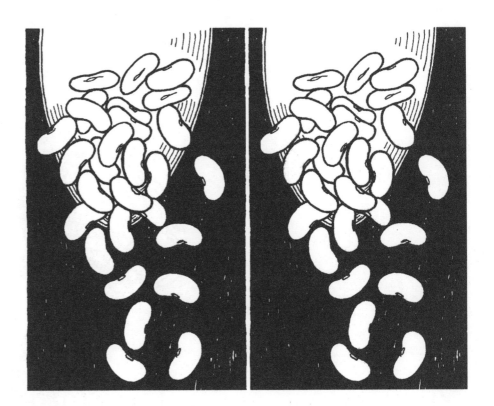

Quick Rye Mushroom Pilaf

Serves: 2–3   Time: 20 minutes

1. Heat the oils in a skillet. Add the thyme, onion, and garlic and sauté over medium heat until the onion is almost tender. Add the rye flakes and stir over medium-high heat until the flakes are lightly toasted and emit a nutty fragrance, about 3 minutes longer. Add the mushrooms and stir.

2. In a small bowl, mix together the tamari and the water and pour the mixture over the flakes in the skillet. Cover and reduce the heat. Simmer for about 10 minutes or until the liquid has been absorbed.

3. Add the parsley and toss. Serve with a salad for a light lunch or as a side dish to accompany some baked or fried tofu or tempeh.

1 teaspoon vegetable oil

1 teaspoon toasted sesame oil

1 teaspoon thyme

*1 cup chopped onion
(1 medium onion)*

2 cloves garlic, minced

3/4 cup rye flakes

*1 1/2 cups sliced mushrooms
(about 7 medium mushrooms)*

1 tablespoon tamari

1 1/2 cups water

1/4 cup chopped fresh parsley

Kasha Varnishkes

An easy and hearty dish from Eastern Europe.

Serves: 3–4   Time: 25 minutes

1. Heat the oil in a skillet. Add the onion, garlic, and thyme. Sauté over medium heat for about 3 minutes. Add the mushrooms and sauté 2–3 minutes longer. Add the buckwheat and stir. Add the water and cover. Reduce the heat to low and simmer for about 15 minutes or until all the water has been absorbed.

2. While the buckwheat is cooking, bring a large pot of water to a boil and cook the noodles al dente. When the noodles are done, reserve 2 tablespoons of the cooking water, then drain the noodles through a colander. Return the noodles to the pot in which you cooked them.

3. In a small bowl or cup, mix together the noodle water and the tamari and add it to the drained noodles. Add the cooked buckwheat and mix well.

For an authentic peasant meal, serve with sauerkraut or some steamed cabbage.

1 tablespoon olive oil

*1 cup chopped onion
(1 medium onion)*

3 cloves garlic, minced

1 teaspoon thyme

*2 cups sliced mushrooms
(about 10 medium mushrooms)*

1/2 cup toasted buckwheat

1 cup water

Water for cooking noodles

8 ounces whole grain noodles

*2 tablespoons water from
cooking noodles*

3 tablespoons tamari

Bulgur with Vegetables and Spicy Peanut Sauce

Serves: 2–3   Time: 30 minutes

1 tablespoon oil

1 cup chopped onion
(1 medium onion)

2 medium carrots, cut into
matchsticks

1 cup bulgur

2 cups water

1 teaspoon tamari

1 medium yellow squash and
1 medium zucchini, cut in
1/2-inch slices (or 2 yellow
squashes or 2 zucchinis)

1 recipe Spicy Peanut Sauce
(see page 101)

Garnish: fresh parsley or finely
chopped scallions

1. Heat the oil in a large skillet. Add the onion and sauté over medium heat until it begins to become tender. Add the carrots and bulgur.

2. In a small bowl, combine the water and tamari and pour the mixture over the bulgur and vegetables in the skillet. Place the squash on top of the bulgur-vegetable mixture and cover. Bring to a boil, then reduce the heat and simmer for about 10 minutes, or until all the liquid has been absorbed.

3. While the bulgur-vegetable mixture and squash are cooking, prepare the sauce.

4. Lightly fold the squash into the bulgur-vegetable mixture. Transfer to individual serving plates. Pour generous helpings of sauce over each portion, garnish with parsley or scallions, and serve immediately.

Bulgur with Corn and Red Peppers

Serves: 3–4   Time: 25 minutes

1 tablespoon oil

1 cup chopped onion
(1 medium onion)

1 red bell pepper, chopped

1 teaspoon basil

1 cup bulgur

1 3/4 cups water

1 tablespoon tamari, or to taste

1 cup corn, cut off the cob

1. Heat the oil in a large skillet. Add the onion and sauté over medium heat for about 5 minutes or until it is almost tender. Add the pepper and the basil. Sauté with the onion for a minute. Add the bulgur and mix well.

2. In a small bowl, combine the water and tamari and pour the mixture over the bulgur and vegetables in the skillet. Stir once, reduce the heat, cover, and simmer for about 10 minutes. Place the corn on top of the other ingredients. Cover and continue to simmer for about 5 more minutes or until the water has been absorbed.

This is a good side dish to accompany beans.

Bulgur and Leeks with Soy Cheese Sauce

Serves: 3–4   Time: 30 minutes

1. Heat the oil in a large skillet. Add the chopped leeks and the herbs and stir over medium heat for 2–3 minutes. Cover, reduce the heat, and cook, stirring occasionally, for about 5 more minutes.

2. Add the bulgur, water, and salt. Turn the heat to high, stir briefly, and cover. When the mixture boils, reduce the heat to low and cook for 10–15 minutes longer or until the water has been absorbed.

3. While the bulgur cooks, prepare the sauce .

4. To serve, fluff bulgur with a fork, place on serving plates, and top with the sauce. This dish is good with sliced tomatoes or a yellow vegetable.

*For information on cleaning leeks, see Sautéed Leeks on page 147.

1 tablespoon olive oil

2 leeks, white and tender green part only, cleaned and chopped* (about 4 cups)

1 teaspoon herbes de Provence (see page 102)

1 cup bulgur

1¼ cups water

¼ teaspoon sea salt

1 recipe Soy Cheese Sauce (see page 100)

Black Beans with Pasta

This recipe is especially good with corn pasta shells, but other kinds of pasta will work in this South-of-the-Border dish.

Serves: 2–3   Time: 25 minutes

1. In a large kettle, bring water to boil for cooking the pasta.

2. Meanwhile, place the tomato purée, corn, salsa, and basil in a medium, heavy saucepan. Mix, cover, and bring to a boil. Reduce the heat and simmer, covered, for 3–4 minutes.

3. Add the beans to the corn mixture. Bring to a boil, then reduce the heat and keep the mixture warm while the pasta cooks.

4. When the water boils, add the pasta and cook it al dente. Then drain it through a colander and toss it with the tomato-bean mixture.

5. Serve with a green salad for a nutritious, inexpensive, and tasty meal.

Water for cooking pasta

8 ounces (about 3 cups) pasta shells

1 medium to large tomato, blended to a purée in a blender or food processor (about 1 cup purée)

1 cup corn (frozen or cut from the cob)

¼ cup salsa (hot or mild, to taste)

2 cups cooked black beans (see page 169), drained and rinsed

½ teaspoon basil

1 tablespoon tamari, or to taste

2 scallions, chopped

Quinoa with Green Beans and Hazelnuts

The contrast of flavors and textures makes this simple dish outstanding.

1 cup quinoa

2 cups water

3 cups cut green beans
(1-inch pieces)

1/2 cup hazelnuts

1 teaspoon oil (preferably
hazelnut oil)

1 tablespoon oil

1 cup chopped onion
(1 medium onion)

3 cloves garlic, minced

1 teaspoon tarragon

1/2 red bell pepper, finely diced

1 tablespoon lemon juice, or to
taste

1/2 teaspoon sea salt

2 tablespoons mirin

1 tablespoon tamari

Serves: 3   Time: 30 minutes

1. Place the quinoa in a medium pan. Add water and swish the quinoa around to wash it. Drain it through a fine wire strainer. Return the washed quinoa to the pan. Add 2 cups water, cover, and bring to a boil. Reduce the heat and simmer without stirring for 15–20 minutes or until the water has been absorbed. Fluff with a fork.

2. While the quinoa is cooking, steam or pressure-cook the green beans until they are just done. In a pressure cooker, let the pressure come up, cook for a few seconds, and then cool the cooker under running water. Uncover the cooked beans so that their color does not fade.

3. While the beans are cooking, place the hazelnuts in a small bowl. Drizzle 1 teaspoon of oil over the nuts, then stir them around in the bowl to coat them with the oil. Bake the nuts at 350°F (a toaster oven works well for this) for about 10 minutes or until toasted.

4. Meanwhile, heat the remaining oil in a skillet. Add the onion, garlic, and tarragon, and sauté over low heat until the onion is nearly tender. Add the red pepper and sauté for 1–2 minutes longer.

5. In a small bowl, mix together the lemon, salt, mirin, and tamari. Pour this mixture over the vegetables in the skillet and sauté for 2–3 minutes longer. Add the toasted hazelnuts and cooked green beans, mix well.

6. Spoon a bed of quinoa onto individual plates. Serve the green bean-nut mixture on the quinoa, including any broth remaining in the skillet.

Quick Scrambled Tofu Curry

Try this instead of scrambled eggs for a quick, light meal.

Serves: 1 generously   Time: 15 minutes

1. Heat the oil in a skillet. Add the bell pepper, carrot, and curry powder. Sauté over medium heat until the vegetables are tender but still firm. Add the scallion and the crumbled tofu. Stir over medium heat until the tofu is heated through.

2. Place the miso in a cup. Add the water and stir until the miso is dissolved. Add the diluted miso to the tofu mixture in the skillet. Mix well.

3. Serve with toasted whole grain bread or on a bed of cooked grain. Accompany with a salad.

2 teaspoons oil, or as needed

1/4 cup finely chopped green or red bell pepper (1/2 small pepper)

1/4 cup grated carrot (1/2 carrot)

1 teaspoon curry powder

1 scallion, chopped

1 cup firm tofu, crumbled

1 tablespoon white or yellow miso

1 tablespoon water

Oat Flakes for Lunch

Who says that oat flakes are only for breakfast? Try this recipe for a quick, hearty, delicious lunch.

Serves: 2   Time: 15–20 minutes

1. Heat the olive oil in a skillet. Add the carrot, celery, and sage. Sauté over medium heat for 3–4 minutes or until the vegetables are almost tender. Add the sunflower seeds and continue to cook, stirring constantly, until they are lightly toasted. Add the oat flakes and stir until they are lightly toasted. Add the scallions, water, and the tamari. Stir once, cover, and lower the heat. Simmer for about 5 minutes or until the liquid has been absorbed.

2. Fluff with a fork and serve with a green salad.

*Rye, barley, or wheat flakes may be used in place of the oat flakes.

1 tablespoon olive oil

1 medium carrot, cut into matchsticks

1 stalk celery, finely chopped

1/2 teaspoon sage

1/4 cup sunflower seeds

3/4 cup oat flakes*

2 scallions, chopped

1 1/2 cups water

1 tablespoon tamari

Seitan Stew

2 large or 3 medium potatoes, scrubbed and diced (about 3½ cups)

4 medium carrots, scrubbed and sliced (about 1½ cups)

1 cup chopped celery (2 stalks)

2 bay leaves

1½ cups water

1 tablespoon oil

1 cup chopped onion (1 medium onion)

1½ cups sliced mushrooms (about 7 medium mushrooms)

2 tablespoons whole wheat pastry flour

¼ cup tahini

1 tablespoon natto miso (optional)

½ cup water

2 tablespoons tamari

Dash of cayenne pepper, or to taste

6 ounces seitan (about 1¼ cups) in bite-sized pieces

This recipe tastes like an old-fashioned beef stew.

Serves: 3–4   Time: 30 minutes

1. Place the potatoes, carrots, celery, bay leaves, and 1½ cups water in a pressure cooker.* Cover and cook over high heat until the pressure regulator jiggles. Remove the pressure cooker from the heat and let it cool down on its own for a minute or two. If the pressure is still up, place the pressure cooker in the sink and run cool water over it so that that the vegetables do not overcook.

2. Meanwhile, heat the oil in a small, heavy saucepan and add the onion. Sauté the onion over medium heat until it is almost tender, then add the mushrooms. Continue to cook the mixture, stirring occasionally, until the mushrooms are tender.

3. Add the flour to the onion mixture and mix well while continuing to cook. Add the tahini and the natto miso, and mix well. Add ½ cup water and stir vigorously until smooth.

4. Add the mushroom mixture to the potato mixture and mix well.

5. Add the tamari, cayenne pepper, and seitan. Bring to a boil, then reduce the heat and simmer for a minute or so until the sauce thickens.

6. Serve with whole grain garlic bread or Parmesan Bread (page 136) and a green salad for a hearty meal. This stew is good made in advance and reheated just before serving.

*If you don't have a pressure cooker, place the potatoes, carrots, celery, bay leaves, and water in a large kettle. Cover and simmer about 30 minutes or until the vegetables are tender. Follow the rest of the recipe as given, adding more water if the mixture becomes too dry or the sauce too thick.

For an autumn feast, try Buckwheat-Stuffed Acorn Squash (page 211).

For a Far-Eastern flair, try Asparagus Orientale (page 219) with Umeboshi Cream (page 91) and Quinoa Nori Rolls (page 158).

Teff and Tempeh Stew

Serves: 4   Time: 30 minutes

1. Brush the tempeh with 1 tablespoon tamari. Cut the tempeh into small cubes and place them in an oiled baking dish. Bake at 350°F for 20 minutes.

2. Meanwhile, heat oil in a heavy kettle. Add the onions, celery, garlic, and ginger. Sauté over medium heat until the onions are tender.

3. Add the teff, water, and tamari to the vegetable mixture. Cover and bring to a boil. Reduce the heat and simmer, stirring occasionally, for 15 minutes.

4. Add the tempeh and simmer for about 5 minutes longer or until the mixture has thickened.

5. Serve over brown rice or millet accompanied by a green vegetable.

8 ounces tempeh

1 tablespoon tamari

1 tablespoon oil

2 cups chopped onions (2 medium onions)

1 cup chopped celery (2 stalks)

3 cloves garlic, minced

1 tablespoon grated fresh ginger

1/3 cup teff

2 cups water

2 tablespoons tamari

Spinach in Cream Sauce

This is an easy and delicious sauce to serve over pasta or your favorite grain.

Serves: 2–3   Time: 20 minutes

1. Heat the oil in a large, heavy kettle. Add the onion and the herbs, and sauté over medium heat until the onion is nearly tender. Add the spinach. Stir over high heat until the spinach begins to wilt. Cover, reduce the heat, and cook for about 2 minutes or until the spinach is just tender.

2. Blend the tofu and the miso together in a blender or food processor until smooth and creamy. Add the mixture to the cooked spinach and stir over medium heat until hot.

3. Serve on a bed of pasta, rice, or millet. Top with the pecans and sprinkle with a little Parmesan cheese or tofu-Parmesan, if desired.

2 tablespoons olive oil

1 cup chopped onion (1 medium onion)

1 teaspoon herbes de Provence (see page 102)

10 ounces fresh spinach, washed and chopped

1 package (10 1/2 ounces) firm silken tofu

2 tablespoons white miso

2–4 tablespoons chopped pecans

Grated Parmesan cheese or tofu-Parmesan (optional)

Tempeh Chick Pea Curry

Serves: 4   Time: 30 minutes

8 ounces tempeh

1 tablespoon tamari

2 tablespoons oil

1 cup chopped onion
(1 medium onion)

3 cloves garlic, minced

1 tablespoon grated fresh
ginger

1 tablespoon curry powder

1 large red bell pepper, sliced
into strips

1 cup cooked chick peas
(see page 169)

1 cup water

1/4 teaspoon sea salt, or to taste

1. Brush the tempeh on both sides with tamari. Cut the tempeh into small cubes and place it on an oiled cookie sheet. Bake at 350°F for 20 minutes.

2. Meanwhile, heat the oil in a skillet. Add the onion, garlic, and ginger. Sauté until the onion begins to become translucent, then add the curry powder and the bell pepper. Sauté for about 3 minutes longer; pepper should still be crisp.

3. Add the chick peas, water, salt, and the baked tempeh. Simmer for 3–5 minutes.

4. Serve over brown rice.

Chick Peas in Spicy Tahini Sauce

Serves: 3   Time: 20 minutes

1. Heat the olive oil in a large skillet. Add the onion and basil. Sauté until the onion is nearly tender, then add the garlic. Continue to sauté until the onion is tender. Stir in the tahini and half the water. Cook, stirring constantly, until the sauce thickens. Remove the skillet from the heat.

2. In a small bowl, mix together the remaining water with the arrowroot, lemon juice, salsa, and tamari. Add it to the mixture in the skillet. Add the chick peas and stir over high heat until the mixture thickens.

3. Serve on a bed of rice, millet, or pasta and top with garnish. Accompany with a green salad.

1 tablespoon olive oil

1 cup chopped onion (1 medium onion)

1 teaspoon basil

2–3 cloves garlic, minced

1/4 cup tahini

1 cup water

1 tablespoon arrowroot

1 tablespoon lemon juice

2 tablespoons salsa, hot or mild to taste

2 tablespoons tamari, or to taste

2 cups cooked and drained chick peas (see page 169)

Garnish: sliced roasted red peppers, chopped fresh tomatoes, and minced fresh parsley or cilantro

Spicy Pintos and Corn

Serves: 4   Time: 20 minutes

2 tablespoons olive oil

1 cup chopped onion
(1 medium onion)

1 teaspoon basil

1/4 teaspoon oregano

2 teaspoons chili powder

1 teaspoon cumin

3 cups cooked pinto beans,
drained of their cooking liquid*
(see page 169)

2 cups corn (frozen or cut from
2 ears)

1 medium–large tomato puréed
in a blender or food processor
(about 1 cup purée)

3 tablespoons tamari, or to
taste

1 tablespoon lemon juice

Garnish: slices of avocado,
minced fresh parsley or
cilantro, and hot or mild salsa.

1. Heat the oil in a large skillet. Add the onion, basil, oregano, chili powder, and cumin. Sauté over medium heat for 4–5 minutes or until the onion is tender. Place 1 cup of the beans in a small bowl and mash them with a fork. Add them to the skillet with the onion, then add the remaining beans, and the corn, tomato purée, tamari, and lemon juice. Cover and simmer for about 5 minutes.

2. Serve on a bed of rice surrounded by the avocado and sprinkled with the parsley or cilantro. Serve the salsa on the side and accompany with a big green salad.

* For this dish I used beans that were sprouted one day before cooking. Sprouting is not necessary, but if you wish to do so, see page 74.

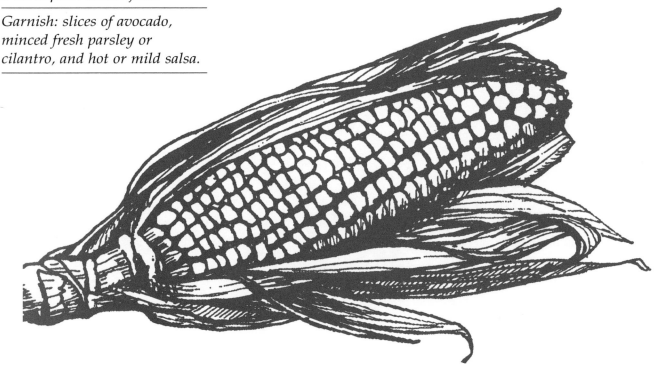

Red Lentil Curry

A jar of red lentils in your cupboard can come in very handy when you need to prepare a meal in a hurry because they cook in about 15 minutes.

Serves: 3   Time: 30 minutes

1. Heat the oil in a heavy, medium-sized pan or large skillet with a tight-fitting lid. Add the onion, celery, and curry powder. Stir and sauté over medium heat for about 5 minutes or until the vegetables are just beginning to become tender. Add the bell pepper and stir for about 1 minute longer. Add the lentils, mix well, and add the water. Stir and cover. Bring the water to a boil, then reduce the heat and simmer, stirring occasionally, for 15–20 minutes or until the lentils are tender and the water has been absorbed.

2. Remove the pan from the heat and add the miso. Mix well.

3. Serve on a bed of brown Basmati rice and sprinkle with the garnish. Add a salad of fresh leafy lettuce, ripe tomatoes, and chopped scallions, topped with Sweet Red Pepper Dressing (page 90).

2 tablespoons oil

1/2 cup finely chopped onion (1/2 medium onion)

1/2 cup finely chopped celery (1 stalk)

1 tablespoon curry powder

1 red bell pepper, chopped

1 cup dry red lentils, rinsed and picked over

2 cups water

2 tablespoons white miso

Garnish: chopped fresh parsley or cilantro

Refried Beans

Make this when you have some leftover beans.

Serves: 3–4   Time: 20 minutes

1. Heat the oil in a skillet. Add the onion and sauté for about 4 minutes or until it begins to become tender. Add the bell pepper and sauté for about 3 minute longer. Add the chili powder, cumin, basil, and oregano and sauté about 2 minutes longer.

2. Add the beans, cooking liquid, tamari, and lemon juice or vinegar. Simmer for about 5 minutes. With a potato masher or large fork, mash the beans, adding a little more water if the mixture gets dry. Add the cayenne pepper or hot sauce.

3. Serve with warm corn tortillas and a salad of lettuce, tomato, and avocado. If you like, toast the tortillas in a toaster oven, spread with the beans, and top with chopped tomato, onion, lettuce, and mashed avocado.

*Kidney, pinto, and Anasazi beans all work well (see page 169).

1 tablespoon olive oil

1 cup chopped onion (1 medium onion)

1/2 bell pepper, diced

2 teaspoons chili powder

1 teaspoon cumin

1 teaspoon basil

1/2 teaspoon oregano

2 cups cooked beans*

1/4 cup bean cooking liquid

2 tablespoons tamari (if the beans are not salted)

1 tablespoon lemon juice or vinegar

Dash of cayenne pepper or hot sauce, or to taste

Adzuki Walnut Croquettes

Yield: 4 croquettes; serves 2–4   Time: 25 minutes

1 cup whole grain bread crumbs

1/2 cup walnuts

1 cup cooked and drained adzuki beans (see page 169)

1 tablespoon vegetable broth powder

2 teaspoons tamari

1/4 teaspoon sea salt, or to taste

1/2 teaspoon cumin

1/4 cup minced onion (1/2 small onion)

1 egg

1–2 tablespoons oil, or as needed to brown patties

1. Place the bread crumbs in a medium bowl. Coarsely grind the walnuts in a blender or food processor and add them to the crumbs. Coarsely grind the adzuki beans in a food processor or mash them with a fork and add them to the bowl. Add the remaining ingredients, except for the oil, and mix well.

2. Shape the mixture into four patties. Heat the oil in a skillet and fry the patties over medium heat until they are brown on the bottom. Turn them over and brown the other side.

Good with catsup, rice, and a salad or with a sauce and steamed vegetables. Or serve them on whole grain burger buns or English muffins with mustard, slices of tomato, pickle, and lettuce.

Bean and Bulgur Burgers

This is a good recipe to use up some leftover beans.

1/2 cup bulgur wheat

1 cup water

2 cups cooked and drained pinto beans (see page 169)

1/2 cup finely chopped onion (1 small onion)

2 tablespoons natto miso*

2 cups natural whole grain corn flakes

2 tablespoons oil, or as needed to brown patties

Yield: 8–9 patties; serves: 3   Time: 30 minutes

1. Place the bulgur in a saucepan with the water. Cover and bring to a boil. Reduce the heat and simmer about 10 minutes, or until the water has been absorbed.

2. Place the beans in a food processor and blend, or mash with a potato masher. Place the cooked bulgur in a large bowl. Add the bean purée, onion, and miso. Mix well.

3. Crumble in the corn flakes. Mix well. Shape the mixture into patties. Heat the oil in a skillet. Place the patties in the skillet (about four at a time) and cook over medium heat until they are brown on the bottom. Turn them over and brown the other side.

4. Serve plain or with a sauce. Add some steamed vegetables and a green salad.

*Natto miso gives a mild, spicy flavor to these burgers; you may substitute barley miso or any other miso.

Vegetable Croquettes

Serves: 3   Time: 30 minutes

1. Pour the soymilk into a small saucepan and bring it to a boil. Place the oat flakes in a large bowl. Pour the hot soymilk over the oat flakes. Mix and then let stand for about 10 minutes.

2. Add the carrots, celery, onion, garlic, sage, and potato flakes to the oat mixture. Mix well.

3. Grind the sunflower seeds coarsely in a food processor or blender and add them to the oat-vegetable mixture. Add the tamari and mix well. Shape the mixture into patties.

4. Heat the oil in a skillet. Slowly brown the patties three or four at a time, adding more oil as needed to prevent sticking.

*Arrowhead Mills Potato Flakes include the nutritious skins.

1 cup soymilk

1½ cups oat flakes

1 cup grated carrots

⅔ cups finely chopped celery

½ cup finely chopped onion

2 cloves garlic, pressed

1 teaspoon sage

½ cup potato flakes*

½ cup sunflower seeds

2 tablespoons tamari

1 tablespoon oil, or as needed to brown croquettes

Teff Burgers

If you have never tried teff, try this easy recipe. Teff's mild, subtly sweet flavor and distinctive texture are very appealing.

Yield: 6 burgers; serves 3–4   Time: 30 minutes

1. Place the teff, water, thyme, garlic, and salt in a medium sauce pan. Bring to a boil. Cover, reduce the heat, and simmer for 15 minutes. Stir the mixture a couple of times toward the end of cooking.

2. Place the teff in a shallow pan to cool. When it's cool enough to handle, add the scallions and mix well. Shape into six patties.

3. Heat the oil in a skillet and fry the patties until they are brown on the bottom. Turn patties over and place a thin slice of soy cheese or dairy cheese on each patty. Cook until the patties are brown on the bottom and the cheese is melted.

4. Serve the burgers on the buns with lettuce and tomato. If you like, spread the buns with mustard and top with sliced pickle.

VARIATION:

Omit the cheese, lettuce, tomato, mustard, and buns and serve with a sauce such as Tahini Brown Sauce (page 97), or Creamy Tomato Sauce (page 95).

1 cup teff

3 cups water

1 teaspoon thyme

2 cloves garlic, pressed

¼ teaspoon sea salt

3 scallions, chopped

2 tablespoons light sesame oil

6 slices soy cheese or dairy cheese

6 Burger Buns (see page 118)

6 slices tomato

6 lettuce leaves

Mustard or pickles (optional)

Leftover Corn Bread and Beans

I won't give quantities for this easy dish; just use what you have.

Leftover or stale corn bread

Cooked beans in their cooking liquid (see page 169)

Soy cheese

Salsa, to taste

Garnish: chopped cilantro, parsley, or scallions

Time: about 15 minutes

1. Use any corn bread. The best beans are pinto, kidney, Anasazi, or black beans cooked and seasoned to taste with salt or tamari, chili powder, cumin, and basil. Don't drain the beans; keep them in their cooking liquid, enough to make the beans juicy but not soupy.

2. Cut pieces of corn bread in half and place them in an oven-proof dish. Toast them under the broiler or in a toaster oven for about 3 minutes or until they are lightly browned.

3. Heat the beans and their liquid in a heavy saucepan. Pour the beans over the corn bread and sprinkle with soy cheese. Broil to melt the cheese and top generously with salsa and garnish.

Hot Tofu and Tahini Sandwich

Tofu and tahini make a great combo in this nutritious sandwich.

1 tablespoon tamari

2 slices firm tofu sliced from the wide side of the block, each a little less than 1/2 inch thick

1 1/2 tablespoons nutritional yeast

2 teaspoons toasted sesame oil

4 slices whole grain bread

1 tablespoon tahini (approximately)

Fresh Boston lettuce

Yield: 2 sandwiches   Time: 10–15 minutes

1. Place the tamari on a small plate. Drop the slices of tofu, one at a time, into the tamari, and turn them over to coat both sides. Sprinkle the nutritional yeast over both sides of each slice of tofu.

2. Heat the oil in a skillet (nonstick works best). Place the slices of tofu in the skillet and cook over medium heat until brown on the bottom. Turn over and cook on the other side. If there is any leftover tamari, dribble it over the browned tops of the tofu slices while the bottoms cook.

3. Lightly toast the bread and spread two of the toasted slices with tahini. Place the browned tofu on the tahini, top with the lettuce, and top with the remaining slices of toast. Serve immediately.

Open-Faced Bean Sandwich

I like to make this for a quick lunch when I have some leftover beans and no cooked grain to go with them.

Serves: 1   Time: 10–15 minutes

¹/₂–1 cup seasoned leftover beans (any kind)

1–2 slices whole grain bread

1. Leave the beans in their cooking liquid. If they have not been seasoned, add tamari or salt, garlic, scallions, herbs, or chili powder and cumin to taste.

2. Heat the beans in a saucepan and spoon them over the bread. If you like, you may toast the bread first.

3. Serve with a big green salad and perhaps some slices of tomato and avocado.

Open-Faced Collard Sandwich with Hummus Sauce

My husband and I both love this sandwich, weird though it may appear. It makes a healthful and delicious lunch.

Yield: 5 sandwiches   Time: 20–35 minutes

1 pound collard greens

1 recipe Hummus Sauce (see page 100)

5 slices whole grain bread, toasted

1. Wash the collards and chop them. Steam or pressure-cook until tender. To pressure-cook, bring the pressure up and cook for 1 minute. Then let the pot cool down on its own.

2. Prepare the sauce.

3. Drain the cooked collard greens and place a generous helping on each slice of toast. Top with the sauce and serve.

Seitan Sandwich

This is a satisfying sandwich that my husband enjoys for lunch.

2 slices whole grain bread

1 teaspoon white or yellow miso

1 tablespoon tahini

Thinly sliced seitan

Thin slice of onion

Slice of tomato

Lettuce or sprouts

Yield: 1 sandwich   Time: 10 minutes

1. Spread one slice of bread with the miso, and spread the other slice with tahini. Cover one slice with seitan. Top with a slice of onion, a slice of tomato, and a leaf of lettuce or some sprouts. Top with the remaining slice of bread.

2. Serve with soup and salad.

Cashew Burgers

Serves: 4   Time: 30 minutes

1 cup raw cashew pieces

1 cup grated carrots
(2 small carrots)

$1/3$ cup minced onion
(1 small onion)

1 cup whole wheat bread crumbs

2 tablespoons nutritional yeast

1 egg

2 tablespoons tamari

$1/2$ teaspoon celery seeds

1 teaspoon basil

1–2 tablespoons oil, as needed to brown patties

1. Place the cashews in a blender and grind them coarsely. Transfer them to a medium bowl, add the remaining ingredients, except for the oil, and mix well.

2. Shape the mixture into patties. Heat the oil in a skillet. Place the patties in the skillet and fry over medium heat until they are brown and crisp on the bottom. Turn the patties over and cook the other side.

These burgers are delicious with Quick and Light Fresh Tomato Sauce (page 96).

11. DESSERTS

Making the desserts for this book was a lot of fun, as well as a challenge. The main challenge was to keep the recipes as low as possible in fat and concentrated sweetener and still make them look and taste wonderful. Other challenges were to make them dairyless, sometimes wheatless and eggless, too, so that vegans or persons with allergies could enjoy them. No saturated cooking fat, such as butter or margarine, is called for, and the sweetener is usually fruit or malt. Occasionally honey, molasses, sucanat, or maple syrup is used. All these desserts were sampled by several people, and only when a dessert quickly disappeared did I include the recipe for it in the book.

Healthful, homemade desserts are a perfect way to introduce your friends and family to natural foods. Everyone likes a homemade pie, cake, or cookies. Wait until they've tried it before telling them how healthful it is.

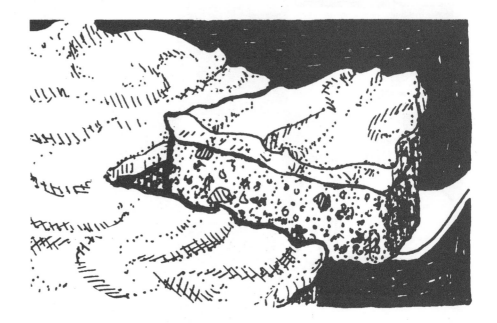

Popcorn Maple Nut Snack

Yield: about 8 cups   Time: 30 minutes

1. In a saucepan, combine the tahini, maple syrup, and vanilla. Mix well and heat, stirring constantly, until thoroughly mixed (3 minutes or less).

2. Place the popcorn and nuts in a large medium bowl. Pour the liquid mixture over it and mix well. Spread the popcorn mixture on unoiled cookie sheets and bake at 300°F for 10–15 minutes or until the tips are browned. Watch carefully lest the popcorn burn. Cool completely and break apart.

This recipe is nice for holiday get-togethers or for a children's party.

2 tablespoons tahini

1/2 cup maple syrup

1 teaspoon vanilla

6–7 cups popped popcorn

1 cup mixed raw unsalted nuts

Almond Candy

This candy is sweet and pretty, perfect for packing in decorative boxes for holiday gifts.

Yield: about 28 pieces   Time: 30 minutes

1. Place the almonds in a blender. Grind them to a powder. Stir them occasionally so that all the almonds are finely ground.

2. Place the ground almonds in a medium bowl. Add the malt powder and mix well. Add the vanilla and mix again. Add the honey. Using your hand and a spoon, mix the ingredients until thoroughly blended. The ingredients should stick together when pressed. If not, add 1–2 teaspoons more honey.

3. Wash your hands before proceeding. Shape the mixture into small balls about half the size of a walnut. Lay the balls on a plate.

4. Wash your hands again. Then place one of the balls in the palm of your hand and press a whole almond into the top. The ball will flatten out somewhat. Press the candy around the almond a bit so that the almond sticks to the candy. Repeat with the remaining balls and almonds.

5. Place the coconut in a plastic bag. Place about five pieces of candy at a time in the bag. Roll the candy around inside the bag until it is coated with coconut. Remove the candy and place it on a plate. Repeat until all the candy is coated with coconut. Store candy covered in the refrigerator or serve immediately.

1 cup whole raw almonds

1/2 cup malt powder

1 teaspoon vanilla

1/4 cup honey (approximately)

About 28 extra almonds

1/3 cup finely shredded unsweetened coconut

Peanut Butter Balls

1/2 cup peanut butter

1 teaspoon vanilla

2 tablespoons fruit-sweetened orange marmalade

1/2 cup raisins (optional)

1/3 cup malt powder (approximately)

1/4 cup finely shredded unsweetened coconut

Back in the 1970s, we used to make a similar recipe, but it contained lots of honey and powdered milk. Here is a version that is a little lighter for today.

Yield: about 16 balls   Time: 15–20 minutes

1. In a medium bowl, cream together the peanut butter, vanilla, and marmalade. Add the raisins, if desired, and mix well. Add about 1/4 cup of the malt powder and mix well, using your hands if necessary. Then add as much of the remaining malt powder as necessary to make the candy firm but not crumbly.

2. Shape the mixture into small balls. Place the coconut in a plastic bag. Place a few balls at a time in the bag and roll them around to coat them with coconut. The candy can be eaten right away but is better after being refrigerated in a covered container for a few hours.

Halvah

1/2 cup tahini

2 tablespoons honey

1 teaspoon vanilla

1/2 cup malt powder (approximately)

1/4 cup finely shredded unsweetened coconut

This tastes even better than halvah that is sweetened with lots of white sugar.

Yield: about 20 small balls   Time: 15–20 minutes

1. In a medium bowl, cream together the tahini, honey, and vanilla. Add 1/3 cup of the malt powder and mix well, using your hands if necessary. Leaving the mixture in the bowl, knead in as much of the remaining malt powder as necessary to make the candy firm.

2. Shape the mixture into small balls about half the size of a walnut. Place the coconut in a plastic bag. Place a few balls at a time in the bag and roll them around to coat them with coconut. The halvah can be eaten right away but is better after being refrigerated in a covered container for a few hours.

Fruit and Nut Squares

I once brought this simple recipe to a potluck, and it was gone before the fancy whipped-cream desserts were even touched.

Yield: 32 two-inch squares

Time: 20 minutes to prepare; 25 minutes to bake

2 cups date pieces

1 cup raisins

2 teaspoons vanilla

1¼ cups peach nectar or other fruit juice

2 cups walnuts

½ cup oat flour

½ cup barley flour

½ cup malt powder

1 teaspoon cinnamon

¼ cup oil

1. Place the date pieces, raisins, vanilla, and peach nectar in a saucepan. Bring to a boil. Cover, reduce the heat, and simmer for about 5 minutes or until the liquid has been absorbed and the dates have formed a purée. Set aside.

2. Place 1 cup of the walnuts in a blender or food processor and grind them. Place the remaining nuts on a cutting board and coarsely chop them with a sharp knife.

3. Place all the nuts in a medium bowl. Add the oat flour, barley flour, malt powder, and cinnamon. Mix well. With a fork, slowly stir in the oil and mix until the oil is thoroughly incorporated into the mixture. The mixture should look like coarse crumbs.

4. Sprinkle a little more than half of the crumb mixture evenly into a lightly oiled 8-x-8-inch baking dish. Spread the date purée evenly over the crumb mixture, and sprinkle the surface with the remaining crumb mixture. Lightly press the crumb mixture into the date purée.

5. Bake at 350°F for 25 minutes. Cut into 2-inch squares. Let cool for about 30 minutes before removing from the pan.

Lazy-Day Blackberry Cobbler

This recipe is fun to make; the fruit starts out on the top but ends up on the bottom after baking.

Serves: 5–6

Time: 20 minutes to prepare; 30 minutes to bake

¼ cup oil

¾ cup sucanat

1 cup whole wheat pastry flour

1 teaspoon baking powder

¾ cup soymilk

2 cups blackberries

½ cup walnuts

1. Place the oil in the bottom of a 7-x-11-inch baking dish.

2. In a mixing bowl, combine the sucanat, flour, and baking powder. Mix well. Add the soymilk and beat until smooth. Pour this batter over the oil in the baking dish, but do not stir.

3. Arrange the blackberries over the batter and sprinkle with the nuts. Bake at 350°F for 30 minutes.

VARIATIONS:

Substitute sliced raspberries or blueberries for the blackberries.

Blueberry Crumble

Serves: 4

Time: 15–20 minutes to prepare;
20–25 minutes to bake

1 pint blueberries

1 tablespoon arrowroot

1/4 cup concentrated fruit sweetener

1/2 cup barley flour

1/2 cup oat flour

1/2 cup malt powder

1/4 teaspoon nutmeg

1/4 cup oil

1 teaspoon vanilla

1. Wash, stem, and drain the blueberries. Place them in an oiled loaf pan, 4 1/2 x 8 1/2 x 2 1/2 inches. Add the arrowroot and the fruit concentrate and mix well. Set aside.

2. In a medium bowl, mix together the two flours, malt powder, and nutmeg. Add the oil and vanilla and mix well with a fork until the oil is distributed evenly throughout the mixture. Sprinkle the flour mixture evenly over the blueberries in the loaf pan.

3. Bake at 350°F for 20–25 minutes or until the crust is golden brown and the blueberries are bubbly. Serve warm or cool, plain or topped with ice cream (or Rice Dream).

Peach Crumble

This quick and easy dessert drew raves from everyone who tried it.

5 cups sliced peaches (5–6 medium peaches)

1/4 cup concentrated fruit sweetener

1 tablespoon arrowroot

1 1/2 cups whole grain bread crumbs

1 cup oat flour

1 teaspoon cinnamon

2/3 cup sucanat

1/3 cup oil

Serves: 4–6

Time: 20 minutes to prepare; 30 minutes to bake

1. Place the peaches in a lightly oiled 2-quart baking dish. In a small bowl, mix together the sweetener and the arrowroot. Pour this mixture over the peaches. Set aside.

2. In a medium bowl, combine the bread crumbs, oat flour, cinnamon, and sucanat. Mix well. Stir in the oil and mix until the oil is evenly distributed throughout the mixture. Sprinkle this mixture evenly over the peaches in the baking dish.

3. Bake at 350°F for 30 minutes or until peaches are tender and the top is brown. Serve either warm or cold.

No-Bake Apple Pie

This pie is delicious with Pecan Pie Crust (page 138).

Yield: 9-inch pie   Time: 15 minutes to prepare;
1½ hours to chill

1. If the apples have been sprayed, peel them; if they were grown organically, you may leave the peel on, but wash them well. Cut the apples in quarters, remove the core, and cut flesh in thin wedges.

2. Pour the soymilk into a heavy saucepan. Add the vanilla and the agar flakes. Stir, then add the sliced apples. Bring to a boil, stirring constantly. Cover, lower the heat, and simmer, stirring occasionally, for about 5 minutes or until the agar flakes have dissolved and the apples are just tender. Be careful not to break the apple slices while stirring. Remove the pan from the heat and gently transfer the apples to a medium bowl with a slotted spoon.

3. In another medium bowl, mix together the applesauce, honey, and the soymilk in which the apples were cooked. Pour this mixture into the baked pie crust.

4. If any apple slices have fallen apart during the cooking, push these down into the applesauce mixture. Arrange the remaining apple slices to overlap in a circle on the top of the pie, pushing them down into the applesauce mixture just enough so that they will hold together when you slice the pie. Sprinkle with cinnamon, if desired. Chill until firm.

3 small–medium cooking apples

1 cup soymilk

2 teaspoons vanilla

1 heaping tablespoon agar flakes

1 cup unsweetened applesauce, at room temperature

¼ cup honey

9-inch baked pie crust

Cinnamon (optional)

Rhubarb Raisin Pie

An old-fashioned dessert made a little healthier.

Yield: 9-inch pie   Time: 20 minutes to prepare;
45 minutes to bake

1. Prepare the pie crust. Line a 9-inch pie pan with the bottom crust. Rub 1 tablespoon of the arrowroot over the bottom and the sides of the crust. Fill the crust with the rhubarb and raisins.

2. In a small bowl, mix the remaining arrowroot with the honey. Drizzle the honey mixture over the rhubarb and raisins in the crust. Sprinkle with the cinnamon.

3. Cover the pie with the top crust. Flute the edges and cut some holes in the top to allow the steam to escape. Bake on the bottom rack of a 350°F oven for 45 minutes or until rhubarb is tender when stabbed with a knife through one of the steam vents and the crust is golden brown.

1 double Whole Wheat Pie Crust (see page 137)

2 tablespoons arrowroot

4 cups sliced rhubarb

1¼ cups raisins

⅓ cup honey

1 teaspoon cinnamon

Donna's Pumpkin Pie

9-inch Whole Wheat Pie Crust
(see page 137)

2 cups cooked, drained, and
mashed pumpkin* (or canned
pumpkin)

1 package (10½ ounces) soft
silken tofu

1 teaspoon vanilla

1 cup date pieces

½ cup rice syrup

1 teaspoon cinnamon

1 teaspoon allspice

¼ teaspoon nutmeg

For Thanksgiving, my friend Donna asked me to make her a pumpkin pie that would neither aggravate her allergies to eggs and dairy products nor contain sugar or honey. The result tasted very similar to a traditional pumpkin pie, and Donna's family loved it.

Yield: 9-inch pie

Time: 30 minutes to prepare;
50–60 minutes to bake

1. Prepare the pie crust.

2. Blend together the remaining ingredients in a blender or food processor. Do this in more than one batch if necessary. Pour the blended mixture into the crust. Bake at 350°F for 50–60 minutes or until a knife inserted into the center of the pie comes out almost clean.

*To cook a pumpkin, cut a hole at the stem end as if you were making a jack-o-lantern. With a large spoon, scrape out the seeds and the stringy parts. Place the pumpkin on a cookie sheet and bake at 350°F for about 1 hour or until it can be easily pierced through the side with a knife. Let the pumpkin cool for easier handling, cut it in half, and then scrape the flesh away from the skin. Drain off any excess liquid and mash the flesh.

Pecan Pie

9-inch Whole Wheat Pie Crust
(see page 137)

1 cup pecan halves

1 cup water

1 rounded tablespoon agar
flakes

1 cup barley malt syrup

½ cup rice syrup

1 teaspoon vanilla

This pecan pie is a little lighter and less sweet than the traditional recipe and even more delicious.

Yield: 9-inch pie

Time: 30 minutes to prepare;
2–3 hours to chill

1. Prepare the pie crust. With a fork, pierce the top and the sides of the crust. Bake at 350°F for about 20 minutes and let cool.

2. Place the pecans in an oven-proof pan and bake at 350°F, stirring occasionally, for about 10 minutes or until they are lightly roasted. You may use a toaster oven for this step.

3. In a medium saucepan, combine the water and the agar flakes. Bring the mixture to a boil, stirring often, until the agar is dissolved. Add the barley malt, rice syrup, and vanilla. Mix well.

4. Pour this mixture into the baked pie crust. Top with the pecans and refrigerate until firm.

Dried Fruit Pie

A rich, fruit-sweetened pie that is perfect for winter.

Yield: 7½-inch pie   Time: 30 minutes to prepare; 2 hours to chill

1. Prepare the pie crust. Let it cool while you make the filling:

2. Combine the remaining ingredients in a saucepan. Bring the mixture to a boil and cook over medium-low heat for about 10 minutes, or until the fruit is plump and the agar is dissolved. Let the mixture cool at room temperature for 15–20 minutes or in the refrigerator or freezer for 5–10 minutes. The mixture should still be more than lukewarm: cool enough to keep the crust from becoming soggy but not so cool that it starts to set.

3. Fill the baked pie shell with the fruit mixture and place the pie, uncovered, in the refrigerator to chill until set, 1–2 hours.

Serve the pie plain or with Tofu Vanilla Whip (page 265).

1 Barley Walnut Pie Crust (see page 140)

2 cups apple juice

1 slightly rounded tablespoon agar flakes

2 tablespoons lemon juice

1 teaspoon allspice

¼ teaspoon coriander

1½ cups raisins

1 cup chopped dried apricots

Tropical Island Pie

This healthful desert is made with fresh, raw pineapple and sweetened with fruit.

Yield: 9-inch pie   Time: 20 minutes to prepare; 1½ hours to chill

1. Prepare the pie crust, let it cool, and place the pineapple in it.

2. Pour the orange juice into a medium saucepan and add the vanilla, date pieces, and agar flakes. Bring the mixture to a boil. Reduce the heat, cover, and simmer for about 10 minutes or until the agar has dissolved and the date pieces have become a purée. Pour the juice mixture over the pineapple chunks in the crust. Sprinkle with coconut. Chill until set, about 1½ hours.

9-inch baked pie crust (the Pecan Pie Crust, page 138, is good)

3 cups fresh pineapple, cut into bite-sized chunks

1½ cups orange juice

2 teaspoons vanilla

1 cup date pieces

1 rounded tablespoon agar flakes

Garnish: raw or lightly toasted grated coconut (optional)

Blueberry "Cream" Pie

1 Pecan Pie Crust
(see page 138)

1 cup pear juice (apple or white grape juice would also be good)

1 slightly rounded tablespoon agar flakes

1 package (10½ ounces) extra-firm silken tofu

⅓ cup honey

1 tablespoon vanilla

1 tablespoon lemon juice

1 teaspoon grated lemon peel

1½ cups blueberries

At the end of every cooking course I teach, everyone brings a dish to share. One time, I made this pie, and it was gone before I had a chance to taste it!

Yield: 9-inch pie   Time: 15 minutes to prepare; 2 hours to chill

1. Prepare the pie crust and let it cool.

2. In a saucepan, mix together the juice and the agar flakes. Bring the mixture to a boil. Reduce the heat and simmer for about 10 minutes or until the agar is dissolved.

3. While the juice mixture is simmering, place the tofu, honey, vanilla, lemon juice, and lemon peel in a blender or food processor. Blend until smooth and creamy. (If you are using a blender, you may have to do this in two batches.) While the mixture is still blending, pour in the dissolved agar mixture. Blend until thoroughly mixed.

4. Pour the tofu mixture into the baked pie shell. Top with the blueberries, pushing them into the surface a little so that they stick to the pie. Chill for at least 2 hours before serving.

VARIATIONS:

Use strawberries, peaches, nectarines, or pitted cherries instead of blueberries.

Pineapple "Cream" Pie

9-inch baked whole grain pie crust, preferrably Pecan Pie Crust (page 138) or Barley Walnut Pie Crust (page 140)

16-ounce can unsweetened crushed pineapple

1 rounded tablespoon agar flakes

1 tablespoon vanilla

⅓ cup concentrated fruit sweetener

1 package (10½ ounces) extra-firm silken tofu

1 cup strawberries or raspberries (optional)

This easy pie is not too rich.

Yield: 9-inch pie   Time: 20 minutes to prepare; 3 hours to chill

1. Drain the juice from the pineapple into a saucepan. Add the agar flakes and bring the mixture to a boil. Cover, reduce the heat, and simmer, stirring often, for about 10 minutes or until the agar is dissolved.

2. Meanwhile, place the vanilla, fruit sweetener, and tofu in a blender or food processor. Blend until smooth and creamy. Stop the machine occasionally and scrape the sides with a rubber spatula so that the tofu is well blended. Transfer the tofu mixture to a medium bowl.

3. Add the dissolved agar and the pineapple to the tofu mixture and mix well. Fill the pie crust with this mixture. Decorate the top of the pie with strawberries or raspberries, if desired, and chill until set, about 3 hours.

Chocolate Almond "Cream" Pie

Dark chocolate with an almond "cream" topping.

Yield: 9-inch pie

Time: 40 minutes to prepare;
2–3 hours to chill

1. In a medium saucepan, combine the Rice Dream and agar flakes. Bring the mixture to a boil. Cover, reduce the heat to low, and simmer, stirring often, for about 10 minutes, or until the agar is dissolved .

2. Add the sucanat and the chocolate chips. Continue to stir until the chocolate is melted.

3. While the agar is cooking, place the tofu and 1 teaspoon of vanilla in a blender or food processor. Blend until smooth and creamy. Stop the machine occasionally and scrape the sides with a rubber spatula so that the tofu is well blended. When the chocolate is melted, immediately pour the hot mixture onto the tofu mixture. Blend.

4. Pour the filling into the pie crust. Chill until the filling is firm, 1–2 hours.

5. Meanwhile, prepare the topping: Combine the water and agar flakes in a saucepan. Bring the mixture to a boil. Reduce the heat and simmer, stirring occasionally, until the agar is dissolved, about 10 minutes.

6. Pour the hot agar mixture into a blender or food processor with the vanilla, honey, and blanched almonds. Blend until very smooth. Pour this mixture over the chocolate filling in the pie crust. Sprinkle with the toasted almonds and chill until firm, about 1 hour.

*To blanch almonds, place the almonds in a saucepan and cover them with water. Bring the water to a boil and boil for 1–2 minutes. Drain the almonds through a colander and rinse with cool water. Press each almond between your thumb and forefinger with a sideways motion; the skin will slip off easily.

**To toast almonds, place them in an oven-proof pan and bake them at 350°F until they begin to brown, about 10 minutes. Stir the almonds occasionally so that they toast evenly.

CHOCOLATE FILLING:

$1/2$ cup Rice Dream beverage

1 tablespoon agar flakes

$1/3$ cup sucanat

1 cup malt-sweetened chocolate chips

1 package ($10 1/2$ ounces) extra-firm silken tofu

1 teaspoon vanilla

9-inch pie crust, baked and cooled (Pecan Crust, page 138, is good)

ALMOND TOPPING:

1 cup water

$1 1/2$ teaspoons agar flakes

1 teaspoon vanilla

2 tablespoons honey

$1/2$ cup blanched almonds*

3 tablespoons sliced or chopped almonds, toasted**

Peanut Butter "Cream" Pie

Make this for your favorite peanut butter fan.

1 Peanut Butter Pie Crust (see page 139), or any other 9-inch whole grain pie crust

1 package (10¹/₂ ounces) extra-firm silken tofu

¹/₂ cup honey

2 teaspoons natural caramel flavor or vanilla

³/₄ cup peanut butter (smooth or crunchy)

1 cup pear nectar or apple juice

1 tablespoon agar flakes

2 bananas

¹/₃ cup dry-roasted peanuts, carob chips, or chocolate chips*

Yield: 9-inch pie

Time: 20 minutes to prepare; about 2 hours to chill

1. Prepare the pie crust. Let it cool while you make the filling.

2. Place the tofu, honey, caramel flavor or vanilla, and peanut butter in a food processor and blend until smooth and creamy. Stop the machine occasionally and scrape the sides with a rubber spatula so that the mixture is well blended. Set aside.

3. In a saucepan, mix together the pear nectar or apple juice and the agar flakes. Bring to a boil. Reduce the heat and simmer, stirring, for about 10 minutes or until the agar flakes have dissolved.

4. With the food processor running, slowly pour the juice-agar mixture into the container with the tofu-peanut mixture.

5. Slice the bananas and place them in the baked pie crust. Pour the blended mixture over the bananas. Sprinkle with the peanuts or the chocolate or carob chips. Refrigerate the pie until it sets, about 2 hours.

*Look in natural foods stores for carob and chocolate chips that are sweetened with malt and dates and that contain no saturated fat.

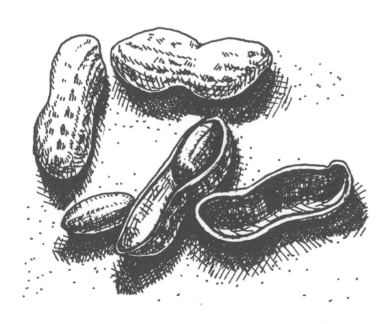

Raspberry "Cream" Pie Supreme

The color of this pie is a gorgeous bright pink, perfect for a special occasion.

Yield: 9-inch pie   Time: 30 minutes to prepare; 3 hours to chill

1. Prepare the pie crust and let it cool.

2. Meanwhile, prepare the filling: Combine the jam, water, and agar flakes in a saucepan. Bring to a boil, reduce the heat, and cook, stirring occasionally, for about 10 minutes or until the agar is completely dissolved.

3. Place the tofu, raspberries, and honey in a food processor. Blend until smooth and creamy. Add the agar mixture and continue to blend until well mixed. Pour the mixture into the baked pie shell. Chill until set, about 2 hours.

4. Meanwhile, prepare the glaze: Combine the jam with the water and agar flakes in a saucepan. Bring to a boil while stirring constantly. Reduce the heat and simmer, stirring often, until the agar is completely dissolved, about 10 minutes. Carefully spread the glaze over the top of the pie. Chill until set, about 30 minutes or more.

*Let frozen raspberries thaw before adding them, with their juices, to the recipe.

VARIATION:

Substitute equal amounts of blackberries or strawberries for the raspberries. If using strawberries, increase the quantity of agar to a heaping (rather than slightly rounded) tablespoon.

---

1 Pecan Pie Crust
(see page 138)

RASPBERRY FILLING:

1/2 cup fruit-sweetened raspberry jam

1/2 cup water

1 slightly rounded tablespoon agar flakes

1 package (10 1/2 ounces) extra-firm silken tofu

2 cups raspberries, fresh or frozen*

1/3 cup honey

GLAZE:

3 tablespoons fruit-sweetened raspberry jam

1/3 cup water

1 teaspoon agar flakes

Oatmeal Raisin Cookies

Yield: about 20 cookies   Time: 20 minutes

1½ cups oat flakes

½ cup barley flour

1 teaspoon baking powder

½ cup sucanat

¼ cup oil

1 egg

2 tablespoons soymilk or fruit juice (approximately)

½ cup sunflower seeds

¾ cup raisins

1. In a large bowl, mix together the oat flakes, barley flour, baking powder, and sucanat. Slowly stir in the oil, mixing with a fork until it is evenly distributed. Add the egg and mix well. Then add just enough soymilk or juice to make the mixture hold together. Add the sunflower seeds and raisins and mix well, using your hands if necessary.

2. Dip a 2-tablespoon measure (such as a coffee scoop) in water to keep dough from sticking to it. Use this measure to scoop the dough onto an oiled cookie sheet. Wet your hand in cool water and flatten each cookie with your palm. Bake at 350°F for 8 minutes.

Oatmeal Molasses Cookies

Yield: about 16 cookies   Time: about 20 minutes

⅓ cup honey

¼ cup molasses

1 egg

¼ cup oil

1 teaspoon cinnamon

½ teaspoon cloves

½ teaspoon baking soda

¾ cup whole wheat pastry flour

1¼ cups oat flakes

½ cup raisins

1. In a large bowl, combine the honey and the molasses. Add the egg and beat. Gradually stir in the oil. Add the cinnamon, cloves, and baking soda Mix well. Stir in the flour, oat flakes, and raisins. Mix well.

2. Drop by the spoonful onto an unoiled cookie sheet. Bake at 350°F for 10–12 minutes.

TIPS FOR BAKING COOKIES

- Preheat the oven.

- Bake cookies on the top rack of the oven.

- Most cookies bake quickly; check them often lest they burn.

- If the tops of the cookies do not brown, turn the oven to broil for a minute or two. Watch carefully so that you don't burn the cookies.

- Leave the cookies on the cookie sheet for about 5 minutes before removing them.

- Let cookies cool completely before wrapping them.

- Store cookies in an airtight tin or in plastic bags in the refrigerator.

Jam-Filled Tahini Cookies

Use your favorite flavor of fruit-sweetened jam to make these cookies.

Yield: 18–20 cookies   Time: 35 minutes

1. In a mixing bowl, cream together the tahini, oil, syrup, and vanilla. Slowly stir in the flour to form a stiff dough. Mix with your hands and knead the dough a few times, if necessary, to make it hold together.

2. Roll the dough into 18–20 balls the size of walnuts. Place the balls of dough on an oiled cookie sheet. Make a well in the center of each cookie by pressing it with your thumb. If you wish, you may shape the well with your fingers (Drawing a). Drop a teaspoon of filling into each well (Drawing b).

3. Bake at 350°F for 15 minutes on the top rack of the oven. If the cookies are not cooked on the top, turn the oven to broil and cook for a couple of minutes more. Watch closely so they do not burn.

| 1/2 cup tahini |
| 2 tablespoons oil |
| 1/4 cup maple syrup |
| 1 teaspoon vanilla |
| 1 cup whole wheat pastry flour |
| 1/2 cup fruit-sweetened jam |

a.

b.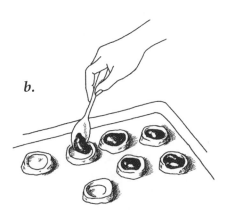

Carob Drop Cookies

These are very moist and delicious. Even my husband, who says he does not like carob, enjoyed them.

Yield: about 30 cookies   Time: 25 minutes

1. Combine the water, oil, maple syrup, and vanilla in a large bowl. Mix well.

2. Sift together the carob powder, flour, and baking powder. Add the flour mixture to the liquid mixture and mix until just blended. Don't overmix. Fold in the chocolate or carob chips and the walnuts, if desired.

3. Drop by the spoonful onto an oiled baking sheet. Leave some space between the cookies for them to expand. Bake at 350°F for 8–10 minutes. Cool on the baking sheets.

| 1/2 cup water |
| 1/3 cup oil |
| 1/2 cup maple syrup |
| 1 teaspoon vanilla |
| 1/4 cup carob powder |
| 1 1/4 cups barley flour |
| 2 teaspoons baking powder |
| 1/2 cup malt-sweetened chocolate or carob chips |
| 1/2 cup chopped walnuts (optional) |

Barley Chocolate Chip and Walnut Cookies

1½ cups barley flour

3½ teaspoons baking powder

¼ cup oil

½ cup rice syrup or malt syrup

2 teaspoons vanilla

1 large egg

1 cup finely chopped walnuts

1 cup chocolate or carob chips*

These wheatless, grain-sweetened cookies are really good, yet not too sweet or rich.

Yield: about 20 cookies　　　　　　　　Time: 20–25 minutes

1. Place the barley flour in a large bowl. Add the baking powder and mix well. Slowly stir in the oil and work it through the flour with a fork until it is evenly distributed. Add the rice syrup or malt syrup, vanilla, and egg. Mix until a stiff dough is formed. Add the walnuts and the chocolate or carob chips and mix until they are evenly distributed throughout the dough.

2. Dip a 2-tablespoon measure (such as a coffee scoop) in water to keep dough from sticking to it. Use this measure to scoop the dough onto an oiled cookie sheet. Wet your hand in cool water and flatten each cookie with your palm. Bake at 350°F for 10–12 minutes.

*Look in natural foods stores for chocolate or carob chips that are sweetened with malt or date sugar and that contain no saturated fat.

VARIATIONS:

• You may substitute ⅓ cup of honey for the rice or malt syrup. The batter will not be as stiff; it will drop nicely from the spoon, and you won't need to flatten it with your hand afterward. The baking temperature and time will be the same.

• *Date Pecan Cookies:* Substitute pecans for the walnuts and dates for the chocolate chips. You may also substitute natural caramel flavoring for the vanilla.

No-Bake Carob Oatmeal Cookies

Yield: about 16 cookies   Time: 25 minutes

1. In a medium saucepan, combine the sucanat, carob powder, soymilk, and oil. While stirring constantly, bring the mixture to a boil. Cook at a rolling boil for 1½ minutes. This cooking is necessary for the cookies to set.

2. Add the peanut butter and the vanilla and mix well Add the oat flakes and mix again. Drop the mixture by the spoonful onto a sheet of waxed paper. Cookies will harden as they cool. They are better after they have set for a while.

1 cup sucanat

¼ cup carob powder

¼ cup soymilk

2 tablespoons oil

⅓ cup peanut butter (smooth or crunchy)

1 teaspoon vanilla

1½ cups oat flakes

Double Peanut Butter Cookies

Yield: about 24 cookies   Time: 20 minutes

1. In a mixing bowl, cream together the peanut butter, oil, malt syrup, vanilla, and soymilk. In another bowl, mix together the sucanat, oat flakes, barley flour, and baking powder. Add the dry mixture to the peanut butter mixture, add the peanuts, and mix well, using your hands if necessary.

2. Drop the dough by the heaping tablespoonful onto an oiled cookie sheet. Flatten each cookie out by pressing it down with a fork. Dip the fork in water to keep it from sticking to the dough. Bake at 350°F for 8–10 minutes.

¾ cup peanut butter

¼ cup oil

½ cup malt syrup

2 teaspoons vanilla

2 tablespoons soymilk

½ cup sucanat

1 cup oat flakes

¾ cup barley flour

2 teaspoons baking powder

½ cup dry-roasted unsalted peanuts

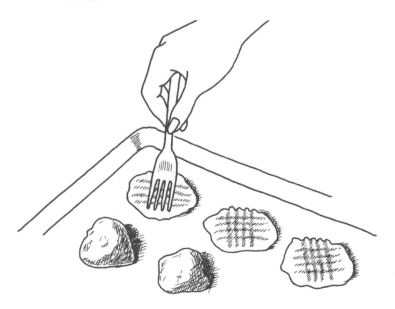

Gingerbread

This eggless, wheatless cake is spicy but not too sweet.

1 cup barley flour

1/2 cup oat flour

2 teaspoons cinnamon

1/2 teaspoon allspice

1/4 cup sucanat

1 tablespoon baking powder

1 package (10 1/2 ounces) firm silken tofu

2 tablespoons oil

1/4 cup molasses

1 rounded tablespoon finely grated fresh ginger

1/2 cup soymilk

1/2 cup chopped walnuts

1/2 cup raisins

Serves: 9　　　　　　Time: 20 minutes to prepare; 30 minutes to bake

1. Sift together the flours, cinnamon, allspice, sucanat, and baking powder. Set aside.

2. Place the tofu, oil, and molasses in a blender or food processor and blend until smooth and creamy. Transfer the mixture to a large bowl. Add the ginger and the soymilk and mix well.

3. Add the flour mixture to the tofu mixture and beat with a wooden spoon just enough to mix well. Fold in the walnuts and the raisins. Transfer the mixture to an oiled and floured 8-x-8-inch cake pan. Bake at 350°F for 30 minutes or until a toothpick inserted into the center of the cake comes out clean.

4. Serve warm or cool. Gingerbread is good plain or topped with either Lemon Mousse Topping (page 265) or Grandma Agnes's Sweet-and-Sour Dessert Sauce (page 262).

Holiday Fruitcake

Everyone who has tasted this fruitcake has loved it. It contains no wheat, added sugar, or oil. There's lots of dried fruit (I favor unsulfured); you'll find it easier to cut with scissors than with a knife.

1 1/2 cups strawberry juice*

1/2 cup chopped dried papaya

1 cup chopped dried pineapple

1/2 cup raisins

1/2 cup chopped dried apricots

1/2 cup chopped dried figs

1 cup chopped walnuts

2 eggs

2 teaspoons vanilla

1 cup barley flour

1 tablespoon baking powder

Yield: 2 loaves　　　　　　Time: 1 1/2 hours to soak fruit;
20 minutes to prepare; 45 minutes to bake

1. Pour the juice into a large bowl. Add the dried fruit and mix. Let stand for 1 hour.

2. Add the walnuts, eggs, and vanilla and beat well.

3. Sift together the flour and the baking powder. Add the flour mixture to the fruit mixture and beat lightly with a wooden spoon.

4. Turn the batter into two well-oiled and floured loaf pans, 4 1/2 x 8 1/2 x 2 1/2 inches. Bake at 350°F for 45 minutes or until a toothpick inserted into the center of a loaf comes out clean. Let cool for 10 minutes in the pans and then place on racks to finish cooling.

*If you don't have strawberry juice, substitute another fruit juice.

Blackberry Cake

This is one of my favorite cakes.

Serves: 9   Time: 20 minutes to prepare; 35 minutes to bake

1. In a large bowl, cream together 1 cup jam and the egg. Add the amasake and 1/4 cup oil, and beat well.

2. In a medium bowl, sift together the barley four, wheat flour, and baking powder. Set aside.

3. In a small bowl, mix together the blackberries, fruit sweetener, and arrowroot. Oil an 8-x-8-inch cake pan with the remaining 2 table-spoons of oil. Evenly spread the blackberry in the pan. Set aside.

4. Add the flour mixture to the liquid mixture and beat just enough to mix thoroughly. Spread the batter over the blackberries in the pan and bake at 350°F for 35 minutes.

5. To make the sauce, combine the remaining cup of jam and the water in a saucepan. Mix well and bring to a boil, stirring occasionally. Serve the cake with the warm sauce.

CAKE:

1 cup fruit-sweetened blackberry jam

1 egg

1 cup amasake

1/4 cup oil

1 cup barley flour

1/2 cup whole wheat pastry flour

1 tablespoon baking powder

1/2-pint box of fresh blackberries (or 1 1/4 cups frozen)

1/4 cup concentrated fruit sweetener

1 tablespoon arrowroot

2 tablespoons oil

SAUCE:

1 cup fruit-sweetened blackberry jam

1/4 cup water

TIPS FOR BAKING CAKES

- Preheat the oven.

- Oil and flour the baking pan before you mix the batter.

- Sift the dry ingredients together into a large bowl. A second sifting may help to make the cake lighter.

- Beat the liquid ingredients well before you add the dry ingredients.

- Add the dry ingredients to the liquid ingredients, and beat just enough to mix well. Beating more than necessary may make the cake tough.

- As soon as the batter is mixed, pour it into the cake pan, then place it immediately in the oven. If the batter stands more than a few moments, the cake will not rise as well.

- Bake cakes on the middle rack of the oven.

- Don't open the oven until you think that the cake is done. When the cake is done, it will spring back when lightly pressed with your finger. You may also test the cake by inserting a toothpick into the center. If the toothpick comes out clean, the cake is done.

- Let the cake sit in its pan for 5–10 minutes, then carefully run a knife around the edges of the pan before removing the cake from the pan.

- If you are going to frost the cake, let it cool first on a clean dish towel or a rack.

- To keep the plate clean when frosting a cake, place pieces of waxed paper under the edges of the cake. Pull them out after you have applied the frosting.

Carrot Cake

Serves: 9

Time: 20 minutes to prepare;
30–35 minutes to bake

1 cup whole wheat pastry flour

1/2 cup unbleached white flour

1 tablespoon baking powder

1 teaspoon cinnamon

1 teaspoon allspice

1/4 teaspoon nutmeg

1/2 cup date sugar

1 egg

1/3 cup oil

1/2 cup concentrated fruit sweetener

2/3 cup soymilk

1 cup grated carrots (2 small carrots)

1 cup raisins

1/2 cup chopped walnuts

1. Sift together the two flours, baking powder, spices, and date sugar. If some of the date sugar remains in the sifter, add it back to the bowl with the other ingredients. Resift.

2. In a large mixing bowl, combine the egg and the oil. Beat with a wire whisk until well blended. Add the sweetener and beat again. Add the soymilk and beat again. With a wooden spoon, gradually stir the flour mixture into the liquid mixture. Beat until the batter is well blended. Fold in the carrots, raisins, and nuts.

3. Turn the batter into a well-oiled and floured 8-x-8-inch baking dish. Bake at 350°F for 30–35 minutes or until a toothpick inserted into the center of the cake comes out clean.

This cake is good plain, with a traditional cream cheese icing, or with Tahini Malt Icing (below).

Tahini Malt Icing

1/2 cup tahini

1/4 cup water

1/4 cup malt syrup

2 tablespoons fruit-sweetened orange marmalade

1 teaspoon vanilla

1/4 cup malt powder

This is a lot healthier than a sugar-and-butter icing, and its flavor is reminiscent of caramel.

Yield: enough to frost 8-x-8-inch cake

Time: 15 minutes

1. In a medium bowl, mix together the tahini and the water. Add the malt syrup and mix again. The mixture will be very stiff. Add the marmalade and the vanilla and mix again. Then add the malt powder.

2. Allow the cake to cool before frosting it.

The texture of this icing is gooier than a traditional icing, but it tastes very good on the cake.

Jean's Birthday Cake

This cake is a raspberry version of the Blackberry Cake (page 259), but it is in two layers with the fruit between the layers and a chocolate almond icing. For my husband's birthday, I took one of these cakes to his workplace, and it was gone in 10 minutes.

Serves: 9   Time: 20 minutes to prepare; 20 minutes to bake; 1–2 hours to cool and ice

1. In a large bowl, cream together the jam and the egg. Add the amasake and beat well. Add the oil and beat again.

2. In a medium bowl, sift together the barley flour, wheat flour, and baking powder. Add the flour mixture to the liquid mixture and beat with a wooden spoon just until blended.

3. Pour the batter into two well-oiled and floured 8-x-8-inch cake pans. Bake at 350°F for 20 minutes or until a toothpick inserted into the center of the cake comes out clean. Turn the cakes out to cool, one onto a serving platter, the other onto a clean dish towel or rack. Make the icing.

4. When both the cake and the icing are cool, spread icing over the top of the layer that is on the serving platter. Add a layer of raspberries over the icing, reserving a few to garnish the top of the cake. Carefully position the top layer of cake and spread the whole cake with the remaining icing. Garnish with the remaining raspberries.

VARIATION:

To make this cake wheatless, substitute oat flour for the wheat flour.

1 cup fruit-sweetened raspberry jam
1 egg
1 cup almond-flavored amasake
1/4 cup oil
1 cup barley flour
1/2 cup whole wheat pastry flour
1 tablespoon baking powder
1 recipe Chocolate Almond Icing (below)
1/2-pint box fresh raspberries

Chocolate Almond Icing

Yield: enough to frost a 2-layer 8-x-8-inch cake   Time: 15 minutes to prepare; 1 hour or more to cool

1. Combine the soymilk, sucanat, and chocolate chips in a heavy saucepan. Stir over medium heat until the chocolate chips are melted and the mixture comes to a boil.

2. Add the almond butter and mix well. Transfer the mixture to a bowl so that it will cool faster. Let the icing cool to room temperature. You may cool it in the refrigerator, but remove it before it becomes chilled and too stiff to spread. Spread over Jean's Birthday Cake (above), or any plain or chocolate cake. The cake should be cool when you spread it with icing.

1/4 cup soymilk
1/2 cup sucanat
1/2 cup malt-sweetened chocolate chips
1/2 cup almond butter (from roasted unsalted almonds)

Applesauce Oat Cake

A fruit-sweetened cake that is good plain or with a sauce.

1 cup unsweetened applesauce

1/3 cup concentrated fruit sweetener

1/3 cup oil

1 egg

1/4 cup soymilk

1 cup oat flour

1/2 cup unbleached white flour

2 teaspoons baking powder

1 teaspoon cinnamon

1/2 teaspoon allspice

1 cup raisins

1/2 cup chopped walnuts or pecans

Serves: 6   Time: 20 minutes to prepare; 30 minutes to bake

1. In a large mixing bowl, combine the applesauce, sweetener, oil, egg, and soymilk. Beat well with a wire whisk.

2. Sift together into a medium bowl the oat flour, white flour, baking powder, cinnamon, and allspice. Add the flour mixture to the liquid mixture and beat with a wooden spoon until the batter is smooth.

3. Fold in the raisins and nuts. Pour the batter into an oiled and floured 8-x-8-inch baking dish. Bake at 350°F for 30 minutes or until a toothpick inserted into the center of the cake comes out clean.

4. Serve warm or cool from the pan, plain or with Grandma Agnes's Sweet-and-Sour Dessert Sauce (below). This cake is also good topped with applesauce.

Grandma Agnes's Sweet-and-Sour Dessert Sauce

The idea for this unusual recipe comes from my friend Louise Hammel, whose Irish grandmother made a similar sauce. It is a simple recipe with a sophisticated flavor.

1 cup apple juice (or an apple-berry combination)

1/4 cup concentrated fruit sweetener

1/4 cup sucanat

1 rounded tablespoon arrowroot

2 tablespoons balsamic vinegar

Yield: about 1 1/2 cups sauce   Time: about 10 minutes

1. In a small saucepan, combine the apple juice, sweetener, sucanat, and arrowroot. Mix well until the arrowroot is dissolved.

2. Stirring constantly, bring the mixture to a boil. Add the vinegar and continue to cook for 2–3 minutes.

3. Serve warm over Applesauce Oat Cake (above) or over any plain cake.

Peach Kanten Cake

A special dessert that is worth the time it takes to make. It is wheatless and dairyless, so it can be enjoyed by persons with allergies to those foods.

Serves: 6   Time: 40 minutes to prepare; 2 hours to chill

1. Sift together the barley flour, oat flour, and baking powder. In a small bowl, beat together the oil, egg, sweetener, 1/2 cup soymilk, and 1 teaspoon vanilla. Stir the flour mixture into the liquid mixture and beat with a wooden spoon until the batter is smooth. Pour the batter into a well-oiled and floured 8-x-8-inch cake pan and bake at 350°F for 15–20 minutes or until a toothpick inserted into the center of the cake comes out clean. When the cake is done, let it cool in the pan for at least 1 hour.

2. Prepare the custard: In a medium saucepan mix together the soymilk and agar flakes. Bring the mixture to a boil, stirring constantly. Reduce the heat and simmer, stirring often, until the agar flakes have dissolved, 5–10 minutes.

3. Place the cup of sliced peaches, the arrowroot, and 2 teaspoons vanilla in a blender and blend until smooth. Add this purée to the soymilk mixture in the saucepan and mix well. Add the malt syrup and bring to a boil, stirring constantly. Reduce the heat and stir over low heat until thickened.

4. Spread this mixture while still hot evenly over the cake. Refrigerate for about 1 hour.

5. Arrange the sliced peaches all over the top of the cake. Push the peach slices down into the custard a little as you place them on the cake. Set aside.

6. Pour the peach juice into a small saucepan. Add the remaining tablespoon of agar flakes and bring the mixture to a boil. Reduce the heat and simmer, stirring occasionally, until the agar flakes have dissolved, 5–10 minutes.

7. Carefully and very slowly pour this hot juice mixture over the custard and peach layer on top of the cake. Refrigerate until set. Cut into squares and serve.

CAKE:

1 cup barley flour

1/2 cup oat flour

1 tablespoon baking powder

1/4 cup oil

1 egg

1/3 cup concentrated fruit sweetener

1/2 cup soymilk

1 teaspoon vanilla

CUSTARD:

1 1/2 cups soymilk

1 tablespoon agar flakes

1 cup sliced peaches

3 tablespoons arrowroot

2 teaspoons vanilla

1/2 cup malt syrup

TOPPING:

1 1/2 cups sliced peaches, as needed to cover cake

1 cup unsweetened peach juice

1 slightly rounded tablespoon agar flakes

Coconut Cake with Grilled Pineapple

This dessert is served warm, with a thick coconut milk sauce.

CAKE:

1 cup finely shredded unsweetened coconut

1 cup barley flour

1/2 cup oat flour

1 tablespoon baking powder

1/4 cup oil

1 egg

1/2 cup maple syrup

2 teaspoons vanilla

3/4 cup soymilk

SAUCE:

2 tablespoons oil

3 tablespoons barley flour

1 1/2 cups coconut milk drink*

1/4 cup maple syrup

GARNISH:

6 round slices cored and peeled fresh pineapple, 1 inch thick

1. Place the coconut in an oven-proof pan and bake at 350°F until lightly toasted, 3–5 minutes. Watch it carefully.

2. Sift together into a medium bowl the flours and baking powder. Add the toasted coconut and mix well.

3. In a large bowl, beat the oil and the egg together. Add the maple syrup and the vanilla and beat again. While continuing to beat, add the soymilk. Add the flour mixture to the liquid mixture and beat until well mixed.

4. Pour the batter into a well-oiled and floured 8-x-8-inch cake pan. Bake at 350°F for 20–25 minutes or until a toothpick inserted into the center of the cake comes out clean. Leave the cake in its pan until you are ready to serve it.

5. While the cake is baking, prepare the sauce: Heat the oil in a saucepan. Add the barley flour and mix well. Slowly pour in the coconut milk while stirring constantly with a wire whisk. Bring the mixture to a boil, then reduce the heat and simmer until thickened. Add the maple syrup and mix well. Keep stirring and bring to a boil again. Set the sauce aside until you are ready to serve the cake, then reheat it. If the sauce becomes too thick on setting, thin it to the desired consistency with a little coconut milk.

6. When you are ready to serve the cake, place the pineapple slices on a cookie sheet and broil for 3–5 minutes. (Alternatively, the pineapple may be cooked on an outdoor grill. Place the slices directly on the rack and grill them for 3–5 minutes.) Cut the cake into six pieces and top each piece with a pineapple slice. Pour the warm sauce over the top and serve immediately.

*Bottled coconut milk drink is available in the juice section of many natural foods stores.

Baked Apple

A simple and healthful dessert.

Serves: 4   Time: 40 minutes

1. Wash the apples, then with a sharp paring knife cut out the stem end, making an opening about 1 inch in diameter. Using a tea-spoon, scoop out the core, leaving the bottom of the apple intact.

2. Place the hazelnuts in an oven-proof dish and bake them at 350°F for about 10 minutes or until they are lightly toasted.

3. Place the hazelnuts, raisins, cinnamon, and allspice in a blender and grind them coarsely. Place the raisin-nut mixture in a bowl, add the sweetener, and mix well.

4. Fill the apple cavities with this mixture. Place apples in a baking dish, cover, and bake at 350°F for 20 minutes or until the apples are tender but still hold their shape.

5. Serve hot or cold, plain or with Tofu Vanilla Whip (variation of recipe below).

4 large baking apples

$1/2$ cup hazelnuts

$1/2$ cup raisins

1 teaspoon cinnamon

$1/2$ teaspoon allspice

3 tablespoons concentrated fruit sweetener

Lemon Mousse Topping

This topping is not nearly as rich as it tastes. Serve it on fresh or stewed fruit, fruit kantens, and pies.

Yield: $1^1/2$ cups   Time: 10 minutes

1. Place all the ingredients in a powerful blender or a food processor. Blend until very smooth and creamy. Stop the machine occasion-ally to scrape the sides with a rubber spatula so that everything is well blended.

2. Chill and serve.

VARIATION:

Tofu Vanilla Whip: Reduce the quantity of lemon juice to 1 teaspoon and the lemon peel to $1/4$ teaspoon. Increase the vanilla to 1 table-spoon.

1 package ($10^1/2$ ounces) extra-firm silken tofu

$1/4$ cup mild-flavored honey

2 teaspoons vanilla

1 tablespoon lemon juice

1 piece of lemon peel, about 1 inch square

Old-Fashioned Bread Pudding

1/3 cup maple syrup

1 egg

2 cups soymilk

1 teaspoon vanilla

2 teaspoons cinnamon

4 cups whole grain bread cut into 1/2-inch cubes

1/2 cup chopped walnuts

1 cup raisins

Save your stale bread in the freezer, then try this easy dessert and watch it disappear.

Serves: 6   Time: 15 minutes to prepare; 45 minutes to bake

1. In a large bowl, beat together the maple syrup and egg. Add the soymilk, vanilla, and cinnamon. Mix well.

2. Add the bread, walnuts, and raisins. Mix well, then transfer to a lightly oiled 2-quart casserole. Bake at 350°F for 45 minutes or until center of pudding is firm and top is brown. Serve warm or cold.

Amasake Millet Pudding with Strawberry Gel

1/2 cup millet

1 1/2 cups water

1 cup almond-flavored amasake

1/4 cup maple syrup

1 tablespoon vanilla

2 cups strawberry juice

2 rounded tablespoons agar flakes

2 tablespoons concentrated fruit sweetener

1-pint box of fresh strawberries, washed and sliced

This looks very pretty when it is cut into squares and arranged on a platter.

Serves: 9   Time: 40 minutes to prepare; 2–3 hours to chill

1. Wash the millet and drain it through a wire strainer. Place it in a saucepan and stir it over high heat until it is dry. Then grind it to a powder in a blender.

2. Place the ground millet in a heavy saucepan with the water, amasake, maple syrup, and vanilla. Bring the mixture to a boil while stirring constantly. Reduce the heat, cover, and cook, stirring often, for about 25 minutes. Pour the millet-amasake mixture into a lightly oiled 8-x-8-inch cake pan. Place in the refrigerator to chill until firm, at least 1–2 hours.

3. When the pudding is firm, combine the strawberry juice, agar flakes, and sweetener in a saucepan. Bring the mixture to a boil. Reduce the heat and simmer, stirring occasionally, until the agar is completely dissolved, about 10 minutes. Let cool for about 10 minutes.

4. Arrange the strawberries over the pudding and pour the agar-juice mixture over it. Refrigerate until firm, about 1–2 hours. Cut pudding into squares and serve plain or with Sweet Almond Sauce (page 267).

Stove-Top Rice Pudding

This simple pudding simmers slowly on top of the stove.

Serves: 6   Time: 50 minutes

Place the cooked rice, Rice Dream, vanilla, sweetener, and raisins in a heavy saucepan. While stirring constantly, bring the mixture to a boil. Cover and reduce the heat. Simmer, stirring occasionally, for about 45 minutes, or until all the liquid has been absorbed.

This pudding may be eaten warm, but it is even better chilled. Generously dust each portion with cinnamon before serving.

VARIATION:

For a creamier pudding, stir in about 1/3 cup of Tofu Vanilla Whip (variation of Lemon Mousse Topping, page 265) after the pudding has finished cooking. Top with the remaining whip.

3 cups cooked short grain brown rice (see page 152)

2 cups original flavor Rice Dream beverage (or soymilk)

1 tablespoon vanilla

1/3 cup concentrated fruit sweetener

1 cup raisins

Cinnamon

Sweet Almond Sauce

A dessert topping with a mild almond flavor that is good on fruit pies, puddings, or cakes.

Yield: about 1 1/3 cups   Time: 20 minutes

1. Place the almonds in a blender with 1 cup of water and grind until smooth. Strain the almond milk through a fine wire strainer into a small saucepan. (The pulp can be added to cookies or cakes.)

2. Add the sweetener, almond extract, and arrowroot. Mix well. While stirring constantly, bring the mixture to a boil. Reduce the heat and stir until thickened. Let cool to room temperature and serve.

This sauce is especially good served on Amasake Millet Pudding with Strawberry Gel (page 266).

*To blanch almonds, place the almonds in a saucepan and cover them with water. Bring the water to a boil and boil for 1–2 minutes. Drain the almonds through a colander and rinse with cool water. Press each almond between your thumb and forefinger with a sideways motion; the skin will slip off easily.

1 cup blanched almonds*

1 cup water

1/4 cup concentrated fruit sweetener

1/2 teaspoon almond extract

1 tablespoon arrowroot

Carob "Cream" Sauce

1 cup unsweetened carob chips

1 cup soymilk

2 teaspoons vanilla

1/3 cup sucanat

This sauce looks like dark chocolate but has a taste that is deliciously its own.

Yield: about 1½ cups   Time: 15 minutes

1. Combine all the ingredients in a heavy saucepan. Stir over medium heat until the chips melt and the sauce is smooth.

2. Serve over plain cake or fresh fruit.

Chocolate and Peanut Mousse

1½ cups soymilk

1 slightly rounded tablespoon agar flakes

1/2 cup malt-sweetened chocolate chips

2 tablespoons peanut butter

2 tablespoons maple syrup

Rich and creamy.

Serves: 4   Time: 20 minutes to prepare; 1 hour or more to chill

1. In a small, heavy saucepan, combine 1 cup of the soymilk and the agar flakes. While stirring constantly, bring the mixture to a boil. Reduce the heat and simmer, stirring often, for about 10 minutes or until the agar is dissolved.

2. Add the chocolate chips and the peanut butter. Stir until the chocolate has melted and the peanut butter is blended. Remove the pan from the heat. Stir in the syrup and the remaining soymilk. Mix well. Pour the mixture into a bowl and chill. To cool it more quickly, place the bowl in the freezer.

3. When the mixture is firm, place it in a food processor and blend until smooth. Serve the mousse immediately or return it to the refrigerator to serve later.

Fresh Coconut Sherbet

Served over slices of ripe mango, coconut sherbet is an exquisite end to a light summer meal.

Serves: 4

Time: 20 minutes to prepare; 4 or more hours to freeze

Liquid from 1 coconut

Soymilk

1 tablespoon agar flakes

1/2 cup rice syrup

1 1/2 teaspoons vanilla

2 tablespoons arrowroot powder

1 cup grated fresh coconut

1. To extract the milk from the coconut, puncture two of the three spots on its end with an ice pick or a sharp, thin knife. Place the coconut, pierced side down, over a cup and let it drain. Strain the milk through a wire strainer to remove any pieces of shell. Reserve the milk to use later.

2. To break open the coconut, wrap it in a towel and place it on a tough, hard surface such as a concrete floor or driveway, then smash the coconut with a hammer. The towel will keep the pieces from flying all over. Unwrap the towel and carefully pry the flesh away from the pieces of shell with a knife. Grate enough coconut to make 1 cup, reserving the rest for other uses.

3. Taste the coconut milk for freshness. If it tastes good, measure it and add enough soymilk to make 1 1/2 cups. If you cannot use the coconut milk, use 1 1/2 cups soymilk.

4. Pour 1 1/4 cups of the the coconut-soy liquid into a saucepan and set the rest aside. Add the agar flakes, rice syrup, and vanilla to the pan. Bring the mixture to a boil. Reduce the heat and simmer, stirring often, for about 5 minutes or until the agar flakes are dissolved. Dissolve the arrowroot in the remaining liquid, add it to the saucepan with the other ingredients, and simmer for 2–3 minutes more or until the mixture thickens slightly.

5. Remove the mixture from the heat and add 2/3 cup of the grated coconut. Mix and pour into a shallow dish such as a small square cake pan. Freeze the mixture until it is solid.

6. Meanwhile, place the remaining coconut on a cookie sheet or in a shallow baking pan. Bake at 350°F, stirring often, for 5–10 minutes or until the coconut is lightly toasted. A toaster oven works well for this.

7. When the sherbet is frozen, break it up with a spatula and place the pieces in a food processor. Whip the sherbet, stopping the machine several times to scrape the sides so that the mixture is well blended. Serve immediately over slices of fresh ripe mango or pineapple. Top with the toasted coconut.

Peach Sorbet

4 ripe peaches

1 cup peach nectar

1 tablespoon agar flakes

¹/₄ cup concentrated fruit sweetener

This peachy sorbet is very light and refreshing.

Serves: 4   Time: 15 minutes to prepare;
                                             4 or more hours to freeze

1. Peel and chop the peaches.

2. Pour the peach nectar into a saucepan. Add the agar flakes and bring to a boil. Reduce the heat and simmer for about 5 minutes or until the agar is dissolved. Remove from the heat and add the sweetener.

3. Pour the peach nectar mixture into a shallow dish such as an 8-x-8-inch cake pan. Add the peaches and freeze.

4. When the mixture is frozen, break it up into pieces with a spatula. Place the pieces in a food processor and whip, stopping the machine several times to scrape the sides so that the mixture is well blended.

5. Serve immediately with slices of fresh peaches and garnish with a sprig of fresh mint, or transfer the sorbet to a container and return it to the freezer to serve later. If it gets too hard, let it stand outside the freezer a few minutes until it is soft enough to scoop.

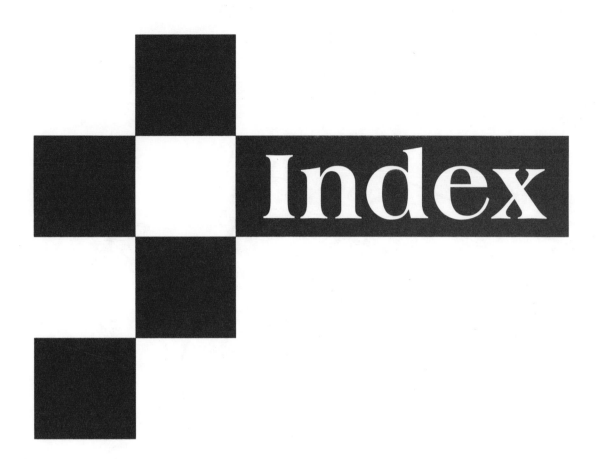

Index